THE NEW SECRET OF SUCCESS

What prevents one person from evolving and adapting to change, and makes another get ahead regardless of obstacles? Are some people naturally endowed with characteristics that lead to success? And what about those of us who may not be so gifted?

INSTINCT reveals how highly successful people leverage certain traits and compensate for those that they lack. Even if you inherited great potential, you need to learn the techniques and entrepreneurial attitude that best build a career.

—from INSTINCT

"A thoroughly original, engaging, scientific, and counterintuitive take on success and entrepreneurial behavior."
—Tom Peters, author of
In Search of Excellence and *Re-Imagine!*

"Harrison shows you how to unlock the abilities you already possess, and how to obtain the ones you don't. A must-read for anyone who's ever dreamed big."
—Earvin "Magic" Johnson, five-time NBA champion and
CEO of Johnson Development Corporation

Instinct

Tapping Your Entrepreneurial DNA to Achieve Your Business Goals

Thomas L. Harrison

Chairman and CEO,
Diversified Agency Services,
Omnicom Group, Inc.

with

Mary H. Frakes

WARNER
BUSINESS
BOOKS™

NEW YORK   BOSTON

Warner Business Books
Hachette Book Group USA
1271 Avenue of the Americas
New York, NY 10020

Visit our Web site at www.HachetteBookGroupUSA.com.

Warner Business Books is an imprint of Warner Books, Inc. The Warner Business Books logo is a trademark of Warner Books, Inc.

Printed in the United States of America

Originally published in hardcover by Warner Business Books.
First Trade Edition: September 2006
10   9   8   7   6   5   4   3   2   1

Warner Business Books is a trademark of Time Warner Inc. or an affiliated company. Used under license by Hachette Book Group USA, which is not affiliated with Time Warner Inc.

The Library of Congress has cataloged the hardcover edition as follows:

Harrison, Thomas L.
    Instinct : tapping your entrepreneurial DNA to achieve your business goals / Thomas L Harrison with Mary H. Frakes.—1st ed.
        p. cm.
    Includes index.
    ISBN 0-446-57684-0
  1. Success in business. 2. Entrepreneurship—Psychological aspects. 3. Insight. 4. Resilience (Personality trait) 5. Businesspeople—Psychology. I Title: Tapping your entrepreneurial DNA to achieve your business goals. II. Frakes, Mary H. III. Title.
    HF5386.H2735 2005
    658.4'09—dc22

                                                                                    2005010566

ISBN-13: 978-0-446-69819-1 (pbk.)
ISBN-10: 0-446-69819-9 (pbk.)

This book is dedicated to entrepreneurs everywhere; your intuitive willingness to follow your instincts creates progress and innovation in every industry. It's also dedicated to all near-entrepreneurs: May you be intellectually prepared for and emotionally open to change, and embrace a new understanding that risk can be redefined as opportunity.

ACKNOWLEDGMENTS

First I want to thank my incredible life partner, Pam, for taking a gamble on a "boy from Maryland," as I often have referred to myself. You had enough faith and love to share every day ever since we had to count pennies when I was a grad student. You have been alongside me and with me during all of my career changes, and supported me as I weighed the risk and opportunity of each one. Even today, you continue to provide your counsel with clarity of thought and laser precision. You are what has made this journey so pleasurable, rewarding, and rooted in confidence. Your advice, support, and love have made my life fabulously satisfying.

I have learned so much about the world and myself from each of the three children with whom I have been blessed. Michael, Matthew, and Lindsay, each of you makes me so proud. You also make me smile every day, laugh every day. I see in all of you reflections of the genetic pool you inherited from your mother and me. I also see the beginnings of a successful businessman or consultant, a successful entrepreneur, and a young lady whose talent will entertain nations of people. (This is all parental conjecture, not a prescription!) Whatever you choose to do in your life's work will be a successful journey, I'm sure.

Dr. Richard P. Sutter, my adviser at West Virginia University, suggested a somewhat shocking life punctuation point while I was working toward my Ph.D. Without his keen observation and counsel, I might never have seen the initial opportunity that started my evolution from scientist to CEO.

Two colleagues from my early days at Pfizer deserve special thanks for assisting in that evolution. Bob Hall, my Pfizer district sales manager, took a chance and believed in me enough to start me in a career of selling. Ron Cohen, my sales representative colleague in those early years, was a mentor of immeasurable importance. I have the utmost respect for how both of you allowed me to express my genetic inclination to sell creatively, honestly, and effectively.

Along my career path, I've enjoyed the luxury of working with many intelligent, intuitive, strategic, and loyal leaders—none more so than John Wren, Omnicom Group's CEO. John's acquisition of the Harrison & Star Business Group for Omnicom was a most significant punctuation point in my career. John provided a global stage on which I could express my style of leadership, my brand of counsel and strategic support for an incredibly strong and diverse array of CEO entrepreneurs who lead the most influential communications companies worldwide today. As a result, I have the opportunity to represent what I believe is the best, most successful, and most entrepreneurial body of talent that resides atop the communications industry today. I'm enormously proud of that association.

All too rarely in one's career do you enjoy the chance to work with someone who helps you develop and express clearly your thoughts, your vision, your ideas—a person who helps make work the rewarding professional experience it's supposed to be. This project has been one of several such experiences I've been lucky enough to have in my life. When I was introduced to Mary Frakes, who co-authored the pages you're about to digest, she immediately embraced the concept of exploring the genetic underpinnings of success, an idea I had wrestled with mentally for several years. When I saw the deep excitement in Mary's eyes as I discussed the theory behind the project, I knew the book needed to be written and that Mary was the one to work with me on it. Mary's skills and clarity of expression turned my thoughts, my input, my hours of thinking, scribbling, dictation, and transcriptions into a volume of which I'm immensely proud, and which I believe will make a significant difference in the lives of entrepreneurs, potential entrepreneurs, and near-entrepreneurs.

I am also grateful to Harry Rhoads, CEO of the Washington Speakers Bureau, for his excitement and support after reading the book treatment. He helped make it easy to interview some of the highly successful entrepreneurs whose personal career stories illustrate so well the concept of success that starts in the genes.

Marybeth Belsito, an entrepreneur, forcefully encouraged me to write this book when I casually explained to her, over a business lunch, the concept of genetic expression of success. Joey Reiman years ago suggested I write a book, though at the time we were talking about a different concept. Thank you, Joey, for your friendship—although I know I don't need to thank you for that. Joey has always been intrigued with my cell biology background, my ability to sell, and my leadership of Diversified Agency Services. You are thought of as an inspiration by so many who know you, who have read your books, and who have heard you speak. You're genetically a Big Thinker.

Thanks also to Rick Wolff, who has edited so many books for Warner, including some of the best business works of our generation. Rick saw the importance, value, and contribution that my book could make, and his interest in what makes superentrepreneurs special was most helpful. Rick, it is a pleasure to count you as a genuine friend and to have had your critical eye on this project. Rob Robertson provided advice as both literary agent and amateur scientist; his insights helped shape the book's exploration of the role of genetics.

Without my many clients over the years, I wouldn't have had the opportunity to express my entrepreneurial genes. Your willingness to encourage innovation and strategic thinking have reinforced time and again my belief that those qualities are what make companies into dominant market leaders. And throughout the many different expressions of those entrepreneurial genes, Diane Bedell, my executive assistant for going on twenty years, has not only helped me manage a hectic professional life but has done it with grace and consistent good cheer.

I have thanked them elsewhere, but I can't stress enough my gratitude to each of this book's interviewees. Their insights and stories have so effectively enhanced, enriched, and informed my thinking about the genetic contribution to success and the entrepreneurial spirit. Your time has been so valuable to the prescriptive thesis expressed throughout this book.

Finally, I'd like to thank all the many entrepreneurs whom I've had the good fortune to meet over my career but whom I did not interview formally. With your ability to see opportunity others don't, to see around corners, to conceive, build, and lead, you have been an unknowing inspiration to this project. You are the building blocks of the foundation on which rests the structure of *Instinct: Tapping Your Entrepreneurial DNA to Achieve Your Business Goals.*

—Tom Harrison

C O N T E N T S

INTRODUCTION

I n 1987, Victoria Chacon left her home in Peru to come to the United States. The twenty-seven-year-old was alone; she had left her young son behind with her family. She spoke no English, knew no one in this country. "I would wake up every day alone, without my family, without my son, without my friends, without my whole world. For several months, believe me, I was crying day and night." She held two jobs as a housekeeper and busgirl at two Atlanta hotels and worked from 6 A.M. to 11:30 P.M., all the while studying her copy of *How to Learn English in 15 Days*.

When a friend told her that jobs available through the Georgia Department of Labor paid far more than the $4.25 an hour she made cleaning rooms, she got someone to drive her there. The recruiter set up an interview at Hormel Food Corp., but warned Chacon that even though she had gotten high scores on the labor department's written exam, her broken English would be a problem. The Hormel manager who interviewed her said the same thing: "I have hundreds of applications from people who speak good English and have experience. Why should I give you this position?"

"I told him, 'All I'm asking is for one opportunity. Let's make a deal. Let me work for you for one week. After that, you can put me together with your best worker, and I'm going to beat them. And if you still don't like my work, you don't even have to pay me.' I guess that moved his heart." She got a nine-dollar-an-hour job on the night shift in the bacon department. She quit one of her two hotel jobs, but still found time to sell kids' shoes on weekends at a flea market.

Months later, a friend said his boss, a builder, needed someone to clean the house they were painting and asked Chacon if she wanted the job. "I asked how much they would pay. He said, 'Well, it's a huge house, so I guess they're going to pay you $1,200.' The builder recommended me to other builders, and that was the beginning of my business."

She hired a couple of her hotel co-workers. For more than three years, she would go from site to construction site with flyers and business cards during the day, and then to her night job at Hormel. When the Olympics came to Atlanta, she started a second company to provide temporary construction workers. In addition to those two, Chacon is now exploring a very different opportunity: "I saw my community growing very fast, and I said, 'At some point we're going to need a publication in order to raise our voice, for the English-speaking community to be aware of what's going on inside the Latino community.'" In May of 2000, she launched *La Vision*, a bilingual newspaper from a Latino perspective that circulates throughout Georgia.

Contrast Chacon's story with that of a former vice president at a subsidiary of a global financial data firm. After the division for which he worked was shut down, he tried to start a small independent consulting business, but never really gave it his full attention. With his severance package gone and the consulting business floundering, he decided he'd like to return to a corporate job. However, he is now over fifty and has been out of the workforce for a couple of years. He has had difficulty finding a job. He's considered overqualified, his experience in a rapidly changing field is outdated, and employers can find people younger who are willing to work for less. And he can't figure out where he went wrong or what to do next.

What prevents one person from evolving and adapting to change, and makes another a Victoria Chacon, who gets ahead regardless of the obstacles that stand in her way? Are some people *naturally* endowed from birth with characteristics that invariably lead to success? And if so, what about those of us who may not be so genetically gifted? Are we doomed to a lifetime of repeated failure if those qualities don't come naturally? Is success the product of something in our DNA or something we learn? Or is it some combination—a genetic, instinctive predisposition that we can enhance at crucial moments in our lives by using learned skills and abilities? With the mapping of the human genome, scientists have begun answering those questions. Every day, new research is overturning assumptions about how much of our be-havior is acquired and how much is inborn.

I've been at various times an advertising executive, a marketing representative for a pharmaceutical company, an entrepreneur, and now a corporate executive—an intrapreneur. It's been quite a ride for a small-town boy whose father owned a grocery story in Maryland. How-ever, my original training was in cell biology. My evolution from re-search scientist to CEO demonstrates how anyone can take the building blocks they've been given and make something completely unexpected from them—creating an addiction to success in the process. As my ex-ample demonstrates, careers do not need to be—and often are not—linear.

Today I'm the chairman and CEO of Diversified Agency Services (DAS), the largest, most profitable, and fastest-growing division of a multibillion-dollar corporation called Omnicom Group Inc. Our group includes more than 150 distinct—and often quite distinctive—profit centers. DAS has hundreds of offices worldwide, and we're responsible for just over half of the parent company's revenues. DAS functions as a holding company of talent that we can deploy in virtual, flexible, strate-gically aligned teams to represent our client's specific initiatives. In a way, DAS is like a receptor nerve cell for Omnicom. We try to serve as an intake mechanism, strategically acquiring companies that will keep DAS and Omnicom leaders in each discipline in which we choose to compete, that will strengthen our global talent offering, or that will open up profitable new markets for continued growth.

As I worked with entrepreneurs over the years, I began to realize that there was something that set successful entrepreneurs apart from most other people I dealt with—or even from less successful entrepre-neurs. We all know people of whom others say, "He (or she) is a born entrepreneur." Indeed, it did seem as though these people had always had certain characteristics that came as naturally to them as their hair color (in some cases, even more naturally!).

Instinct: Tapping Your Entrepreneurial DNA reveals how highly suc-cessful people have leveraged certain inherited personality traits and learned how to compensate for those that they lack. Many of the peo-ple interviewed for this book happen to be entrepreneurs, but the qual-ities they embody are needed by everyone in business today. Even if you inherited great potential, you need to learn the techniques and mind-set that help you turn it into the entrepreneurial attitude that best builds a career. Regardless of where we work, each of us needs to approach our careers as though we're a company of one, with a picture of personal success.

If you think you got shortchanged in the genetic lottery, you can still be successful—but only if you know what you're starting with and, more important, how to make up for what you may not possess. This book provides a road map to the attitudes and behaviors that can help you capitalize on the genetic foundation you inherited and compensate for what you feel you lack. Understanding how to activate your "success genes," compensate for your weaknesses, and make better instinctive decisions constitutes what I call "the DNA of success." Businesses have marketing plans; you need one, too. The DNA of success is that personal marketing plan. Doing these things will help you, your employees, and your organization perform at the highest level and achieve their greatest potential.

Using real-life examples and the latest scientific discoveries about the connections among genetics, biology, evolution, and psychology, this book demonstrates how success in career, business, and life often depends on using your instincts to evolve and adapt to changing circumstances.

To develop the DNA of success, you must:

• *Do a genetic inventory.* Understanding your genetic heritage and natural abilities gives you a starting point from which you can grow and develop strategies for achieving success. In Chapter 1, you'll find an Entrepreneurial Personality Quiz that can help you understand how your genes affect your personality.

• *Unlock your inborn strengths to help yourself manage your weaknesses.* Even good genes are useless unless you put them to work. Everyone has certain innate advantages, but it's essential to know how to unlock them and compensate for what you may lack. Seven key behaviors serve as "Success Promoters." Without them, your genes probably won't be enough. With them, you can make the most of what you've already got to compensate for what you feel you may be missing.

• *Use those Success Promoters to improve your decisions.* Our actions are where "what we're born with" intersects with "what we've learned." Using what you know about yourself, good decisions become a "virtuous circle." They can teach you what works, and train your instincts to become better decision-making guides in the future.

Instinct: Tapping Your Entrepreneurial DNA to Achieve Your Business Goals draws on the experiences of a variety of people whose track records of success speak for themselves. Many are among the most recognized names in American business; with others, their achievements may be more recognizable than the names themselves. Still others are incredible success stories of entrepreneurs who are not widely known. Some fit the traditional definition of an entrepreneur, such as Sam Zell, founder and chairman of Equity Group Investments LLC, the United States' largest commercial and residential landlord; or Sam Wyly, who has either launched or headed ventures in a variety of fields, including computing, restaurants, mining, energy, and craft retailing. Still others have certainly demonstrated the traits of successful entrepreneurs in a corporate context, whether they are turnaround whizzes like Barry Gibbons, formerly of Burger King; intrapreneurs like John Patrick, who was IBM's Internet evangelist; or corporate innovators like American Airlines' Robert Crandall. Their stories about how they have learned to unlock their potential and overcome obstacles can help identify the psychological markers that predict success as well as the actions and experiences that cancel out weaknesses. By suggesting practical steps that anyone can take, these stories can help us perform a kind of mental "genetic re-engineering" on ourselves to develop and encourage the traits and ideas that enable us to adapt, survive, grow, and be successful. After all, even a strong inborn entrepreneurial desire and personality can be blocked if we fail to recognize and use it strategically.

Evolution is what it's all about—in business, careers, and life. There might seem to be a certain discontinuity in my career as I went from molecular biologist to sales and marketing to entrepreneurial agency owner to CEO. However, in retrospect I can see the evolutionary threads that tie my various incarnations together. Trying new things. Communicating well with others. A personality that attracts others. Doing what comes naturally and trusting my innate instincts. Understanding my own limitations and hiring people to complement my own attributes. Pursuing something I liked. Being willing not only to assume risk but to look at risk as opportunity. Being unquestionably honest in my relationships with clients and colleagues; without this, all the rest would have been meaningless. Those threads are not unique to me; the people in this book exhibit them just as clearly. You can, too. Their stories and advice will help you unlock the power of your genetic potential to achieve your own kind of success.

Evolution has refined our genetic instructions over centuries to help us survive as a species. The DNA that has been passed on is the DNA that worked. In the same way, the advice of these high achievers can be passed on as a sort of "DNA of ideas"—the traits, attitudes, behaviors, and decisions that made them so successful. We may not have their genetic code, but we can take advantage of their experiences and knowledge to maximize our own.

I'll make a bold prediction here: If you have this "entrepreneurial DNA," you *will* be successful. Not necessarily in the way you predict, not necessarily in the time frame you expect, but you will succeed— whatever that means for you. And if you adopt the Success Promoters that nourish entrepreneurial DNA, you'll do better at whatever you attempt.

I'll be the first to admit that I'm not trying to pursue rigorous scientific inquiry in this book; I left the lab long ago. However, I've tried to present both scientific research and anecdotal evidence I've observed over the years that suggest that entrepreneurs have an inborn predisposition to thinking in a certain way that contributes to their success. That predisposition needs to be switched on by certain behaviors, but it's there from the beginning. It's instinctive. It doesn't necessarily guarantee success, but lacking it seems to be a pretty clear marker for failure in any entrepreneurial endeavor. Research in this area is in its earliest stages, but already there are indications that lab science will increasingly confirm my own day-to-day practical experience and observations.

To those in my life who could have been entrepreneurs, who should have become entrepreneurs but didn't, I apologize that this book has not been published earlier. Perhaps it could have provided the incentive you needed to just take the short-term risk. You absolutely would have experienced the long-term rewards.

It may not be too late. Mapping the human genome is only, as

Human Genome Project leader Francis S. Collins has said, "the end of the beginning." Discoveries about how our genes affect the way we learn, grow, and behave are in their infancy. Just as the information in your DNA has to be decoded and replicated so that your cells can use it, this book can help you decode your own "DNA of success." For all of those near-entrepreneurs who are thinking about taking the leap, read this book, take a deep breath, take the risk, and be truly happy in your own career—not someone else's or one that someone else prescribes for you. Prescribe your own future. Enjoy your own success.

Instinct

CHAPTER 1

The Critical 50 Percent:
Doing Your Genetic Inventory

When Kay Koplovitz was three years old, she begged to be allowed to accompany her older sister to kindergarten. "I'd ask my mother, 'Why can't I be in kindergarten too? I know my way; I can find it.' So I went off on my own." Teachers tried to send her home. It didn't work, says Koplovitz: "I'd turn around and come right back."

That same kind of determination later led Koplovitz to be ahead of her time in another way when she founded the USA Network, becoming the first woman to head a television network. Koplovitz didn't have a traditional background for becoming a corporate leader; like me, she studied science in college. But that led her to spot an opportunity: the idea of delivering broadcast programming via satellite to cable companies instead of over telephone lines, as the three broadcast networks did.

Koplovitz may not have gone to business school, but she had an entrepreneur's belief in her idea and her ability to make it successful. "I didn't think it was risky," Koplovitz says. "You could just see the opportunity. For me it was as though it had already been written, like it was a historical fact, even though it hadn't occurred yet. I was more certain that it would be successful than I was of a lot of other things. I do think there's something innate about people's tolerance for risk."

Personality is determined by many things, but scientists are beginning to find that a lot more of you is built into you when you're born than we used to think. Scientists now believe that roughly 50 percent

1

of the differences in our personalities is inherited.[1] In working with many entrepreneurs and entrepreneurial thinkers over the years, I've come to believe that the inherited combination of personality traits that is unique to each human being is the basis for whether we will eventually become successful.

The DNA of success is really *your* DNA of success. Understanding it can help you make better career decisions and keep you evolving in a direction that can make you successful, no matter how unconventional your career path may seem. The DNA of success is especially important for anyone who is considering being an entrepreneur. Any venture starts with an opportunity, a person, and an idea. Unless that person has entrepreneurial DNA, the idea probably won't get very far.

ARE ENTREPRENEURS BORN OR MADE?

There's some evidence that entrepreneurial thinking tends to run in families. In some cases, families actually produce whole crops of entrepreneurs. One example is that of John Bogle Sr., and John Bogle Jr. Father and son each launched their own separate businesses in the mutual fund industry. In doing so, they were carrying on a tradition that had started generations earlier. Philander Bannister Armstrong, grandfather of Bogle Senior, created Phoenix Mutual Life Insurance Company. Grandfather Bogle was involved in the formation of a canning company. And there may be yet another generation to come. John Bogle Jr. says he sees a contrarian, risk-taking attitude in his daughter. His son is more cautious, but already displays the analytical orientation that characterizes his father and grandfather.

The Bogles are just one example of a family with an entrepreneurial streak. One Seattle family includes nine entrepreneurs spread over three generations: Larry Mounger, his two sons and two daughters, and four third-generation cousins. Twin brothers Ted and Fred Kleisner are another example. Fred is the president and CEO of Wyndham International; he was formerly president and COO of Starwood Hotels and Resorts, which includes the Westin, Sheraton, and St. Regis chains. Ted is president and managing director of the world-famous Greenbrier Resort. Not only are the two men leaders in the same industry, they are also third-generation hoteliers.

I even see it in my own family. Both my sons have already demonstrated entrepreneurial instincts. As college freshmen, they studied to get real estate licenses so they could make some money during their student years, and one has already told me he wants to start a company after he graduates. My daughter has produced a CD of her own music and is selling it. In fact, all of my three children may be born entrepreneurs. They used to sell seashells at the Cape May, New Jersey, seashore. People could walk on the beach and pick them up themselves, but for some reason they bought them from my kids.

Multiple studies have shown that having at least one self-employed parent increases the chances that a person will be self-employed.[2] Are genes at work here? If so, how? Or is it simply a case of learning by example—imprinting, as we trained scientists say? Is the entrepreneurial instinct created before baby's first breath, or when Mom or Dad helps set up a lemonade stand in the front yard, as Pam and I did for our three children?

Being exposed to an entrepreneurial environment early in life clearly is important; we'll look at how and why in Chapter 2. And it's true that some entrepreneurial skills must be learned. No one is born knowing how to put together a good business plan, get financing, or juggle the myriad tasks involved in a start-up.

However, environment doesn't explain everything. Many of the successful people interviewed for this book said they grew up watching entrepreneurial behavior in their family, but just as many said exactly the opposite. When you deal with a born entrepreneur, you usually know it.

"For those who do it over and over again, I think there's probably something innate about them," says Thomas Kinnear, executive director of the University of Michigan's Zell Lurie Institute for Entrepreneurial Studies. "Somewhere down in those chromosomes there's gotta be something. My brother's an entrepreneur, my grandfather was an entrepreneur, his father was an entrepreneur. What is it? I've been involved in nine start-ups. Even though I'm a teacher, I can't seem to let go."

Time and time again I have seen eager people come into my office with what seems like a good idea. They may have a great proposal, they may be a lot smarter than I am, they may even be very personable. But the ones who eventually succeed seem to have something else—something that goes beyond smarts, an idea, and being willing to work hard.

Where does that come from? To begin to get at that question, it helps to think about the difference between entrepreneurial *behavior* and the entrepreneurial *personality*. My dad ran a neighborhood grocery store; that's entrepreneurial behavior. People who exhibit entrepreneurial behavior may or may not be successful, and entrepreneurial behavior isn't necessarily passed on. The entrepreneurial spirit can be expressed in many ways that have nothing to do with starting a business.

"Nobody's yet found [a specific genetic link], but anecdotally you sort of see it. Even though children of entrepreneurs tend to regress to the average, they probably are more entrepreneurial than the standard average, at least for a few generations," says Kinnear. "Of course, if they get too rich, then they become Paris Hilton."

Where biology may play a role is in creating a genetic foundation for personality. Instinctively pouncing on opportunity, being unstoppable in pursuit of a vision, being able to persuade others of the value of your idea—those are some of the marks of thinking like an entrepreneur. They're also the qualities that help make you successful today, whether you run a grocery store, lead the development and launch of a major product or division, need to revive an ailing corporation, or spearhead a community project.

At this point, no one can provide a definitive answer to the nature-versus-nurture question—certainly not me. But scientific research is beginning to confirm what I've suspected for a long time, based on my exposure to hundreds of entrepreneurs and other highly successful people over the years: that it's not all learned behavior. In the 1950s, many scientists thought we were simply a product of our environments—little rats in boxes being trained to press a lever for rewards. However, there is more and more evidence that some aspects of personality are partly genetic. Even if you didn't come from a family of entrepreneurs, you may still have basic personality traits that give you a head start in entrepreneurial thinking.

It shouldn't come as a big surprise that genes play an enormous part in our personalities. After all, the basic genetic code we all share controls everything from eye color to our risk of having certain diseases. It only makes sense that those genetic instructions might also affect how each individual brain absorbs and responds to what's going on around it.

THE SCIENCE BEHIND INHERITING AN ENTREPRENEURIAL PERSONALITY

To understand how the entrepreneurial spirit might get inherited, let's step back and look at how genes affect us generally. Genes contain the recipe for how every cell in our bodies develops. Every cell has a copy of all the information necessary to produce an entire human being; that's why Dolly the sheep could be cloned from a single cell. Genes don't just affect hair color, height, and whether we go bald. The role of genes in increasing the risk of diseases such as cancer, diabetes, and heart disease is becoming clearer every day.

It's easy to see that genes influence physical problems and traits. However, scientists are now discovering that our genes affect how we behave, too. The success of the Human Genome Project has enabled scientists to begin to connect what happens in our cells and what happens in our brains. They have found links between genes and increased risk of alcoholism, schizophrenia, bipolar disorder, obesity, depression—even smoking.

We've only begun to explore just how our genes create a predisposition to such behaviors. Some scientists believe it's because genes direct how our brains develop, before and after we're born. Genes may program some of us to develop more circuitry in certain parts of our brains than others. For example, women have been found to have more connections between the right and left sides of their brains than men do. Others believe mechanical processes are more important than developmental ones. Genes guide our brains in producing and processing the chemicals, such as dopamine, that affect our moods. Some believe it's a combination.

Whatever the process, the most important point is this: Our understanding of just how important our genes are and how they shape our day-to-day behavior is in the infant stages. With the decoding of the human genome, we've just started to unlock these secrets. Companies are already marketing genetic tests to consumers who want to know how vulnerable they are to illness, or how well their bodies process nutrients, drugs, or environmental stresses. I believe by the time my yet-unborn grandchildren are my age, we'll all know parts of our genetic code and what they mean for our lives in the same way we now know our cholesterol levels.

GENES AND PERSONALITY

I heard a story a while back that reminded me of the mystery of genetics. A man was watching his four-year-old son do what kids do: show off. As the father watched, something seemed strangely familiar about the dance the little boy was doing. Suddenly he realized that the boy's movements were exactly the same as the dance the man had watched his own father do as an elderly man. Since the boy's grandfather had died thirty years before the child was born, he couldn't have somehow learned the steps.

As I said earlier, scientists have found that roughly 50 percent of the differences in our personalities are linked to our genes. Any parent knows that some children are born with a sunny disposition, physical gracefulness, or a thirst for learning—and others, even in the same family, simply weren't. Children display a personality early on that can't necessarily be explained by their upbringing. (I can hear every parent out there heaving a huge sigh of relief.)

Researchers in the emerging field of behavioral genetics have begun to turn up some fascinating examples of just how strongly inheritable our personalities are. Countless studies have demonstrated striking similarities between twins separated at birth. Here's a brief sample of the kinds of discoveries scientists have made in recent years:

• In one famous example, identical twins who were reared separately tended to have similar occupations, senses of humor, habits, and opinions.[3]

• A person's overall level of happiness and well-being seems to be largely genetically determined. Researchers found that they could predict a twin's happiness better by looking at the other twin's happiness than by looking at educational achievement, income, or status.[4]

- Genes seem to affect the tendency to start and to continue smoking.[5]

- Differences in how one specific gene gets copied seem to affect anxiety levels. One variation of that gene has been linked to self-confidence and cheerfulness; a different variation seems to promote chronic anxiety.[6]

- One switched letter on yet another gene seems to affect whether someone tends to be chronically depressed. That is even more remarkable when you consider that we have an estimated 20,000 to 30,000 genes, and roughly half of those are considered "junk DNA."[7]

- In one study of men in New Zealand who were treated badly as children, the activity level of a specific gene seemed to affect whether the men later became criminals. Those in whom the gene was very active turned out okay; those with less activity were four times as likely to become criminals.[8]

- Scientists have been able to make mice more aggressive by knocking out entirely the functioning of one gene. Replacing it calms the mice down.[9] (And before you say "I'm a human, not a mouse," remember that we share roughly 98 percent of our genes with mice.)[10]

- One study of 700 teenagers and their parents found that genetics accounted for anywhere from *71 to 89 percent* of a teen's score on antisocial behavior, depression, school performance, and social responsibility. (Ironically, the study had intended to show the impact of friends and other influences, not genes, on teen behavior.)[11]

Some scientists are even beginning to go beyond saying that our personalities are influenced by our genes. They've started linking certain aspects of our personalities to specific genes. For example, a craving for novelty has been linked to the long version of the D4DR gene, although this finding has not yet been fully confirmed.

One recent study is particularly interesting. Comparing leadership behavior and personality characteristics in twins, researchers have found that genes account for roughly 30 percent of the differences between people in terms of having a track record of leadership. Almost all of the rest was accounted for by what's called "non-shared environmental influences"—in other words, life lessons, events, and the impact of other people outside the family. In fact, family seemed to have very little statistical connection.[12]

My days in the lab are long behind me, so I'm not in a position to validate scientifically any individual research project. But they demonstrate that we have only begun to understand just how strong that influence is. Collectively they make a case for genetic influence on our personalities and behavior.

And they certainly support my own observations over the years that some people naturally have an innovative bent, work habits, risk-taking tolerance, and problem-solving talents that contribute to business success. These people may have learned skills that enhance those tendencies. They may also have had an environment that encouraged those tendencies through either positive or negative reinforcement. But like ivy climbing a wall, those learned skills and that environment also had something on which to build. Having that foundation doesn't mean those lucky people are predestined to become successful. It simply means they probably started out with an extra helping of certain qualities that tend to promote success.

"My mom has told me, 'The older you get, the more you're like your dad,'" says Herman Cain, former chairman of Godfather's Pizza. "Both my mom and dad were people persons. I inherited that orientation toward people. My dad was more of an extrovert than my mother; he was like a magnet. He would walk into a room and people would be attracted to him. Quite frankly, I inherited that."

Richard Branson is known for outrageous behavior to promote the Virgin Group. As a young adult, Richard Branson's mother demonstrated similar daring. She became a chorus girl—"My parents were shocked"—and persuaded a flight instructor to let her pilot a glider ("He said I could do it as long as I dressed like a man."). To make money to help support her family, she made and sold objets d'art.[13]

"Arthur had that tenacity," says Molly Blank, mother of Home Depot co-founder Arthur Blank. So did she. After her husband died, she took over the pharmaceutical supply company he had started and ran it successfully before eventually selling it.[14]

"[Tom] was a catalyst; he was the ringleader," says Jane Scott of her son Tom, co-founder of Nantucket Nectars.[15]

"It's something genetic," says Robert Crandall. The former chairman of American Airlines was referring to the indomitable spirit of a seventeen-year-old girl who was the subject of a story in the *New York Times*. The story depicted her struggle to keep up her good grades at school despite having been born into poverty. "Maybe she's a descendant of Attila the Hun, who was a very determined person."

Let me make clear that all of this has nothing to do with intelligence—at least not in my view. For one thing, intelligence is even more highly affected by learning and environmental influences than personality is. And intelligence isn't the same thing as the "success genes." Take it from me. I worked like a dog all through school, but if I had had to rely solely on grades for success—well, let's just say I'm a lot happier tackling business problems instead of written exams. What I'm talking about here is the personality traits that give someone a leg up in achieving what they want to achieve.

WHAT'S YOUR STARTING POINT?

So why is any of this relevant in a business book? Well, given all this new scientific information about how our genes affect our personalities and behavior, doesn't it make sense to understand and use your genetic background to increase the odds of your being more successful? If you were born with a predisposition to being analytical or outgoing or emotional, doesn't it make sense to take advantage of those natural strengths instead of trying to fit yourself into a mold that forces you to work against who you are?

There are five broad aspects of our personalities that scientists say are highly inheritable. Everyone has a unique combination of these traits. The terms used to describe them by researchers beginning as early as 1957 have varied: the "Big 5," the "five-factor model," and so on. They're the basis for much scientific research as well as many of the personality tests often administered by human resources departments; they also inspired the Entrepreneurial Personality Quiz later in this chapter.

These traits don't work like on-off switches. Personality is not a case of "you either have it or you don't." With each trait, you may have a lot, very little, or be somewhere in the middle. Each of the Big 5 traits also has multiple aspects, and you may have more or less of each one of those as well.

In each of us, those traits and subtraits combine in a unique way. Even without any environmental influences, the number of possible combinations is enormous. And when you throw in how our environments affect those genetic qualities, it's easy to see why each of us is unique.

The Big 5 Traits are easily remembered by their acronym OCEAN, attached to them by National Institute on Aging researchers Paul Costa Jr. and Robert McCrae:

Openness to Experience: Measures how receptive a person is to new experiences and ideas. Someone who prefers buying a new car every couple of years to sticking with the old one, and traveling to new places rather than visiting familiar haunts year after year, probably would be highly Open to Experience. Innovators, researchers, entrepreneurs, even some marketers all tend to score high on Openness (some personality researchers refer to it as Intellect).

LOW OPENNESS IS ASSOCIATED WITH . . .	HIGH OPENNESS IS ASSOCIATED WITH . . .
Being focused on the here and now	Being imaginative and creative
Preferring the routine and familiar	Preferring variety and novelty
Having few interests	Having many interests
Preferring the conventional	Preferring originality
Mistrusting emotion	Valuing emotion
Being dogmatic	Being flexible

Conscientiousness: Measures a person's motivation and deliberate approach to accomplishing tasks. Being disciplined, organized, methodical, reliable, and persistent are hallmarks of someone who's highly Conscientious. The accounting profession probably is filled with highly Conscientious people. (Before you say "What about recent financial scandals?" remember that in psychological terms, Conscientiousness isn't the same as ethics. You can be extremely Conscientious in pursuing a questionable goal.)

Low Conscientiousness is associated with being . . .	High Conscientiousness is associated with being . . .
Spontaneous	Methodical
Disorganized	Organized
Late	Punctual
Irresponsible	Dutiful
Unmethodical	Self-disciplined
Unambitious	Driven to achieve
A procrastinator or abandoning tasks quickly	Persistent
Unreliable	Reliable

Extroversion: Measures how attracted a person is to activity and people. If someone you know is always on the go, loves to party, likes to dominate the conversation, and seeks out adventure, chances are they're highly Extroverted (salespeople are the classic example).

Low Extroversion is associated with . . .	High Extroversion is associated with . . .
Being a loner	Preferring groups
Being unlikely to reach out to others	Being outgoing
Being a very private person	Assertiveness
Not being a thrillseeker	Craving excitement
Being less exuberant	Being prone to positive emotions
Preferring a relaxed pace	
Passivity	A high energy level
	Liking to dominate

Agreeableness: Measures the ability and desire to cooperate with others and avoid confrontation. Someone who is self-sacrificing, tends to defer to authority, generally trusts other people, and hates to argue is probably pretty Agreeable (administrative assistants couldn't do their jobs without having a high degree of Agreeableness).

Low Agreeableness is associated with being . . .	High Agreeableness is associated with being . . .
Skeptical	Trusting
Having a sense of superiority	Modest
Guarded	Candid, frank
Arrogant	Eager to defer to authority
Uncooperative	Cooperative
Objective, ruthless	Altruistic and tender-hearted
Aggressive	Disliking confrontation
Competitive	Self-sacrificing

Neuroticism: Sometimes labeled Emotional Stability or Emotional Control, this measures a person's overall tendency to feel chronic negative emotions such as depression, anxiety, and hostility. Being generally pessimistic, easily upset, and anxious characterize someone who's Neurotic (artists often are stereotyped as having a high degree of Neuroticism.)

Low Neuroticism is associated with being . . .	High Neuroticism is associated with being . . .
Calm	Easily upset
Fearless	Anxious
Unemotional	Easily angered
Resilient	Easily depressed
Self-possessed under stress	Vulnerable under stress
Resistant to immediate temptation	Impulsive
Unselfconscious	Nervous in social situations

After about age thirty, all five traits tend to stay relatively stable.[16] Your behavior may change over the years as you learn skills and make mistakes, but these aspects of your personality will tend to color your perspective on the world and your automatic reactions to it. The research that demonstrates this only confirms the opinions expressed by many of the interviewees for this book. Former Philadelphia 76ers president Pat Croce's comment is typical of most of their answers: "I don't think you can change your basic personality. People can cope, they can bend, they can learn to deal with things, but rarely do they change. I think your hard drive is wired, just like a computer is wired, but you can change the personal path you take."

That's why, regardless of whether you're a one-person business or a leader in a Fortune 500 corporation, understanding how these traits affect performance is important—not just for you personally, but for the people who work with you. Managers have to match employees to the right tasks in order to give them their best chance for success. Looking at inherited personality traits gives managers more powerful tools in making hiring and training decisions and getting the most from employees.

Taking an individual's genetic strengths into account doesn't mean discrimination. Researchers have shown that the Big 5 traits function across cultural, gender, and racial lines. However, it does mean that managers may need to screen personality traits specific to a given job and recognize which aspects of personality will likely stay the same regardless of training or exposure to new experiences. Understanding the Big 5 traits can help you manage people of varying strengths and personality types. Knowing them can help you identify employees who may need extra help in specific areas, or who are likely to adapt and evolve in certain roles. And that knowledge can certainly help you understand how to manage yourself to success.

"But I'm Not Like My Family!"

I can hear you saying "But if genes are so important, how come I'm so different from the rest of my family? My dad was a lazy slob; does that mean I'm doomed to be one, too?"

Not at all. Here's why:

• *Genes can be recessive.* Physical traits often skip a generation. It's logical to assume that personality traits can, too.

• *Genes don't operate in a vacuum.* The way a gene functions can be affected by when and how its instructions get switched on and carried out. As science writer Matt Ridley points out in his book *Nature via Nurture*, scientists are discovering that genetic instructions are more like a recipe than a blueprint. If you put all the right ingredients into a cake batter but you set the heat too low or leave it in the oven too long, things can go wrong. Genes function in much the same way. The environment you grew up in may be very different from the environment your dad grew up in. Even if your personalities were identical, you have learned different things than your parents did, and your genes will express themselves differently.

• *Genes aren't photocopies.* You're a mix of two sets of genes: your mother's and your father's. Each of them inherited a combination of genes from their parents, each of whom also inherited two sets from their parents. It doesn't take a math genius to see that the number of ways those genes can be combined, even in the same family, is enormous.

• *Genes affect your environment—and vice versa.* If your genes give you a personality that's slightly different from a brother or sister, you may react and behave differently in your environment. That behavior will probably lead people—including your parents—to treat each of you a bit differently, no matter how hard they try to be evenhanded. The different treatment can reinforce any differences in siblings' personalities.

• *Genes may behave differently, depending on whether they come from your father or your mother.* Research on mice shows that certain genes, called "imprinted" genes, function only if they're inherited through the father; others work only if they came from Mom. Maternal imprinted genes seem to influence the parts of the brain that deal with thinking; paternal genes have more impact on development of the emotional, limbic parts of the brain.[17]

Researchers have found that living in the same family has less to do with personality than genes do; an estimated 10 percent or less of the differences in our personalities can be attributed to shared environments such as family.[18] And after a certain age, that family environment has less and less to do with who we are.[19]

Your Genetic Inventory

Want to know where you stand on each of the Big 5 personality traits? This quiz can give you a general idea of what strengths and weaknesses may be highly influenced by your genes. Knowing them can help you understand how they might help or impede you as an entrepreneur. It can also show you areas you may need to supplement, either through experience or finding other ways to obtain what you lack. There are no right or wrong answers; what counts is your individual combination of traits and how you develop, use, and apply them. This is not designed to be a formal psychological examination. It is only intended to give you a general idea of your genetic starting point.

ENTREPRENEURIAL PERSONALITY QUIZ

Answer the questions by checking either A or B. Once you've answered all questions in each section, total the number of checkmarks in each column.[20]

SECTION I	A	B
You find it more enjoyable to (a) deal with real-life, concrete situations, such as closing deals, winning new clients, and reviewing data, or (b) imagine new products that don't yet exist and daydream about how you might be able to develop them.		
You (a) are not terribly absorbed by natural or artistic beauty; you relate more to people, things, and information, or (b) respond powerfully to beauty and often find it in things others don't, whether in the arts or nature.		
You generally (a) make sure you keep your emotions from affecting your business decisions, or (b) are very aware of how your behavior and decisions are influenced by what you feel.		

	A	B
When you hit an obstacle in reaching a goal, are you more likely say to yourself, (a) "If I just stick to my game plan and persevere, I'll get there; I've done it before," or (b) "Maybe there's another way to reach my goal; besides, I'd rather try something new anyway"?		
When a conversation at a business gathering turns to abstract ideas such as philosophy or a discussion of aesthetics, would you tend to (a) find another conversation; you can't be bothered with all that irrelevant debating, or (b) find yourself interested in hearing various ideas and opinions, and perhaps even join in the conversation?		
Which concept appeals to you most: (a) "A tradition of excellence" or (b) "Think different"?		
Total for Section I	_____	_____

Section I: Openness to Experience

This aspect of personality measures how receptive you are to new experiences and ideas. If you had a lot of As in this section, you probably tend to focus on the here and now, the concrete, the norm. You are more comfortable with tradition, routine, and the familiar than with questioning the status quo. You may dislike ambiguity and prefer having a few well-defined interests. You often get impatient with things you perceive to have little usefulness or connection with the real world. Having a low degree of Openness can be valuable in enforcing regulations or focusing on well-defined, specific goals, such as sales.

If you had mostly Bs here, you tend to think creatively, try new things, and have many different interests. Generally, you are intellectually curious, aware of your own emotions, and open to reexamining ideas and beliefs. A high score here can be an asset in recognizing new opportunities and alternative ways of doing things. Many entrepreneurial personalities, especially those who actually start their own companies, exhibit a high degree of Openness.

SECTION II

	A	B
Which statement has been more applicable to your career? (a) "If I can believe it, I can achieve it," or (b) "The only believable victories are probably the temporary and partial ones."		
If you had to organize your own daily schedule and calendar, you would (a) be fine; you're highly organized about most things, or (b) miss or be late for a lot of meetings.		
If you're forced to break a promise to your best friend, would you be more likely to say to yourself (a) "I'll either find a way to keep my promise eventually or make it up to him somehow," or (b) "Well, we're good friends; he'll understand."		
What you accomplish in your life defines who you are: (a) I agree, or (b) I disagree.		
Which statement best describes what you do when faced with a task you dislike? (a) "The sooner I get this out of the way, the sooner I won't have to think about it anymore," or (b) "I know I've got to do it sometime—just not now."		
When you use your intuition in making a decision, you (a) do so only after you've spent some time thinking through all the issues first, or (b) rely on your initial gut reaction, which usually proves to be the right one anyway.		
Total for Section II	____	____

Section II: Conscientiousness

Conscientiousness examines your ability to control impulses and plan to achieve your goals. If you had mostly As, you probably have a sense of your own ability to get things accomplished and control your own destiny. Your obligations to others are important to you. You probably are considered dependable, persistent, prudent, and tend to act and/or think in an organized, methodical way. If you are extremely high in Conscientiousness, you may even be a perfectionist and a workaholic. Finally, you may have a high desire for achievement and recognition. Scoring high on Conscientiousness indicates an aptitude for actually following through on an entrepreneurial idea.

If you had mostly Bs in this section, you tend to act on your impulses, sometimes without thinking things through. People may see you as spontaneous, flexible, and free-spirited; they may also see you as inconsistent, scattered, and unreliable. You may have long-term goals but be relaxed or even indifferent about pursuing or achieving them. You may also be easily distracted by a new or different goal, or procrastinate about the steps necessary to achieve it. Entrepreneurs who are low on Conscientiousness will need to find ways to provide themselves with some impulse control, focus, planning, and organization.

SECTION III

	A	B
When you meet someone whose company you enjoy, you are more apt to (a) invite them over to your house for a social engagement, or (b) wait for them to indicate an interest in getting together.		
After you've been to a party with a lot of other people, are you more likely to feel (a) energized, maybe even sorry to leave the party, or (b) tired and ready for some quiet time alone?		
When a meeting you're involved in but not responsible for seems to be drifting and ineffective, you (a) try to take charge and focus the discussion, or (b) wait to see if the discussion becomes more productive and something valuable will emerge.		

On vacation, would you prefer to spend more time (a) going, doing, and seeing as much as possible, or (b) relaxing, reading, and kicking back?		
If you were a car, would you prefer to be (a) a Ferrari Modena, racing from Paris to Dakar, or (b) a classic Bugatti, carefully tended and pampered by your owner?		
People often comment on your ability to create an atmosphere of joy and cheerfulness: (a) True, or (b) False?		
Total for Section III	_____	_____

Section III: Extroversion

Extroversion looks at how comfortable you are with actively seeking out and connecting with other people. If you had mostly As here, you enjoy socializing and talking with others. People see you as assertive, energetic, and high-spirited; you may even be considered the "life of the party" type. You enjoy being busy and feel restless if you're not. In general, you probably think of yourself as a pretty happy person much of the time. You tend to prefer excitement and stimulation to peace and quiet. Extroversion can be an asset for an entrepreneur who must constantly sell his or her product.

If you had mostly Bs, you probably tend to be somewhat low-key and quiet. This does not mean you dislike people or are antisocial. You simply don't need as much stimulation and excitement as an extrovert does, and are less likely to seek it on your own, though you may enjoy it if someone else initiates it. You have less difficulty being alone than others, and less need to dominate a conversation. When you do socialize, you probably prefer smaller groups. People may think of you as a bit reserved. Entrepreneurs with a low Extroversion score need to understand how to make sure that their reserve or lack of exuberance is not misinterpreted as unfriendliness or arrogance.

SECTION IV

	A	B
When working with a new client, do you tend to (a) go ahead and get started on the work based on a handshake, or (b) begin only once all contracts have been finalized and signed?		
If you had to reschedule a client meeting because something more important came up, would you be more likely to (a) be straightforward about why you have to cancel, or (b) give the client a flattering reason, even if it's only partly true?		
When colleagues come to you with a problem not of their own making, are you more likely to (a) enjoy doing what you can to help, saying, "We've all been there," or (b) help but secretly feel that they should be able to handle their own problems?		
If a group of your colleagues insisted on pursuing a plan you absolutely knew would create problems for your company, would you (a) quietly point out the problems but agree in advance that you'll do whatever everyone else wants, or (b) fight for your idea, even if it means some serious confrontation?		
When you've been successful at something, it's been mostly because (a) you've had a lot of help from others, great opportunities, and a little luck, or (b) you've worked harder and smarter than a lot of other people.		
When you watch a presenter stumble through harsh questioning from an audience, do you mentally (a) sympathize with the person, or (b) criticize them for being ill prepared?		
Total for Section IV	____	____

Section IV: Agreeableness

Agreeableness is connected to your ability to cooperate with other people. If you had mostly As here, harmonious relationships and getting along well with others are probably a high priority for you. All the Boy Scout virtues—helpfulness, generosity, the ability to compromise, the ability to trust and be trusted—are related to Agreeableness. A high score here means you're probably extremely well liked—a valuable trait. However, being overly agreeable can be just as problematic for an entrepreneur as not being agreeable enough. Too much Agreeableness can prevent an entrepreneur from defying popular opinion to pursue a vision, or making tough decisions, especially if they involve confrontation or conflict.

If you had mostly Bs here, you may have difficulty with compromise and getting along with others. You may frequently be suspicious of other people's motives or actions, and they may in turn see you as uncooperative and self-involved. You may hear yourself saying "Business is not a popularity contest" a lot. Being low on Agreeableness can help an entrepreneur fight for an unpopular idea or make tough calls, but it can also prevent seeing ways to achieve consensus and collaboration.

SECTION V

	A	B
When you make a decision, you tend to (a) make it quickly and move on, or (b) worry a lot about the worst-case scenario so you'll be prepared if it happens, and worry afterwards about the consequences.		
If you lost a competitive bid and found out that the client had given the winner inside information that wasn't available to you, would you be more likely to feel (a) glad you aren't going to do business with a dishonest client, or (b) angry and resentful that the bidding was unfair?		

	A	**B**
When it comes to having "the blues," you tend to (a) shake them off easily when they happen, which isn't often, or (b) lose energy, get discouraged, and have trouble getting yourself motivated again.		
You are (a) rarely nervous in social situations; you're not generally worried about the impression you make on others, or (b) very aware of what other people think about you, and conscious that others watch and evaluate you constantly.		
If you see something you love but aren't sure you can afford, you're more likely to (a) resist the craving until you're sure the purchase won't affect your other financial plans and dreams, or (b) go ahead and get it; you'll figure out later how you'll pay for it.		
When you're under stress, you (a) feel a weird sort of clarity and resolve; pressure often brings out the best in you, or (b) battle to fight off feelings of panic, confusion, and helplessness.		
Total for Section V	____	____

Section V: Neuroticism

Neuroticism measures how strongly and negatively you react to the stresses of life. If you had a lot of As in this section, your emotions tend to remain relatively stable; you don't tend to have wild mood swings. You may not always be happy or cheerful, but you don't tend to be overwhelmed if you occasionally feel depressed, anxious, or angry. You're less likely than others to worry constantly or suffer over your problems. Entrepreneurs who score low on Neuroticism have an advantage in not letting obstacles get them down.

If you had mostly Bs, you may have difficulty coping with day-to-day stress that other people seem to sail through. You may have strong emotional reactions to problems and take a long time to get over bad moods, anger, or hostility. You often feel anxious or depressed, and other people may see you as a worrier. Frequent, strong, persistent negative emotions and difficulty coping with them can leave you easily discouraged. An entrepreneur with a high degree of Neuroticism needs to understand how this trait can affect the ability to persist in creating or pursuing a vision.

WHAT YOUR ANSWERS MEAN FOR THINKING LIKE AN ENTREPRENEUR

None of these traits is an unmixed blessing. Depending on the situation, each can help, hurt, or simply be irrelevant. Even if you read the description of, say, Agreeableness and think it sounds like an admirable personality trait, it can also be problematic. Each one, taken to an extreme, can become a problem.

For example, Openness to Experience sounds like a great idea for an entrepreneur, right? But Openness without some balance of Conscientiousness can mean you leave a lot of things unfinished, distracted by whatever bright, new shiny idea crosses your path. Someone who is highly agreeable may automatically defer to others, unwilling to trust his or her own judgment. And Neuroticism may sound awful, but if you *never* feel anxiety, anger, or depression, you may seem a bit robotic to other people.

To understand how these traits can help you be successful, let's think about the role of a CEO. I believe there are various types of CEO. Some are what I call "builder CEOs." These are the folks who have the great idea, launch companies or divisions, shift those ol' paradigms, and try to change the world. Chances are a builder CEO would probably be high on Openness to Experience. Then there are the "maintenance CEOs." These are people whose strength is in brilliant execution rather than a novel strategy, and who are in established companies in relatively stable industries (if there is such a thing anymore). Their personality profile might be even stronger on Conscientiousness than a builder CEO's. There are "turnaround CEOs"; I would guess their traits are probably closer to those of the builder CEO, since they need to choose a new course for the enterprise.

Each can be successful at the right time in the right place—if there's a good match between personality and opportunity. A maintenance CEO in a company that really needs a builder CEO can leave the company trailing its competitors. A builder CEO can get so caught up in moving forward that the core business gets neglected. A turnaround CEO would probably get bored at a company that doesn't demand Herculean efforts to succeed.

Another thing to remember about your answers is that how you behave is affected not only by individual traits but by your combination of them and how your environment affects their expression. For example, let's say you feel angry much of the time—an important component of Neuroticism. If you're also highly agreeable, you may not express that anger because you want to avoid confrontation. Without a good dose of Agreeableness, someone who's highly conscientious may get too wedded to a rigid system and have difficulty accommodating other people's needs. And of course, behavior can be modified by adopting specific behaviors and mental attitudes; it's called learning (duh!).

The interactions remind me of the building blocks of chromosomes, which are organized in what are called "base pairs." The nucleotides A and T are always paired with each other; so are C and G. In the same way, the human expression of two combinations of personality traits seem to be especially powerful.

• *Openness/Conscientiousness:* A good balance between the two of these allows you to be receptive to new ideas, yet gives you the discipline to pursue a goal. I scored high on Openness, but I've always remembered—and lived by—something my dad said to me: "Tom, never start anything that you don't finish." That's the best advice he could have given me; it helped bring out my natural Conscientiousness.

• *Extroversion/Agreeableness:* Balancing these two gives you the energy that entrepreneurial thinking demands, but offsets it with the ability to work with others.

In each paired-up combination, one trait helps counteract the potential problems that a strong dose of the other trait can create. That's why I call these two combinations Power Pairs. Just as base pairs are the building blocks of our DNA, Power Pairs are the building blocks of success.

Entrepreneurial thinking can benefit from certain aspects of all four of these qualities. However, most people won't score equally highly on all of them. Knowing which ones affect you most powerfully helps you understand which ones you need to balance in another way. For example, many people who start their own businesses are high on Openness, but they need to partner with someone who can supply the Conscientiousness required for operational effectiveness.

The trait that presents the greatest challenges for thinking like an entrepreneur is Neuroticism. If you're naturally anxious, you may have difficulty taking risks. If you're easily upset and lack the ability to rebound from the punches life throws, you will have more difficulty persevering in the face of obstacles. And being easily overwhelmed by a negative outlook or emotions—for example, when a potential customer says "Not interested!"—makes it more difficult to stay on forward focus and spot new opportunities. If you scored high on Neuroticism, you may be saying to yourself about now, "Well, I should just give up; it's hopeless." Keep on reading. There are habits and structures you can develop for yourself that can help you tackle challenges that might otherwise swamp you.

GENES AND BEHAVIOR

Now what? What if you've taken the test and you don't like your results? If you scored low on Extroversion, does that mean you might as well give up and hide out in your one-hundred-square-foot noisy cubicle forever?

No way. Genes aren't fate. If genes were all there were to it, you could stop reading this book now. Even people with great genes can't be successful if they don't do something with what they've got. And great genes are no guarantee of success. No one ever got to the corner office by attaching a map of their DNA to their résumé. You have to know how to use your own combination to your best advantage.

The way a gene delivers its instructions is called its expression. A gene produces a result only when it gets expressed. How the gene is expressed determines how those genetic instructions get implemented. Events can interfere with or promote that expression.

Though it's not a formal scientific process, I like to think of personality traits as functioning in much the same way. How a personality trait gets expressed makes a difference in the impact it has on your ability to succeed. And just as there are things that can promote or interfere with genetic messages, so there are behaviors, attitudes, and techniques that can make the most of what you start out with. In upcoming chapters, we'll talk in more detail about those behaviors and attitudes. Using them to unlock the hidden power of your own set of personality traits can help you overcome the challenges we all face in thinking like entrepreneurs.

C H A P T E R   2

Imprinting Pleasure:

Creating An Addiction to Success

When I was a kid, one of my father's entrepreneurial ventures was buying and driving the local school bus. Every kid in Cascade, Maryland, rode to school on that bus, including me. My earliest taste of being an entrepreneur was sweeping out that bus every night from age ten until I graduated from high school. I got a quarter a week. It felt like big money at the time, especially in our part of the country. Every week I put that quarter into a brown manila envelope. When I was fifteen, I bought my first car. It was just a used 1950 four-door Plymouth—robin's-egg blue—but I was the only fifteen-year-old in my little hometown who had a car. I was so proud of it that I washed and waxed it at least once a week. I paid $175 for it, and every cent came from the 700 quarters I had saved up from cleaning out my dad's school bus.

People think that when we say something is "in our genes," that means it's carved in stone. Wrong. The way a gene works can be changed by other genes, timing, or even external factors or environmental influences. Here's an example. The temperature outside an incubating crocodile egg determines whether the croc will become a male or female, not the croc's chromosomes. Males are created at 34 to 36 degrees Centigrade, females at 26 to 30 degrees.[1] External factors affect how the genes that control sex get expressed—in other words, the way their instructions get carried out. Those messages are turned on and off or are distorted all the time.

In the same way, even if you've got entrepreneurial spirit in your genes, it will only get you so far. You may be at genetic risk for getting a disease, but it doesn't mean you necessarily will get it. And you may have certain genetic advantages, but unless you learn to unlock them, they may never develop to the fullest—or even get expressed at all. Certain behaviors help trigger your genetic predisposition (or improve your chances of beating it).

For example, perfect pitch, the ability to recognize a musical note without its being connected to anything else, seems to be inherited. It tends to run in families, and one study has even found a link with a specific gene. But unless a child gets music lessons by the time he or she is roughly six years old, the ability never gets developed. Something happens in that musical training that switches on the child's innate perfect pitch.[2] Without the training, the genetic ability is useless. A study of people with hostile-personality traits found that they are more likely to become dependent on nicotine than less hostile people.[3] However, if they never try cigarettes, their chances of becoming a chronic smoker drop to zero. If I hadn't had to be an entrepreneur at an early age, cleaning out that school bus every night, who knows whether I would have made the switch from cell biology to selling—even if I had the genes for it?

More and more studies are exploring the genetic component of addiction. Researchers have found that identical twins tend to have the same smoking habits. Multiple studies have linked addictive behavior to genes that affect levels of dopamine and serotonin in the brain.[4] Another example: Researchers have found that genes seem to affect how likely a heavy drinker is to relapse into alcoholism despite counseling and medication.[5] This kind of research reinforces a theory I've had for a long time: that we can become addicted to success—yes, addicted to success—by putting ourselves in situations that take advantage of our genetic assets.

Addiction to drugs or alcohol actually rewires the physical structure of our brains to crave the pleasure of a cigarette or a drink. I think we can also get rewired to crave success in much the same way. Achievement can give us feelings of pleasure that are just as strong as any drug. That pleasure creates connections in our brains that lead us to seek out and create even greater success. Success that's based on who we are genetically becomes a kind of perpetual-motion machine. Enjoying the pleasure that results from making a successful decision trains our instincts to function better the next time. And good instincts increase the chances that we'll succeed again.

Former Major League Baseball commissioner Peter Ueberroth learned about the pleasures of success as a kid when he used to go to local parks to play in pickup games:

> "I was always going to a different park, 'cause I went to eight different grammar schools in six different states. I'd go to the park to play, and there were always pickup games. You had to try to get along with the people so you'd get picked. I'd have the chance as a nine-year-old to bat against a thirteen-year-old, who would scare the pants off me and fire that ball faster than I could imagine and strike me out. I'd also as a nine-year-old get to bat against eight-year-olds, and I'd hit the ball very solid and I could have success. And I got a lot of chances to bat. On an average Saturday, I'd bat thirty times in a day against kids from fourteen to nine. Wow. That's a lot of experience; that's more than a Little Leaguer will get in a full season. . . . So you had lots of failure, you had lots of successes, you had fear. But you started to look forward to running down to that park so you could get picked. All of that prepares somebody for life. In my case I failed a lot and succeeded a few times. I liked succeeding better than failing, so I began to rely on myself rather than the excuses that were around me."

I think repeated exposure to success can make the same kind of permanent, but more useful, connections in the brain that a chemical addiction does. The longer you've smoked, the more your brain is wired to crave nicotine. The more we experience success, the more we train our brains both to crave it and to look for ways to create or recreate it. And we improve our odds of feeling that pleasure by using whatever genius is already in our genes.

NATURE FINDS NURTURE

I was born with a brain that's geared toward analyzing things. One of my earliest memories is of getting a chemistry set for Christmas. I loved to fool around with combining different formulae. Sometimes I would follow the guidebook that came with the kit, but usually I would just start combining and experimenting—often until fumes started rising out of my little glass beaker. I became known in my family as the scientist; my mother sometimes called me "the doctor." She used to say she could tell that I always had something going on in my head—always busy, always thinking. People began to treat me like the kid God sent to cure people's sicknesses. They began to assume I was smart. Because they assumed that, I liked doing things that made me smarter, such as chemistry.

Many of the direct effects of genes are obvious, such as having red hair or being six feet tall. But genes have indirect effects, too. They're trickier to prove, but they can be just as powerful as the direct ones. Let's say your genes gave you a beautiful face, athletic ability, or a love of figuring things out. People probably began to treat you a certain way because of your looks, your ability to run bases faster than anybody in the schoolyard, or your analytical tendencies. If your family sees you as "the outgoing one" or "the entrepreneurial one" because of some inborn personality traits, they're probably going to behave differently toward you than they do toward a brother or sister who is "the shy one" or "the slow one." And you begin to learn things about yourself and the world from their behavior.

My mother always painted me into a picture of success. She used to say, "Tom, I don't worry about you. You're going to be a millionaire someday." She treated me as a millionaire in the making because of my inborn habit of analyzing things and constantly figuring out how to make or acquire the things we couldn't afford. And because she treated me that way, those habits got reinforced—habits that helped me achieve her picture of me.

Genes also play another important role in creating early experiences of thinking like an entrepreneur. Let's say you have a genetic predisposition to seeking out novelty. Because it's in your genes, you'll tend to seek out situations in which novelty seeking thrives. Entrepreneurial endeavors might be one of them, but they could be anything that demands putting yourself in new and challenging situations. That means you're likely to get more experience with risk taking at an earlier age than someone without the "novelty-seeking" gene. That experience makes you even more confident and comfortable with taking still more risks—and the more you enjoy that, the more likely you are to do it again. You select what you're already genetically programmed to enjoy and be good at. Being good at it makes you want to do it some more. And doing more makes you even better at it.

Another example: If you're genetically outgoing, you'll have more experience at getting along with people than someone who's genetically shy. Shyness can lead someone to avoid people, so they get little experience at making friends. That lack of experience in turn can make them even more uncomfortable with other kids. Bingo—they become even more shy.[6]

Entrepreneurs are the same way. They're born with certain personality traits that let them experience success early. It doesn't have to be the proverbial lemonade stand (or cleaning school buses). It can be anything that takes advantage of their genetic assets. That success guides them into behaving in ways that help them be successful as adults. It helps "switch on" their genetic assets and develop an addiction to success.

When I was a kid, even though we had very little money, I felt fortunate. After all, my dad was not just the only school-bus driver but the local grocer, which meant I could have all the candy bars, potato chips, and Cokes I wanted. I might have had less money than other kids, but I often had more responsibility. In addition to sweeping out my dad's bus, I was captain of the patrolmen in grade school and a school-bus crossing guard. I felt important. I took care of my toys as though they were jewels; I still have my first baseball and baseball glove and some of my toy guns. One year for my birthday, my parents told me I could have either a motorized go-cart or an *Encyclopedia Britannica*. I chose the encyclopedia, and made my own go-cart by bartering with a friend for wheels and axles and using two wooden Coca-Cola crates from my dad's store for the front and rear end of my go-cart. I thought I'd look smarter with the books on my shelf. I remember being proud that I had figured out a way to have everything I wanted. It was an important early lesson for me in how I could achieve success—even if at that point success was nothing more than having *both* the go-cart and the encyclopedia. (I still have that set of 1960 *Britannicas* today.)

"I was always a responsible kid when I was young—maybe at too

young an age to be that responsible," says Vanguard founder John Bogle
Sr. "I was sort of a nerd, I suppose. I was always treasurer of everything
I touched." Another example of nature finding nurture was the contrarian instinct that helped him become a pioneer in selling mutual
funds directly to investors instead of through brokers. "I was always an
argumentative kid. I like to challenge existing ideas. Around the time
that the United Nations came into existence right after World War II, I
was at Blair Academy, and we had a peace group, a United Nations–
oriented group, and I had a group that I started called the Realist group.
We had debates about whether anything as idealistic as the UN would
work. I argued that it wouldn't . . . and history has not yet spoken
clearly on that point." Sounds like a contrarian to me! That spirit
helped bring him success in the investing world, he says: "The investment things that everybody's talking about—say, the new Internet
world—you better believe that if everybody's talking about it, it's not
going to happen."

From the time he was twelve, Home Depot co-founder Bernie Marcus worked and bought his own clothes. "I worked hard, but I kind of
enjoyed it. Whatever I did, I tried to do the very best I could. Whatever
I did, I always did it well enough that it paid off for me. When I started
out as a busboy and a waiter in the Borscht Belt circuit in the Catskills
and worked my way through college, I always ended up with the best
station. A lot of it had to do with my personality, the fact that I wasn't
a shrinking violet. . . . I always believed I was going to be successful. I
remember walking down the street when I was sixteen years old and
saying to one of my friends, 'Okay, I'm gonna be rich one day. I know
I am.' I had a lot of faith in myself."

These are only two examples of nature—Bogle's contrarian outlook,
Marcus's forthright personality—finding nurture in what they did. That
nurture, that experience, helped enhance their natural gifts.

CREATING AN ADDICTION TO SUCCESS

When Marcelo Claure was a little boy in Bolivia, he used to sell mar-
bles in the schoolyard; when his mother went to the market, he would
stay outside and sell cans of milk. Claure grew up to found Brightstar,

the second Hispanic company in the United States to break $1 billion in annual revenues. He has gone from selling cell phones out of the trunk of his car to becoming the largest reseller and distributor of cell phones in Latin America. He's planning to replicate his success in the Americas in India, China, Africa, and Eastern Europe—in other words, pretty much everywhere.

"We always realize that what we do doesn't have a destination. Once you achieve a goal—something you thought you could never get that result, that in life you couldn't believe you could get there—once you're at that point, you realize what you've got, and you set yourself up with another of these crazy, faraway goals. I guess we are never happy with what we have. We've got to continue to get more, from a financial, personal, and business perspective. . . . We're not going to be satisfied until we're the leaders in the world, and I guess once we become the leaders in the world, I don't know; I guess we'll want to do it again in some other industry."

Some people seem to be addicted to success. To some extent, addiction is in our genes as a species. Evolution designed our brains to make decisions that give us pleasure; if we didn't enjoy food, sex, and staying warm, we wouldn't have survived as a species. When someone enjoys puffing a cigarette, biting into chocolate, or drinking wine, his or her brain releases a chemical called dopamine. This neurotransmitter sends a message to the nervous system that says, in effect, "Hey, I like this!" It cues the limbic system—the part of the brain most closely linked to emotion—to want to experience that pleasure again. Even environments associated with that pleasure can trigger this sort of craving. Anyone who's ever stopped smoking can tell you that being around other smokers can trigger a desire for a cigarette.

These chemical reactions can start to affect our decision-making abilities. When a drug—nicotine or cocaine, for example—causes the limbic system to pump out too much dopamine over and over, the brain eventually changes physically. It loses its ability to produce dopamine and experience pleasure on its own, without that cigarette or drug. It needs more wine, more cigarettes, or more drugs to induce that dopamine-specific pleasure. Even worse, it also becomes unable to enjoy anything else. The cigarette or drug has hijacked the brain's ability to experience pleasure.

Some people seem to make that neurochemical connection more easily than others. One group of researchers found that by knocking out a particular gene, dubbed "Homer," they could turn mice into cocaine addicts.[7] A study of 688 twins found that smokers with a variation of the Epac gene were more likely to get hooked on nicotine.[8] Other studies have tagged genes governing the D2 dopamine receptor as likely culprits in promoting addictive behavior. Our genes seem to affect how quickly our body uses dopamine; the faster you metabolize it, the easier it is to become dependent on that cigarette.[9]

Addiction is a complex issue, of course, and science hasn't yet tackled the concept of addiction to success. But it's clear to me that some people's systems get wired to need constant hits of success. Their genes just seem to crave the pleasure that comes from new challenges. When they don't get it, they experience psychological withdrawal symptoms. We used to talk about people being Type A personalities. What if part of that Type A personality was the result of an addiction to success?

I've got what my wife says is a mild addiction to cars, and I think one reason is that they were associated with success for me as a kid. Because my dad somehow always managed to drive new, flashy cars—always Buicks, never a Ford or a Chevy—I felt rich even though we weren't. His car was his symbol of success. Behind it there really wasn't much, but the façade was shiny. I grew up wanting those trappings of success, too, but I wanted them to come from substance. I knew I had to work harder, smarter, be crafty but honest. I wanted to make a mark at every step and become a millionaire, just as my mom always said I would.

GETTING YOUR BRAIN REWIRED TO WIN

For born entrepreneurs, pleasure comes from winning. We get high on overcoming roadblocks. We may even begin to welcome them, because they're another chance to get our success highs. And that feeling gets developed early on.

Like many of the people in this book, Barry Gibbons had to overcome enormous hurdles as a child. His mother died when he was three; his father was a single parent in the industrial north of England. "It wasn't an easy time for me or my father. This is not a poverty thing, or 'log cabin to the White House.' I just felt outside the society I was in; I was in it but not of it. And there were a lot of barriers that [created for] me. I was really alienated for a long period." Not exactly what you'd call pleasure. And yet his brain must have gotten wired to relish the reward that came with taking on a challenge and winning—even if it wasn't much fun at the time.

"I can't say I basked in any great pleasure," says Gibbons, who shepherded the turnaround of Burger King in the 1990s. "I think what happened is, once you got over one hurdle, the jaw squared up even more, the teeth gritted even more. You realized that you could succeed. Challenges become addictive. It almost becomes like a weekly sports match. I was a competitive team sportsman—soccer—well into my thirties. I can't say I got great pleasure out of victory, but I got great pleasure out of realizing that it could be done and going for the next one."

For many successful people, obstacles seem to switch on whatever genetic assets we have. They let us learn about ourselves, about our ability to win and our behavior when we lose. My earliest understanding of what success feels like and how I could achieve it for myself in the world came from overcoming obstacles, such as a childhood that was short on anything beyond the necessities. I learned that the greatest pleasure often comes from succeeding at the toughest tasks. And I got hooked on it.

ARE YOU ADDICTED TO SUCCESS?

Do you constantly seek out new challenges?

Do you believe in your ability to get whatever you want?

Do you love what you do?

Do you sometimes say "I'm gonna show them"?

Do you get bored by routine?

Do you enjoy putting your skills to a test?

What really clinched my belief in the concept of being addicted to success was hearing about an experiment I think of as the "marathon mice" experiment. (I just can't seem to get away from those lab rats!) Researchers were trying to figure out why certain mice seemed to want to run longer and faster than others. They bred a strain of mice that craved running a lot more than ordinary ones and let them run as much as they wanted to for six days. On the seventh day, they kept some of the mice off the treadmill, and measured the activity of the Fos gene, which gets expressed in the brain in response to excitement. Researchers thought they'd see the most brain activity in mice who were allowed to run as long as they wanted to. To their surprise, the most brain activity showed up in the marathon mice that were *prevented* from running. Even more interesting was *where* the activity showed up: in the brain circuits involved with cravings and rewards such as food, sex, and drugs. The patterns resembled those of drug-addicted rats who were denied their fix of cocaine, morphine, alcohol, or nicotine.[10]

Just like those "marathon mice" seem to be addicted to running, entrepreneurial brains are hardwired to seek out the next opportunity to give themselves that "success high." But you have to get exposed to success to get addicted. The mice had been allowed to run for six days, covering more ground than their slower counterparts. Those six days were what helped get them hooked. For true entrepreneurs, not being able to tackle new challenges leaves them as frustrated as "marathon mice" prevented from running. People who get that experience early and do well at it begin to develop the habits and attitudes that let them experience the pleasure of success repeatedly.

I think the addiction to success that comes from overcoming obstacles begins very early to unlock the power of inherited personality traits. I think it also helps explain why the children of entrepreneurs are more likely to become entrepreneurs. I think it's not just that they're exposed to the entrepreneurial life early. It's that they develop an early addiction to the psychological rewards of overcoming a challenge. An entrepreneurial family may be more likely to create challenges that are entrepreneurial, but addiction to success can come from overcoming any kind of challenge.

DEVELOPING SUCCESS PROMOTERS

Creating addiction to success requires that we learn how to "switch on" our genetic assets. There is a part of each gene that basically tells the rest of the gene what to do. In science lingo, it "promotes" how that gene gets expressed, how it functions; it's sort of a "gene of genes." These so-called promoters act much like a dimmer switch on a light, cranking up or turning down genetic activity. That action can be pretty powerful. Take, for example, an experiment done with a type of rodent called a vole. By inserting a specific promoter into the genes of meadow voles, scientists have transformed promiscuous rodents into more selective, monogamous romantic partners.[11]

Certain attitudes and habits do the same thing for our inherited traits and abilities. I call these attitudes and habits the Success Promoter genes. Like biological promoters, they either help us take advantage of entrepreneurial personality traits we're born with or buffer the impact of less advantageous ones. Without them, all the potential in the world can't make you into a successful entrepreneur. They're the behaviors that nourish entrepreneurial thinking; they help you create a vision for yourself, take risks to achieve it, spot opportunity, and make better decisions.

THE SUCCESS PROMOTERS

★ The "Early Scar Tissue" gene

★ The "Picture-Painting" gene

★ The "Forward Focus" gene

★ The "Seeing Around Corners" gene

★ The "Cold Call" gene

★ The "Whac-A-Mole" gene

★ The "POHEC" gene

★ The "Nice Guy" gene

In biology, promoters help drive evolution. They create large-scale changes in entire species from a relatively small number of genes. (Did you know plants actually have more genes than humans do?) Computer code is generated from two numbers: 1 and 0. Everything after that depends on how the 1s and 0s are combined. Genes function in much the same way with four letters: ACTG. Using them, promoters can create an incredible number of variations in how every single one of our 20,000 to 30,000 genes works. As the variations that help us survive eventually add up and get passed on, the species evolves.

In the same way, Success Promoters create evolutionary change in an individual. They take genetic raw material and use it to create a successful person.

SUCCESS PROMOTER: THE "EARLY SCAR TISSUE" GENE

We all know people who have been hit by adversity and simply implode, like a building being destroyed from within. Still others muddle along all their lives, not really miserable but never really able to make themselves happy, either. And then there are those who seem to succeed against all odds, despite obstacles that would seem to be insurmountable. Early success at overcoming obstacles may serve as one Success Promoter. I have a friend who likes to hike in the mountains. He truly believes that the more you have to struggle to get to the top, the more you enjoy the view. It's the same idea.

Ueberroth has a great phrase for it: "creating scar tissue." From attending eight different elementary schools, he learned how he could succeed despite constantly being the "new kid":

> "You meet the same people, whether you're in an inner-city Chicago downtown school or a Davenport, Iowa, country school. You meet the class bully, and then you meet the people who are trailing the class bully. Eventually they would goad the bully into picking a fight with you. By the time you go to the third school, you have enough brains that you say, 'I'm the new kid, I'm gonna find this guy, and the first rumor I hear that the bully's going to beat me up, I'm going to find him alone and say, "Everyone says you have to beat me up, and you probably can. I'm sure you can. But if you're going to have your friends force you into doing it, why don't you do it now? It's just the two of us and we'll get it over with—if you have to do what people

tell you to do.' ' And the result is, he says, 'No. Nobody's going to tell me what to do.' So the next time he's encouraged to go beat up the new kid, the other kids who have encouraged that get his wrath and are wondering what the heck happened this time. You learn [that tactic is] probably a good thing to do, so you take that and lay that on life."

When I heard him tell that story, it seemed clear to me that those experiences had served as promoters to crank up a profound inborn talent for understanding how to motivate other people. A lot of us have been victims of bullies—schoolyard or otherwise—but how many understood at that early age the smart way to prevent it from happening the next time? However, Ueberroth says, the same kind of setbacks can be a much bigger problem for someone who first learns about them later in life. "[How about when] you've graduated from graduate school and you're in your new job and everything's going along fairly well and there's the bully. And it's not fair. And you don't know what to do. That first experience shatters people, but the scar tissues don't heal over so quickly then."

Ueberroth's story also reminds me of how important timing is to a promoter's impact on a gene. A promoter controls when the gene delivers its instructions, and for how long. Our genes affect our tendency to have twins. However, the way identical twins develop depends on when a promoter tells the fertilized egg to divide. If it happens in the first four days, each twin gets its own separate placenta and amniotic sac, and they are usually healthy. If the egg splits eight to twelve days after fertilization, the twins share one amniotic sac, and their umbilical cords often get tangled. Splits after the twelfth day seem to produce conjoined twins who share organs and limbs.[12]

Timing seems to be important with Success Promoters, too. Early experiences with success at overcoming obstacles begin to teach you about yourself—what helps you beat another kid at checkers, fight back against an abusive parent, or persuade somebody else to do something. By calling on your genetic assets and helping you learn what those assets are, they may literally begin in your childhood to wire your brain for success.

Teenagers may be more sensitive to addictive drugs than either adults or newborns, and therefore more likely to get addicted. Research with adolescent mice has demonstrated that chronic exposure to drugs actually changes the level of a certain protein in the brain, most dramatically in teens.[13] Those molecular changes may affect how genes get expressed in creating associations and patterns in the brain. I think early experiences such as Ueberroth's have the same effect in a more positive way. They addict us early on to the feeling of success and whatever produces it for each of us.

Positive experiences also can create an addiction to success. Real estate magnate Sam Zell remembers being assigned as a young boy to speak at a Friday night religious service: "I sat down, wrote the speech, and I got up and I gave it. I had the room . . . you could hear a pin drop. That was the first time I recognized that I could command other people. That was the educational childhood experience that had enormous implications for me. It's very reinforcing, especially if you think you have unique talents and the rest of the world doesn't necessarily recognize them." The Motley Fool's David Gardner learned about success from doing well at typical school activities. That feeling of achievement was helped by attending a school with only eighty people in his senior class: "It was easier to be a starter on the football team." The key seems to be not *what* produces the feeling of success, but the experience itself—understanding what it is about you that produces the results you want.

PRACTICING SUCCESS

Unlike genes, Success Promoters take practice. Maybe you didn't get a head start from inheriting great genetic raw material or learning early about the experience of success. Success Promoters can help you figure out strategies that let you work with what you've got. If you're not a natural risk taker, for example, maybe you take risk in increments. Maybe you make contingency plans six ways from Sunday. Or maybe you simply create a life for yourself that minimizes risk as much as possible. After all, nobody said not thinking like an entrepreneur makes you a bad person. But it doesn't help you cope with the way the world works now—and besides, it's just not as much *fun*.

To develop an addiction to success, you have to ingrain the Success Promoter habits in ways that suit you. Practicing the Success Promoters helps you understand what you can count on yourself for, and how you'll naturally react in a given situation. That lets you develop career strategies and business practices that work for you. If you inherited a tendency to look on the dark side of life, you may have to adopt habits that help you overcome it. And if you've got a natural optimism, you need to understand how to balance that so that it doesn't leave you starting ventures without finishing them.

Knowing how to create an addiction to success is especially important for business managers, who are responsible for the development and success of their employees. Managers who understand which personality traits are most resistant to change will have less difficulty matching people and responsibilities.

If you haven't yet developed an addiction to success, START NOW! Unless you've really tested whatever genetic assets you've got, you may not know what you're capable of. In 1999, researchers at Princeton, MIT, and Washington University gave young mice extra copies of the NR2B gene to soup up their ability to learn new things. The "Doogie Howser" mice (named after a precocious teenage television M.D.) beat the pants off of other mice at adapting to new environments. They also remembered what they learned better than non-Doogie mice. However—and this is the important part—the gene didn't start working until the mice were actually tested by putting them into a new situation.[14]

You may have a genetic predisposition to becoming addicted to success. You may not. But how will you know unless you constantly test yourself? How will you know what you can handle—and how much *more* you can handle? Using your genetic assets as a guide increases your chance of overcoming whatever challenges you face. And using the Success Promoters in the following chapters will help start to rewire your brain to recognize, remember, and crave that feeling of success.

The Challenge of Defining the Future: Painting an Evolving Picture for Yourself

In April 1975, two young girls stepped off the plane from war-torn South Vietnam. With only her little sister to accompany her, TiTi Tran had come to the United States to try to make a new life for herself and her little sister. She had her work cut out for her. She knew no one here. She had no money, no friends. She got a full-time job as a computer programmer and went to school at night. In her heart, she knew all along that she wanted to start her own business. "I went to school to get my master's degree so that when I became a CEO, I would look good. I would have the credentials, I would have the experience. . . . No obstacle was going to stop me. No money problems, I don't care how bad. No time problem. I gave up a lot of things.

"I always had that yearning desire to do something big. I didn't know what it was at that time, but I just had this thing nagging inside and an image hanging over my head that I wanted to be somebody. I have tremendous, tremendous energy. In Vietnam I had worked with my mom in her little deli at age nine. So I had already dealt with difficult people, people who didn't pay bills. I had to get her inventory and help her in the kitchen. On top of that I had to baby-sit three younger siblings. I was like almost twice my age. You combine that tremendous energy to learn more, to do more, and wanting to be somebody, and there was born an entrepreneur."

TranTech, the company she founded in 1991, has won numerous awards as one of the leading minority-owned government contractors. The former refugee, now TiTi Tran McNeill, has been named an Entrepreneur of the Year by Ernst & Young. "I never felt a moment in my life 'Oh, this is too tough, I'm going to give up and forget about it,'" she says. "I kept going at it, going at it. I have a piece of rock on my desk that says Never Never Quit. My friends said to me, 'Life is too short; you need to stop and smell the roses.' They didn't see that there were only three things in my mind: I want to succeed. I must succeed. I will succeed. I only have one life to live and I need to do something with it while I'm still alive."

GENES, AMBITION, AND CURIOSITY

You can be smart. You can be ambitious. But there's something that goes beyond either of those things. It's something intangible that marks people who are driven not only to become successful but to move from success to success. It's a drive to do more, to want more, to try more. I've always known I had it; so do the other people in this book. It's something that can't be explained by family, environment, or experience. It seems to be built into people's DNA. Many are aware from an early age that they are somehow different. Others usually recognize it, too. And I think that difference starts at the level of our genes.

Before you can dare, you have to dream. Some people seem to be able from an early age to dream a future for themselves that's better than what they've got, and then pursue it wholeheartedly. How can adversity "switch on" some people's determination to succeed yet cause others simply to implode?

A couple of studies seem to confirm that some children are better at rising above their circumstances than others. One study looked at the criminal records of roughly 1,000 men born in Dunedin, New Zealand, to families of similar socioeconomic and racial backgrounds. Some of the men had been abused as children. Not surprisingly, many of those had histories of violence and trouble with the law. However, the study also found that others among the abused youngsters had grown up relatively trouble free. The researchers found that the law-abiding adults had a particular variation of the MAO-A gene; it seemed to give them some protection from their circumstances. On the other hand, abused children who had a different variation of the MAO-A gene committed four times the number of violent crimes as abused children without it. The connection raises the possibility that the good form of the MAO-A gene may have a role in helping children survive their disadvantages, while abuse may help "switch on" a genetic predisposition to criminal behavior.[1]

Another study of more than 1,000 five-year-old twins raised in poverty also sees a link between genes and resilience. Identical twins, who share the same genes, were more alike in how well they performed on intelligence and behavioral tests than fraternal twins, who don't. But how well the parents nurtured the children also played an important role; the mother's warmth and whether she was active in helping the child develop was critical.[2] A nurturing environment clearly is vital, but genes may help explain why some people seem to survive a bad one better than others.

An inborn curiosity also helps people dare to dream. There's a story about Thomas Edison that says a lot about thinking like an entrepreneur. When Edison was asked to sign a guest register, he entered his name and address. Then he came to a column that asked "Interested in?" The great inventor is said to have written: "Everything."[3]

Curiosity lets you do more than cope with change. It can help you anticipate it. An entrepreneur has to deal with a lot of challenges all the time. Someone whose mind can go in a lot of different directions is more prepared to deal with the myriad twists and turns that can hit in a single day than someone who is more one-dimensional. Curiosity also does more than help you deal with today's challenges. It allows you to say, "This is where we are today, but where is my company (or my client) going to be in one year? Two years? Five years? What is the brand going to be? Who might the competitors be? What will the marketplace look like?"

I'm sure you know people whose curiosity seems to be in their DNA. They'll take something apart just to see how it works. When they think about going on vacation, they see themselves exploring the Sierra Nevada, not lounging around the backyard. They're the first to check out the latest controversial movie or try an unfamiliar cuisine. They love to explore new ideas. They're the early adopters that technology companies fall all over themselves to recruit as users. They're always asking, "What if?" They don't manage change; they lead it by seeing tomorrow today.

Sam Wyly is not only one of the country's most successful entrepreneurs, he may well be one of its most diverse. What do a software company, Bonanza Steakhouse, the Michael's arts and crafts retail chain, Green Mountain Energy, a telecom company, a hedge fund, and a silver-mining company have in common? Not much—except that they've all been founded or led by Sam Wyly.

Curiosity and Openness to Experience are part of Wyly's DNA. "I never sat down and said, 'I'll start more than one business,'" Wyly says. "Everything was done one at a time based on its own individual makeup. Partly, I'm like an artist, a painter, a writer, or a creative person in some other area. I enjoy the creative aspects of entrepreneurship, both the analysis and the synthesis of opportunities. It's sort of the intellectual challenge, the entrepreneurial game I play, if you will. It's basically something I enjoy. For me work is fun."

Wyly comes by his Openness to Experience naturally.

"My mom Flora was courageous enough to go to her small-town Louisiana banker to borrow enough money to go to New York City to study dancing in 1929 and come back home and form the Flora Evans School of Dance. She was also the first woman to serves as women's warden at the Angola State Penitentiary in Louisiana. My mother and dad were born entrepreneurs. They farmed a cotton plantation. My forebear grandmas and grandpas were in the Silicon Valley of the 1850s, which was the black land along the Mississippi River. They were among the top cotton producers in 1860 when the Civil War came. We had to struggle with the tag ends of the Great Depression. Trying to hold on to the land, they quit farming to take cash-paying jobs to pay down debts and save money and ultimately buy the *Delhi Dispatch*, a weekly newspaper in Delhi, [pronounced "Del-High"] Louisiana. My seventh-grade-and-up years were spent with my parents running this small business, which was a newspaper. It was a very small town based on cotton farming and was becoming an oil-patch town because recent wildcat drilling had discovered the Delhi Field, the largest discovery in the state up to that time. They had the Western Union telegraph franchise and they also had an insurance agency."

Wyly's instinctive curiosity may have been "switched on" by his family's migrating to each new opportunity: "We would move to new places where I had to adjust to new sets of people, new sets of circumstances where I left one set of people relationships and entered another. Even though I had a sense of family and a sense of self that stayed with me everywhere, I was always the new kid in town. I got very okay with being *in* the crowd, but not of it. I was used to being separate in my own thoughts, to never needing other people as a sense of security, and not being overly bothered by what other people said or thought.

"I vividly remember lying awake one night in my freshman dorm bunk when I was running for class president. I was troubled about bad-mouthing of me from the opposing camp. Thinking it through, I finally concluded that all I could do was to speak or take action in accordance with my own highest standards of what's right. Having done that, I must simply hold myself above being made uncomfortable by negative thoughts coming from elsewhere. Then I slept serenely."

He took the first computer science course ever offered at the University of Michigan ("Nobody knew what to call it. They hadn't invented the term 'computer science.' The class was called 'statistics' for lack of any other bucket to put it in. No business-school professors could teach it, so an engineering-school fellow taught it, which had the extra dividend of helping me learn how engineers had a different perspective than accountants or marketers.") He's also an avid reader, particularly about history. And his business life is about as diverse as it gets. Sam Wyly has built an empire in part by being steeped in the Big 5 inherited personality trait of Openness to Experience.

If you scored high on Openness to Experience (Section I) of the Entrepreneurial Personality Quiz in Chapter 1, you've got a head start in being able to create an ever-evolving vision that can help guide your decisions, keep you on forward focus, and make you more successful. To understand why, let's look at what makes up the trait of Openness—and of people who are able to dream big:

• *Imagination.* To borrow a phrase, this is the ability to "dream of things that never were and ask 'Why not?'" It lets you envision something that doesn't yet exist.

• *Attunement to aesthetics.* Linked to intellectual curiosity is an awareness of and appreciation for aesthetics and the experience of beauty, whether artistic or natural. Such appreciation can help you make unusual connections that can lead to more creative ideas.

- *Awareness and expression of emotion.* People who are open to experience tend to be aware of their own thought processes and comfortable with feeling emotion. How they handle that emotion may depend on other factors, but they aren't closed off from their own feelings.
- *Action/adventure orientation.* Openness often means seeking out experiences—especially new experiences—for their own sake, not just as a means to an end. This tendency promotes a love of novelty and comfort with risk taking.
- *Comfort with abstraction and ideas.* An interest in ideas and intellectual activity—whether that means business concepts, brain teasers, or riddles—can help with making a case for something or debating a theoretical question.
- *A tendency to question conventional values and wisdom.* Openness to Experience sometimes means bending or even breaking the rules. It lets you be comfortable with ambiguity and a certain amount of messiness; you don't always need things spelled out in black and white.

THE VOICES OF OPENNESS TO EXPERIENCE

	LOW OPENNESS	HIGH OPENNESS
Imagination/fantasy	"You're crazy. Show me some historical data that proves it."	"I'm betting the market will look entirely different five years from now. Here's how I see it. . . ."
Attunement to aesthetics	"Aesthetics, schmaesthetics. All I need is something with the prices on it."	"I'm no expert on brochures, but the design's too cluttered, the logo's too small, and the colors stink."
Action/adventure orientation	"How safe is it?"	"I don't know if it will work out, but it'll be a hell of a ride either way."

	LOW OPENNESS	**HIGH OPENNESS**
Awareness and expression of emotion	"I never get angry, dammit. Where's my Tagamet?"	"I'm really angry about not getting that account. This one really hurt to lose, but I know there will be another account."
Comfort with abstraction and ideas	"Don't give me some pie-in-the-sky theory. All I want is the numbers."	"Let me explain the idea behind this, and why it makes a difference in your strategy."
Comfort with questioning conventional values and wisdom	"Just follow the procedures manual."	"Do whatever it takes to satisfy the customer's real needs."

It's easy to see why people who are very open to experience have a head start on "the vision thing." They don't just think outside the box; they don't know the box exists. Looking into the future, imagining a career or role that doesn't exist now, being willing to experiment with trying new things, being sensitive to how you react emotionally to events, being comfortable with proving conventional wisdom wrong—all of these can help you paint a picture of a future for yourself that may look nothing like your present.

As I said earlier, these aspects of your personality are highly influenced by your genes, but they don't function like light switches. They're not either on or off. They're more like dimmers that slide up or down, gradually increasing or lowering the brightness level. Each of us falls somewhere on a sliding scale between having a lot of, say, Openness to Experience and not much at all. Even if you score high overall in terms of your Openness to Experience, you may score high on some of its aspects and low on others. For example, the arts don't do much for me, but I enjoy debating ideas.

SUCCESS PROMOTER: THE "PICTURE-PAINTING" GENE

Successful people may have something extra in their DNA, but they aren't born fully grown. Entrepreneurs don't usually show up in the delivery room yelling, "I smell opportunity here!" In fact, their careers often aren't very linear at all. Their progress can resemble a pinball bouncing from success to success; you know it's going to rack up a big score, but you can't be sure exactly which bumpers it's going to light up and how many points it will score with each one.

What successful people usually do have is a sense that they want to do something great—no, that they will *be* something great—or at least unique. Their Openness to Experience lets them find the right opportunity to live into that picture of greatness. A friend tells a story about what his schoolteacher mother used to say to condemn a student who was misbehaving: "He's just trying to be different." In the eyes of a Southern mother in the 1950s, "being different" was definitely not a good thing; it meant you were an early prototype for Bart Simpson. But for entrepreneurs, "just trying to be different" is where it often starts out.

Having a vision, even if it's a short-term vision, is the cornerstone of all the Success Promoters. It can help "switch on" an innate Openness to Experience and makes it useful by keeping it channeled toward what you really want. I have always had strong goals and ambitions, even though they've evolved from one venture to the next. So has Sam Wyly; so have most entrepreneurs. Many of them, myself included, will say they couldn't initially have envisioned what they have achieved. Yet they always knew they would succeed, and devoted themselves wholeheartedly to the vision they were pursuing at the time.

The greater your level of inherited Openness, the more instinctively you'll see opportunities to evolve in your career. I like to think of it as painting a picture of who and how you want to be in the world. Painting that picture for yourself and seeing yourself in it shows you what you need to do to live into that picture, to make it a reality. Twenty years ago, I wanted a BMW 320i. I could see myself driving one—and eventually I bought it. It wasn't a complete vision by any means, but it was a great motivator.

If you're low on Openness, you have even greater need of an organizing vision. It can help you see possibilities for personal evolution that you might not otherwise notice. To understand how this works, think about the last time you wanted to buy a new car and had your heart set on a particular model. Chances are you began noticing that model on the road every time you turned around. When I wanted that BMW, it seemed like every other car I saw was a 320i. It's not that there were suddenly more of them on the road; my desire simply made me notice them more. In the same way, your desire helps focus your attention on your vision.

That picture needs to be compelling enough personally to power you past the obstacles that pop up as you move forward. Remember, thinking like an entrepreneur means watching the highway instead of the rearview mirror. When you find your right calling, you're pulled into what you can be with a magnetic force. That's the picture you need to paint of yourself—for yourself. And again, it doesn't need to have a ten- or twenty-year time horizon; it just needs to be a picture that keeps you moving forward.

The part that often gives people trouble is the need to fit that vision to who you are. It's not enough to create a vision of the future you desire. You can paint any picture you want, but if that picture isn't right for you, you'll never achieve the kind of success that's possible when you're fueled by your inborn personality, skills, and instincts. Those attributes have the greatest chance of producing your addiction to success.

If your vision ignores who you are, or if it's someone else's vision, one of two things will happen. Either you'll be successful but miserable, or you'll reach a point at which you look around and say, "What happened? Why haven't I gone farther?" Understanding and using who you are lets you know whether you would actually feel comfortable in the role you're envisioning for yourself. It helps you set your own agenda and strategy instead of letting others set it for you.

MARKERS FOR THE "PICTURE-PAINTING" GENE

- You know why you want to be successful.
- You can envision yourself in a new role that stretches you but still aligns with your DNA.
- You understand what personality traits let you be comfortable in each new picture of yourself.
- You are comfortable with a nonlinear, nontraditional career path.
- You embrace change instead of fighting it.
- You know whether you are motivated more by seeking out pleasure or avoiding pain.
- You actively seek out new experiences.

In my case, once I began to imagine myself as something other than a cell biologist, I began a lifelong process of painting pictures for myself. Each picture showed me what the next step in my career could be, why that picture felt right for me, and what I needed to do to live into it. I can't say that I knew as a newly minted pharmaceutical rep that I would become a CEO in a Fortune 500 company. What I did have was a good vision of how my abilities could create the next steps in a path to success that would suit me. Each step of my evolution from cell biologist to sales to marketing executive to agency owner to CEO has been a new picture for me.

Developing a vision that suits you and being able to experience it fully is a key Success Promoter. But what if you think your supply of Openness tends to run pretty low? There are things you can do to jump-start your entrepreneurial thinking in this area. To paint a picture of yourself that can guide your next steps into your future, you need to ask yourself two key questions:

- Why do you want what you want?
- Are you comfortable—really comfortable—in that picture?

Even if you're off the charts on Openness, you still need to under-stand your answers to these questions. Those answers will probably evolve over time, especially if you're one of those novelty-seeking, in-tellectually curious, highly open people, but you need a starting point. Answering each question requires a focus on the future—whether that future is two years away or twenty. The answers need to be vivid and clear so that your image of the future is just as real and important to you as anything in the past—and just as real as all the problems that will try to blot out that picture.

WHY DO YOU WANT WHAT YOU WANT?

It's not enough to want to be successful. Let's face it. If just wanting to be successful made it so, you probably wouldn't be reading this book. For that matter, you wouldn't need to read any book. You'd just want it and bing! The Career Fairy would sprinkle success dust over your bank account. You'd have it made.

You need to answer the question "What does success *feel* like for me?" Ask successful entrepreneurs what, as children, they wanted to be when they grew up, what their vision of themselves as adults looked like. Very few will say, "Why, I wanted to be an entrepreneur, of course!" What they usually do know is (1) that they want to be some-thing special, and (2) *why* that's important for them. They know the psychological and financial payoffs they want, and the inner hungers that having those things will answer.

In my case, a big motivator was being able to protect and provide for my mother, to make her life more comfortable. As a kid, I remem-ber overhearing a discussion between my mother and my father over what they would get me for Christmas that year. All of my friends had toy guns, and I wanted one desperately. My mother wanted to buy it for me; my father argued that we couldn't afford it. It cost all of $1.50. I grew up wanting not just financial security but the ability to provide for myself and the people I loved anything I possibly could. For me, suc-cess has always meant more than just not having to struggle to put food on the table. It has meant being able to provide my loved ones with the best of what life had to offer. I never wanted to be up in the middle of the night, wondering whether I could afford to buy my son a $1.50 toy gun for Christmas.

Once I was in graduate school, it became even more clear that financial security was an important motivator for me. As a researcher, I had a fellowship that paid $333.33 a month. For someone who had been used to earning quarters by mowing lawns and cleaning out the school bus, that seemed like a lot of money at the time. But subtracting $255 a month for rent didn't leave a lot for anything else, including food. My wife, Pam, was going to school during the day and working the night shift at McDonald's to help make ends meet, but it was still personally painful.

You've heard the expression "We counted our pennies"? Well, we literally did. One Friday night, Pam and I were both exhausted from a long week and wanted to go out for pizza. We emptied out our pockets on the living room floor and counted every last bit of change around our apartment to see if we had enough to get not just pizza but a *salad* too! Then it became a question of whether we could afford to have olives (!) on the salad. At that point, I said, "Something's got to change. I've gotta get out of here." It didn't seem fair to either of us to continue on a path that meant sweating for a long, long time over whether we could afford olives on a salad. It was my parents' toy-gun dilemma all over again.

I was ready to paint some kind of new picture for myself, and I can't give Pam enough credit for supporting me in that evolution of my vision for myself. She made clear that if I decided to continue my studies, she would support that, too. Her support freed me to pursue whatever vision suited me best. She understood why I wanted what I wanted.

Herman Cain feels strongly that he shares his desire for success and his appetite for risk with his dad. But there was an enormous difference in why they wanted what they wanted.

"My father's definition of success was different from mine. He walked off a farm at age eighteen with just the clothes on his back. His definition of success was making enough money for his family to live comfortably, help his sons get a little more education than he had, and having enough money so that my mother wouldn't be left with nothing if anything should happen to him. He had zero financial equity, zero wealth. His focus was always on how he could create some financial security. His definition of success was not becoming a millionaire or a jillionaire; he wanted to make sure his wife would not be left with nothing, or that they would not be in poverty in his old age.

"My definition of success revolved around a certain amount of financial security, not just to ensure that the basic necessities were taken care of, but also that certain discretionary things were available, like being able to take a real vacation. My father was not going to spend his security money on a vacation. I wanted to do things like learn how to play golf, travel, have a comfortable home, provide for my kids to go to school, have more leisure time than my dad.

"At one point he worked three jobs to jump-start his quest for success; he was passionate about achieving that. After I got out of college, I didn't work three jobs; I worked a lot of hours on one job. But I wanted an additional layer of what I call success. The thing that was common was our desire for success and our appetite for risk.

"To say that if you have the DNA called passion you'll be successful is not enough. It has to be your definition of success in order for you to be passionate about it. If you don't have the passion to achieve it, I don't care what your DNA is; you won't achieve it. And if you have the passion but don't know what your dream is, you aren't going to achieve it, either."

Developing a vision is especially tricky when the rug keeps getting pulled out from under entire professions and industries. That's why your personal definition of success is so important. It gives you a target, but it leaves you lots of options for how to reach it. Your dream, your passion for it, and your DNA must be aligned in perfect synchronicity.

Even though she cried "day and night" after coming here alone from Peru, Victoria Chacon knows precisely why she came to this country, worked two jobs, and then launched three separate companies: love of her family.

"Many, many times, like a lot of immigrants, I'd find myself asking, 'What am I doing here? Maybe over there I don't have work, but at least I have my family. My whole world is there. What am I doing here?' But at the same time, later I was thinking, 'The only way my son has to find something there is if I'm still here, so I should keep working hard.' Because of the love I feel for them I need this. There were no options. I had to just keep moving ahead, thinking always on them. At one point, if you love someone, you aren't first anymore; they are. They were for me. I'd ask myself, 'If I go back, I might feel better, but what is going to happen with my son, with my family? Who's going to give them the opportunity to have a better life? I'm their only choice, so I don't have any excuses to go back.' "

Chacon's son is now attending Georgia State; her sister and two daughters also are here. "I feel very happy, very grateful, because they are living here. That was my commitment: to provide them a better lifestyle. At this point I can say I did."

ENTREPRENEURIAL MOTIVATORS

You may have all of the following needs; you may have only one or two. Whatever the case, you need to make sure you understand the relative importance of each one for you. Those rankings may change over time, but that's less important than having a basis from which to create your vision.

- Freedom to explore
- Financial security
- A lifestyle you enjoy
- Power or influence over others and events
- Control over your own destiny
- Sheer creativity
- Excitement and freedom from boredom

Your vision has to be connected to your emotions, to what you want and need. (This is another reason Openness to Experience is important; it helps you be aware of your own feelings.) Even if your motivation is simply making big boatloads of money, you need to know what having all that money represents to you. Is it freedom from fear? Is it the envy of others? Is it the ability to get others to love you? Whether those motivations seem admirable or not, you need to be brutally honest with yourself about what they are. Without that emotional connection, the vision won't power your actions. With any enterprise, whether it's starting a business or chairing a community project, you're going to bump up against lots of obstacles. Your mind can get you over the obstacles you'll face, but your heart is what will make you *want* to get over them—and make your gut churn until you do it.

By the way, this vision isn't a static thing. You need to redefine it constantly. Don't just ask what success looks like as an end point. Ask, "What does success look like in my current role?" Challenge yourself to think about the next step. You need to be looking constantly for your next success. Ask yourself, "When I succeed here, what opens up for me?" You won't necessarily know what this success will lead to. However, you should definitely be aware of what new pictures of yourself become available to you as a result of it—and which ones seem most attractive.

SEEING YOURSELF IN YOUR PICTURE

When forensic scientists do tests to compare two samples of DNA, they overlay a transparent diagram of each of the twenty-three chromosomes onto a diagram of the twenty-three chromosomes of the second sample. If the two patterns align, they've got a match. In the same way, you need to overlay the DNA of your vision—all the things you've imagined that would be needed to see yourself in that picture—with your own DNA. The demands of the career you overlay on your personality traits need to line up with who you are.

Well-known children's author Maurice Sendak tells a story that illustrates the value of matching one's vision to one's own strengths. He had gotten a contract to write and illustrate a book called *Where the Wild Horses Are*. However, when he sat down to do the book, he ran into trouble. He discovered he couldn't draw horses.

He went to his editor and said, "I can't do this book. I can't draw horses." Irritated, his editor asked, "Well, what can you draw?" Sendak replied, "I can draw . . . things." The "things" he had in mind were goblin-like creatures who reminded him of his aunts and uncles. And that was how the book became the best-selling *Where the Wild Things Are.*[4]

Simply painting a picture of who you want to be isn't enough. You need to try on that picture mentally to see if you're comfortable in it. The original vision for Sendak's book got shaped to take advantage of his own abilities. You don't want to paint a Picasso if your style is more like Renoir. If you feel as though you fit into the puzzle—if your answers feel right and natural—then the picture may be right for you. That doesn't mean you have all the skills or knowledge you need to do the job. It just means that, taking into account your genetic personality traits and what you've made of them so far, you can see yourself living in that role, meeting its demands and challenges, and aligning it with your own personality. The DNA of your vision and the DNA of your personality have to match.

That's how my evolution from research scientist to CEO began. When I was in grad school in the early 1970s, the impact of the double helix, the underpinning of cellular and molecular biology, was becoming increasingly clear, and the field seemed to offer almost limitless intellectual possibilities for a budding research scientist. Every day yielded new discoveries in genetics, disease, and medicine. My work as a budding cell biologist was fascinating. But it was clear that scientific research was a slow and arduous process; even minor breakthroughs take years. And I was getting really tired of scrounging in the couch cushions for pizza money and having Pam come home exhausted at 2 A.M. smelling like a french-fry machine.

I was finishing up my master's degree when my graduate faculty adviser took me aside one day. He told me that I wasn't the typical lab scientist. "Tom, I've been watching you. I see how people come in and gravitate around you. You have people skills that most researchers just don't have. You should think about getting out and using those skills. They can help you make more money than you'd ever make working in a lab." He suggested I might be happier in a career that took advantage of my innate personality, in which I would work more closely with people and less with rats. I began to think about finding a career with a faster track to financial security.

A couple of days later, I was at the university's medical center when I noticed a group of doctors in their white lab coats. They were listening intently to a well-dressed man carrying a beautiful alligator leather briefcase. He was speaking to them in scientific terms. I was impressed that anyone could get that much attention from a group as notoriously skeptical and elite as those academic docs. I found out the man worked for one of the major pharmaceutical houses, educating doctors about his company's products so they could recommend or prescribe certain medications for their patients. Aha, I thought. This might be the answer to the pizza-money problem.

As a trained scientist, I knew what to do: I researched the field. I went to the *Physicians' Desk Reference* (PDR), which is basically a collection of the information that is FDA-sanctioned with all prescription drugs. It includes chemical descriptions of each drug, what it's used for, the potential side effects, its mode of action, and potential drug interactions. In essence, it tells why the doctor would prescribe the medication for a patient. Browsing over page after page, I knew that with my background in cell biology, not only could I master such information, but I could also convey it easily and in my own way to others.

I began to narrow my PDR search to drugs that were most interesting to me from a scientific point of view, such as antibiotics, psychotropics, and drugs that worked on the metabolism. At that time—1974—Pfizer seemed to have an especially broad array of products that appealed to me and that I felt I could promote.

I've had a lot of turning points in my life, but this was certainly one of the most significant. It was what I call a "punctuation point": a defining opportunity in your life if you have the instincts to recognize it and the guts to pursue it. I mounted a campaign to become a sales trainee for the company and work in Maryland, near where I had been a bag boy and cashier at a local A&P grocery store. It was to become the start of my path to being a CEO.

The picture you paint for yourself may seem a little unorthodox; mine certainly was. But if it still feels right, you can use your own combination of "success genes" to figure out how to get yourself into that picture.

ARE YOU IN THE RIGHT PICTURE?

Here are a couple of ways to help yourself figure out whether your picture feels right to you:

Size (Up) the Problems You'll Face

Think of yourself not as a résumé or a collection of skills but as a way of behaving, an approach to life. As a start, try asking yourself this question: *What's more important to me—feeling good or not feeling bad?*

At first glance, they may seem like the same thing, but they're really not. If you're a "feel good" person, you'll seek to maximize your pleasure. You'll want to do more, be more, have more; you'll tend to say "Why not?" By contrast, if you're more of a "prevent pain" person, you'll have a greater tendency to avoid stress, stick to the familiar, and minimize potential conflict. You'll tend to ask "Why?" or "What if?" before doing something, because not hurting is more important to you than feeling terrific.

If you're more of a "feel good" person, you're thinking like an entrepreneur. If you're more of a "minimize pain" person, you need to think about whether the effort and risks required to achieve your vision are worth the potential reward. The bigger your dream and the bigger the potential reward, the bigger the sacrifice you may be called on to make. Think again about why you want what you want. If avoiding pain is more important to you than the pleasure of pursuing your dream, you may need to adjust your vision. Little dreams, little problems; big dreams, big problems. Make sure you know which you prefer. If you want to be super-successful, be prepared to supersize your challenges.

Try the Sweaty-Palms Test

When you close your eyes and imagine yourself living your vision day to day, don't forget the downside. Envision not only the big corner office and the limo but the hours you'll spend in airports and board meetings. If your palms get sweaty, if you don't feel comfortable, if you just can't see yourself fitting into that picture, you need to figure out why. Maybe it's just your usual response to a challenge, or maybe your metabolism is trying to warn you of a mismatch between who you are and what you want. But if you can see yourself succeeding—using the innate personality and approach to living that have already let you experience success—then it's a matter of putting together the building blocks that can get you where you want to go.

Experiment

Put yourself in situations that will test a single aspect of your vision. If you're thinking about launching a company, try not spending a paycheck and seeing how anxious you feel. Doing a series of small experiments in living your vision can help you find out whether you're comfortable with it.

If your picture requires you to create a false persona, forget it. People don't change personalities as they grow into the entrepreneurial picture they've painted. Successful people are comfortable staying nice people or concerned people or generous people or creative people as they evolve because what they're experiencing, the picture they've created, really was part of them from the beginning. Rather than demanding that they fight to be something they're not, their picture takes advantage of who they are already.

I'm convinced that being able to see myself as a potentially successful sales rep instead of just another grad student helped me get that first job at Pfizer. I had interviewed with the district manager in Baltimore, who sent me to Atlanta to talk with his regional manager. It was pretty intimidating. For one thing, the chair I was in was low to the ground, so I had to keep looking up at this guy whose desk was perched up on a platform. It was clear that my lack of sales experience didn't impress him. When I got back from Atlanta, the Baltimore district manager asked how it went. "Not so great," I said. I even offered to pay for my own airfare, feeling that I didn't want to embarrass him. He thought a minute, then asked, "Do you think you can do this job?"

"Absolutely," I replied—and meant it. It just felt right to me even though I had never professionally sold anything in my life.

"You're hired," he said.

That's the power of being able to see yourself in your picture.

WHAT DO YOU DO IF YOU'RE SHORT ON OPENNESS?

It's easy to see how to create a vision if you're highly open to experience, but what if that isn't part of your genetic makeup? Does that mean you just give up on having a vision and plod along day after day, hoping that somehow something great will turn up?

Not at all. In addition to answering the two questions we've discussed in this chapter, there are tactical things you can do to help crank up whatever Openness you have. Try a few and see how they can increase your ability to stretch your imagination so it can help you envision new options for yourself.

Build Regular Exposure to New Things into Your Life

Set aside some time at least once a month to confront yourself with a new experience or idea and expand your horizons.

Be Voracious in Reading

Learning about the careers of successful people like those interviewed in this book can stimulate your visionary ability.

Challenge Yourself to Find Something Valuable in an Aesthetic Experience

It could be a work of art, a piece of music—I've always found relaxation and focus in sunsets. Force yourself to find similarities between, say, an abstract painting and a business situation. (Ever felt like you were in the middle of a Jackson Pollock meeting?) It will stimulate whatever creativity you've got.

Use Your Analytical Abilities

Push yourself to pursue thoughts to their logical end—and then a little farther. If you work with clients, ask yourself what they'll need in two, five, or ten years. Use logic to jump-start creative thinking.

Learn to Ask Yourself Questions

Pretend you're a reporter having to write a story about the future of your company. Write an imaginary CV or résumé for yourself. Write a business plan for yourself that you think will confer success. It can expand your visionary thinking about what success means for you.

Even if Openness is naturally part of your makeup, it's not an unmixed blessing. Without other personality traits to balance it, it can still lead to aimless pursuit of the next new thing. You need to channel it to help you imagine a series of futures you want to live into, an evolving vision that puts you into pictures that make the most of who you are. That evolutionary vision is the Success Promoter that channels whatever Openness is in your nature into a productive path. It motivates you to seek out the new challenges that keep you moving, step by step, to get to your ultimate picture of success.

CHAPTER 4

The Challenge of Fighting Fear:
Believing in Your Ability to Survive

'm a baseball fan, and I'm fond of a quote that has been attributed to Mickey Rivers, who played for the Yankees and later for the Texas Rangers in the 1970s. Rivers must have known something about taking risks; in 1975 he led the American League in stolen bases. I've always liked the attitude he expressed when he said, "Ain't no sense worrying about things you got control over, 'cause if you got control over them, ain't no sense worrying. And there ain't no sense worrying about things you got no control over, 'cause if you got no control over them, ain't no sense worrying."

When Bernie Marcus was fired at age forty-nine, being worried about starting a business would have been understandable. He had spent a ton of money suing his former employer; he felt that not only had he been terminated unfairly, but that the firing had been handled in a way designed to inflict the most humiliation possible. It would have been easy simply to take another job somewhere else. But that wasn't Bernie Marcus. He and partner Arthur Blank thought they might be able to create a business by selling every home-improvement supply imaginable at low profit margins to *a lot* of people. Thus was born Home Depot and, with it, the concept of the category-killer store.

Was he terrified at the thought of being middle-aged and risking his entire financial future? "Sure," says Marcus. "It was scary because it was the unknown. But we believed we were right, and we had the fortitude to see it through. We had people who actually bet against us being successful; I mean they put down real money. The odds were way against us. There were people in the industry who said there was no way we were ever going to make it, but they didn't discourage us at all."

Marcus feels he inherited that indomitability from his mother. His family came to this country as refugees who couldn't speak English and had little education, he says. His mother's "undying belief in the human spirit" despite being crippled with rheumatoid arthritis taught him about the entrepreneurial spirit:

> "She was the type of person you couldn't knock down. She had a very positive outlook on life even though life dealt her a very difficult hand. Of all the traits that she had, I consider that to be the most important trait of all. She was always able to see a silver lining in anything that was a negative. Even if somebody died, there was something positive about it: 'He's not suffering anymore.' For an entrepreneur, if the glass is half empty you're dead. That glass has got to be full even if it's three-quarters empty. If you don't believe that, you're not going to succeed. Entrepreneurs have to have this sense that they're going to succeed no matter what, that nothing is going to knock them down. . . . If that's DNA, I guess it is."

One of the most intriguing things about superentrepreneurs like Marcus is their ability to take enormous leaps of faith, not only to be fearless themselves but to inspire others to have that same kind of instinctive belief in their ideas. Thinking like an entrepreneur doesn't mean overcoming fear. It means embracing and minimizing it. If you're waking up in the middle of the night in a cold sweat, you're not going to be very effective in convincing others. In fact, you may make them sweat, too. And who needs or wants more anxiety?

What enables one person to launch a business at fifty when other people, faced with being laid off, simply roll over and give up, or take anything they can find? What keeps some people locked into a job they hate (surely I'm not talking about you here!) and others living into that ever-expanding evolutionary vision of themselves? Again, I think it's in your DNA—the DNA of success. When decision points like these come along, people's inborn personality traits kick in, and they either rise to the challenge, aim themselves toward new horizons, panic, or give up.

One of the trickiest challenges of being an entrepreneur is tailoring your risk taking to your ability to stomach it. That's why your vision, the picture of success that you've painted for yourself, is so important. Knowing why you want what you want can help you want to take the risk. But if you have limited appetite for risk, for change, for evolving, you should probably recognize that your goals should be limited, too. Living into a vision of yourself—whether that means starting a company, looking for a new job, or aiming at the next rung on the corporate ladder—means you're always going to be tackling new things. Having an evolutionary vision means you get to decide which things those will be.

Risk taking is a little like exercising a muscle. You need to do it regularly. You need to prepare yourself for it. And you need to stretch yourself without causing a complete rupture or tear.

I have a friend who works at a large electronics company. He's an incredible salesperson—always at the top of the list in his company. I always used to talk to him whenever I wanted to buy a new TV, VCR, or DVD player. He often said, "I really should start my own business." Sometimes he was talking about a retail store. Sometimes it was a consulting business, helping people like me figure out what they should be buying for their homes or businesses. At one point his company had a massive layoff, and he could have taken early retirement. Perfect, I thought at the time. He could start the business he had always dreamed about. I'd say to him, "George, what's really the downside? You've got an incredible reputation. Everybody in the tristate area knows you, knows your value. Let's do the economics of it. If you consult with me, I'll probably buy X amount of stuff from you. All you have to do is do that fifty times a year, and you'd be taking home more money than your employer is paying you."

"But what if I miss a week, or I don't get a consulting job?" he'd say. "What's the likelihood of that happening?" I'd reply. "You're so busy now on nights and weekends doing exactly the same thing."

It never made any difference. "It's too much risk," he'd say. "I've got two boys going to college, my wife wants a new car. . . . I've got too many bills." His reasons could have applied just as well to me, but we had very different perspectives on the risk involved. To me, the pluses and potential were obvious; for him, there was always a roadblock to pursuing his idea, which I'm convinced would have been very successful.

When I see people struggling with this kind of decision, who would like to strike out in new directions but just don't have the confidence'for it, I feel badly for them. And I want to tell them, "Hey, don't agonize so much. If and when it's right for you, you'll know it." Remember the sweaty-palms test we talked about? If your evolutionary vision for yourself makes you want to take on a risk, great. But not wanting to take risks doesn't make you a weak person. It just means you may be cut out to make a lot of singles or doubles instead of swinging for the fences.

What lets some people have the confidence to take the kind of risks that help them become All-Stars?

SEEKING OUT RISK

I have a friend who is a tad on the sloppy side. Her living room is filled with newspapers on the way to the recycling bin, kids' toys waiting to be put away, half-finished projects waiting for a spare hour of attention. Her husband has coined a name for her happy oblivion to the chaos underfoot: "floor blindness." "On some level, she knows there's stuff lying around on the floor," he says. "But somehow she sort of doesn't see it, and it just doesn't bother her the way it does me." I guess it's just like background noise: eventually you don't hear it.

When it comes to risk, entrepreneurs need a kind of floor blindness—or, I suppose, "risk blindness." People looking at my career see a series of risks. I suppose they're right, but I have to confess that it didn't feel like it. Not at all. *For a born entrepreneur, risk doesn't feel like risk; it just feels like the way the world works.* It's another piece of information to be factored into a decision to go after what's around the corner. Risk is opportunity to the entrepreneur.

I think one thing that helped develop my "risk blindness" for becoming an entrepreneur was the risk I had already taken when I left graduate school. Of Pfizer's 684 sales territories at the time (there are thousands more today), Baltimore was dead last before I was hired. I think maybe the district sales manager there figured there wasn't much risk in hiring a kid with no "street" experience, who in fact had never held a real job outside a university lab. From Pfizer's point of view, Baltimore was like the South Pole: all directions led north. It would be a challenge. The medical community there, dominated by Johns Hopkins University, is one of the most sophisticated in the world. Confronted with a drug-company sales rep who didn't know what he or she was talking about, Baltimore doctors were especially skilled at what I used to call a "cephaloectomy": if you wasted their time, they would tear your head off.

Gulp.

With the name Pfizer behind me, I could get a first date with almost any doc I needed to see. The trick, of course, was to prevent the cephaloectomy—to turn on my knowledge of medicine and science and *become* a salesman. My briefcase was well stocked with the company's very expensive sales materials. However, when I began meeting with doctors in hospital lounges between their appointments, paper napkins became my best sales aids. Armed with an understanding of biology, physiology, and biochemistry, I found myself using the napkins as my classroom chalkboard to sketch out how the compounds worked in the body. Within a year, my territory became Pfizer's most productive, and I became their Sales Rep of the Year—the All-Star Club winner.

I quickly got the chance to move to corporate headquarters in Manhattan to work on pharmaceutical marketing materials—all the stuff I never had much use for in the field. I was a scientist in marketing—what a novel concept. It was an unusual picture, but it proved to be a successful one.

That's not to say that there weren't bumps along the way. I think I had been in my new office for all of one day—a Monday—when my new boss told me to put together a three-year P&L by Thursday. Three years in three days! And at that point, I had only the vaguest idea of what a P&L was. Remember, guys who work with lab rats don't take accounting or finance courses in college. I recall being mystified by how something could be both a profit *and* a loss statement.

Gulp again.

I quizzed some colleagues and cribbed a little from things others had done. I survived the Thursday deadline. I immediately signed up for a "Finance for Non-financial Managers" course. And I knew the risk I had taken had paid off.

ENTREPRENEURS AREN'T RISK TAKERS

For a born entrepreneur, risk feels like opportunity. I'm not out there bungee jumping, but I really am happiest when I'm thinking about what challenges the future might bring and how I can succeed at meeting them. As kids in school, the word "risk" is not like one of those words like, say, "flower"—something that has positive associations. We're programmed not to like risk from the earliest years of our lives. Just look up the definition of risk in *Webster's* dictionary: nothing positive there. But successful entrepreneurs understand that the big rewards they seek come only from growing their ability to take on and succeed at increasingly bigger challenges. And for them, those challenges don't feel like risks.

I've already talked about the leap I took in leaving my planned-on career as a research scientist and college professor to being able to make my sales territory for Pfizer the company's most productive within a year after I joined. But many people would balk at the next step in my evolutionary vision. After honing my marketing skills at Pfizer, I left to work for an ad agency. For several years, it was great. Because Pfizer was like the companies who were the agency's clients, I understood things from the client's perspective. I found that my clients were looking to me not for a great ad campaign but for strategic thinking about their overall marketing efforts.

But after several years, I began to get restless. The agency's CEO had just appointed a new president, so I knew it would be a long time before my next promotion. And it seemed to me that for whatever reason, the culture of that agency was beginning to change. I had never been a believer in the idea that my job was nothing more than wearing a big smile, flashing an American Express card, and taking people to lunch. You know it's time to think about moving on when a client takes you aside and says, "Don't bring So-and-So anymore. He doesn't do anything but irritate us. We just want *you* to come help us think about strategy."

I was beginning to feel my entrepreneurial instincts surfacing. I kept finding myself silently second-guessing decisions, thinking about what I would have done differently if I were in charge. More and more,

I felt that those decisions kept me—kept all of us—from capitalizing on the opportunities for an agency that understood and focused on health care. Clients and colleagues had argued that my sales skills coupled with my brand of strategic thinking about how to market and sell medicines could make a health-care ad agency very successful. The field was not only growing but becoming more intellectually demanding, and I kept seeing potential I knew I'd never be able to pursue where I was.

Whenever I'm faced with a risky decision like this, I try to keep things as simple as possible. I listed the pros and cons of each of my choices. I was making a good living where I was, and I supposed I could have continued to do that—if I'd been willing to get more and more bored and uncomfortable every year. I could move to another agency, but I still wouldn't be the lead dog, able to establish the kind of selling relationships and culture I wanted to spend my days developing. Or I could listen to the encouragement of clients and colleagues and start my own agency. I knew why I wanted what I wanted—not just financial security but control over my own destiny and the opportunity to try something new. I could see the potential for greater reward if we could fill the needs that we knew weren't being met in our industry by specializing in intellectual health-care advertising.

What finally clinched the decision was a conversation I had with my wife, Pam. After all, I wouldn't be the only one taking the risk. At that point, our daughter was three years old, and our twin boys had just been born. Also, we had just finished building a new home. It was the third one since we'd been married, and we had always chosen something a little less than we felt we could afford. This one, however, had become a much bigger commitment than we had planned. After all we'd gone through to get to the point that we didn't have to worry about splurging on olives for our take-out salad, I didn't want to make the decision unless Pam was totally on board with it. We sat around the kitchen table and tried to be very logical about it. We laid out all the what-ifs and tried to think about the potential pitfalls.

Pam summed it up best. "What's the worst that can happen if it doesn't work out?" she said. "You've got a great reputation. You can always get a job with another agency." We talked some more. Finally, at exactly the same moment, we both looked at each other and said, "Let's just go for it!" It felt so right that it *had* to be right. It was the most comforting moment since I had been contemplating entrepreneurship. What a free feeling. I was really at peace—and I never looked back. I just had a very different way of looking at things than my buddy at the electronics company, who focused on the downside. We both had a lot on the line, but only one of us was able to say "Let's do it."

I teamed up with a former creative director I had worked with and started Harrison & Star. We had a lease on 2,000 square feet of office space, two employees (us), one telephone, one fax machine, and no steady revenue. Gulp? Not really. By then I was totally convinced it would work out okay. I saw myself in that picture. My experiences had given me the confidence to weather both change and the disappointment of hearing "No" from potential clients. I actually felt more ready for this than I had felt in my earlier moves.

Still, our confidence was definitely tested. For the first few months, cold calls went unanswered. "Who are you?" a bored receptionist would ask. "And what's the name of your agency again? Well, what clients do you have?" One receptionist and I got to be good friends, joking about how her boss had failed to return any of my twenty-five calls.

We didn't spend any more than we absolutely had to. To keep expenses down, I saved every single paper clip. Do you know how many of those things come in your mail? Believe me, it's a lot. Even though I'm now in a corner office in a Manhattan high-rise, saving paper clips is a habit I have to this day. I bought exactly one box at Harrison & Star; it was the first and only box I've bought in my life.

Our little agency began to take off. My partner and I were a unique team, scientific symbiosis in action. I—the account guy—absolutely knew the science behind the medicine, and how to sell to doctors. Just as important, I knew the needs of our clients; after all, I had been in their shoes at Pfizer. Science and service set Harrison & Star apart from our competitors. Our unique blend won us a lot of business, unparalleled growth, and recognition by an industry trade journal as its first health-care Agency of the Year and the fastest-growing agency ever in the industry at the time. Just unbelievable for a small-town boy from Maryland.

Every person interviewed for this book has risk blindness. The difference between them and my friend who's agonizing about going out on his own is not that they don't *see* potential threats. It's that they don't *experience* them as such. They absorb the downside and then either digest it or spit it out. They're more confident relying on their own ability to control their future than they are relying on someone else to control it.

THE LOVE OF WHAT'S NEXT

What lets a John Bogle Sr. be comfortable defying the mutual fund industry and start selling directly to the public instead of through brokers? What lets Sam Zell buy a piece of real estate that everyone else says he's overpaying for? I believe this welcoming of risk is something that's inborn.

I know a woman who is just incredibly talented, smart, a fantastic salesperson. She's grown her employer's business fivefold since she's headed her division. She'd have a built-in client base for her own company; clients absolutely love and respect her. She's no shrinking violet; she's tough as nails on people who don't do what they're supposed to do. She's said many times, "I could do this for myself." And I think she'd like to—if someone could guarantee her she'd get paid every month. She's what I call an "entreprenear," a near-entrepreneur. She backs off and continues to work for someone else who can't hold a candle to her capabilities. I've urged her to just do it, but something innate holds her back every time. What a shame. She'd be a multimillionaire.

Being comfortable with risk taking is essential to entrepreneurial-style success, and I'm not alone in my belief that it's either hardwired into us or missing from our unique DNA composition. Pharmed's Carlos de Cespedes could have been speaking for virtually everyone in this book when he said, "I think it is inborn. You might go from a one to a four [in terms of risk taking], but I don't think you're ever going to go from a one to a ten."

Is there scientific evidence that self-confidence and comfort with risk taking is inherited? Yes. One study of twins found that about 60 percent of the difference between people when it comes to risk taking was genetic; that's even higher than for most other personality traits, most of which range from 30 to 50 percent.[1]

Perhaps the most extreme examples of entrepreneurial risk takers are people who start multiple companies. I believe there are two kinds of entrepreneurs: those who are drawn into it, and those who seek it out. Being drawn into entrepreneurship means being comfortable taking on risk; the second kind are the ones who aren't comfortable without it. They are the start-up entrepreneurs, the ones who launch company after company, who often move on after the start-up phase is over. They love the next new thing, the next challenge. They're always on forward focus.

The University of Michigan's Tom Kinnear agrees: "The problem with some of the entrepreneurs I see who are more serial is that they get into this habit of trying to best themselves. It's like the guys who found insulin. They were twenty-seven, twenty-nine when they found it. And then they spent the rest of their lives trying to have another medical breakthrough of equal import. They never did, and it bothered them."

Kinnear remembers meeting Jonas Salk while the discoverer of the polio vaccine was a researcher at the University of Michigan. "He basically spent all the rest of his life after the polio vaccine trying to find other antibody, antivirus kinds of things, and he never really did. Entrepreneurs are the same; they thrive on the battle and the success. I had lunch with an entrepreneur friend the other day. I can see him wrestling with what's his next big idea, where's he going next—because he did so well the first time out. He's getting tired of his big boat and his golf clubs."

These chronic, instinctive risk takers may have a specific gene that has been associated with novelty seeking—the desire for a constant stream of exciting experiences. Certain variations of the DRD4 gene have been linked not only with novelty-seeking personalities but with attention deficit/hyperactivity disorder.[2] As many as half of ADHD individuals have one specific variation of the DRD4 gene. ADHD can take many forms. In some cases it simply means difficulty getting or staying focused. In extreme cases, children with ADHD disrupt classrooms, have problems controlling their impulses, and are hyperactive. Sounds just like some of the entrepreneurs I know!

The DRD4 gene may have given the early humans who had it a significant evolutionary advantage, according to genetic researcher

Dr. Robert Moyzis of the University of California–Irvine School of Medicine. He speculates that primitive hunters with ADHD traits such as novelty seeking, aggressiveness, and perseverance were more likely to be successful at surviving and providing for their families. "Survival of the fittest" meant those genes would have been passed down to their children. That may have helped the human race survive, improving our ability to seek new ways of doing more things better—whether that is inventing the wheel, creating the latest biotech drug, or serial tasking. It would certainly be an advantage for an entrepreneur, whose ability to cope with something new and different is constantly tested.

Schumpeter said entrepreneurship creates economic growth. Those variations of the DRD4 gene may do for entrepreneurs what entrepreneurs do for the economy: stimulate us to change, grow, and keep moving forward. They may drive human ability to survive just as they help entrepreneurs take on new challenges that drive businesses forward. Maybe attention deficit disorder isn't so terrible after all. I'd hate to think that the drugs to treat the "disorder" are inadvertently homogenizing the next generation of entrepreneurs. No new entrepreneurs, no new big ideas. What a horrible thought—that by bringing kids down to what some physician calls "normal" behavior, we may be normalizing kids to the point that they can't think for themselves.

It's interesting to read about this research and then talk to Barry Gibbons, who has now launched a coffee company with his sons. "I was a complete shit in my teenage years. I was very lucky to avoid jail," he recalls. Ann Rhoades founded PeopleInk and was a founding executive of JetBlue. She remembers that in second grade, the nuns at her school would call her mother "about why I was constantly debating them on why you couldn't get divorced if you didn't like who you were married to, and why I'd go to hell if I didn't go to Mass on Sunday when I didn't feel like it." Many successful comedians remember being disruptive in class; for that matter, one of Richard Branson's teachers predicted he would either go to prison or become a millionaire. (The teacher only missed it by a billion or so!)

I'm not saying any of these people have ADHD, but it does make me wonder whether the entrepreneurial spirit might be linked to the DRD4 gene. I've certainly had the same questions about myself. Even before I became familiar with the research, I was aware that I have always had a mild form of ADHD; it's part of the reason I had to study so hard in school. I think that restlessness may be part of why as an adult I like to explore new things, push into new territory. I've always said risk taking seems to be part of my DNA. Now I think that was more than just a phrase.

As I mentioned in Chapter 2, the DRD4 gene has also been linked to addictive behavior, such as alcoholism. All of these linkages coupled with the stories of serial entrepreneurs seem to confirm my belief: Some entrepreneurs build on their genetic advantages, and doing so leads to the kind of success that is addictive.

Genetics may also give clues about why some risk takers become chronic gamblers and some become successful entrepreneurs. Certain variations of the DRD4 gene are found more often in heroin addicts than in nonaddicts. However, they're also found in mentally healthy people who tend to seek out new experiences. Though it has received the most attention, the DRD4 gene is only one of ten or so that scientists believe affect our desire to seek out novelty. Someone with all ten might become a heroin addict; others might simply enjoy experimenting and taking risks in more socially acceptable ways.[3]

Some researchers believe the differences might simply be a matter of degree. It may be that having one or two of the novelty-seeking genes makes you effective, but all of them can be a problem. Could that help explain the Bulger brothers of Massachusetts? One became the president of the Massachusetts Senate; the other landed on the FBI's Ten Most Wanted List. It could be that the two inherited different amounts of genes that influence risk taking. As one researcher put it, "A middling genetic load may give you a personality disorder, a lighter one gives you a personality quirk and a still lighter one gives you mainstream America."[4]

Finally, I think it's no coincidence that the family background of many successful entrepreneurs includes people who faced the challenge of immigrating to this country. It takes a certain confidence to uproot your family and come to a country where you may not speak the language. It seems to me that the confidence that helped Sam Zell's parents to leave Germany just before World War II and then later flee Japan was expressed by Sam in starting a business. Events such as the war may have helped switch on an inherited confidence and entrepreneurial instinct for moving on, just as a business idea can switch on the desire to start a company or drive a serial entrepreneur to pursue a new challenge.

SUCCESS PROMOTER: THE "FORWARD FOCUS" GENE

Having confidence and taking risks are circular processes. To take risks requires confidence that you're going to succeed. And that kind of confidence—even if it's inborn—gets developed when you take risks and succeed at them. You need both parts of the formula. The kind of faith in yourself that successful entrepreneurs display is difficult to comprehend for someone who just doesn't have it. It's the part that most often seems to be instinctive.

But what do you do if you were born a little short on self-confidence? Even people who had faith in themselves starting in the cradle recognize that certain techniques let them act confidently in taking risk. One of these is what I call "staying on forward focus." It means constantly keeping your eye on that picture you're living into, and watching for an opportunity to paint the next one.

People aren't really afraid of risk. They're afraid of failing *if they take that risk.* If they knew they were going to succeed, it wouldn't be so scary, would it? That's where staying on forward focus can help. When you're walking a tightrope, you don't want to look down; you want to concentrate on where you're going. What keeps successful people constantly evolving toward greater and greater success? What keeps pulling them into the future, taking risk after risk? Staying on forward focus. It's the Success Promoter that unlocks whatever level of self-confidence your genes gave you.

Sam Zell was confident from a young age. He started his career in real estate while he was still in college, running the largest student-housing real-estate operation in Ann Arbor. He is now chairman of Equity Group Investments LLC, which includes the nation's largest office-building owner/manager as well as its largest real estate investment trust (REIT). "I knew from the time I was very young that I was

---

MARKERS FOR THE "FORWARD FOCUS" GENE

- You understand your personal brand and know what's valuable about it.
- You use commitment as a tool to keep yourself on forward focus.
- You aren't afraid to be wrong sometimes.
- You see risk as opportunity.
- You think about mistakes only in terms of how their lessons can help you do better.

---

different in my thinking; it was pervasive all through growing up and being a teenager. I had different criteria and different interests from most of the other kids I knew. I wasn't into frivolous things. I always dated women who were older than I was. I just had a different kind of perspective. I was riding home once on a train sitting opposite a guy who was a contemporary of my father's. I'd been out of law school maybe two years at this point. I was telling him I had hired this young lawyer to work for me. And then I kind of laughed and said, 'I think he's maybe six months older than I am.' And the guy said, 'Yeah, Sam, but you were born old.'"

Confident? You bet. But staying on forward focus unlocks the power of that confidence when the going gets rough. "I don't ever not think about risk," Zell says. "I look at every investment, every decision I made, and I start by attempting to understand the downside. In the late 1980s, I formed a distressed property fund. I went out and raised $400 million and put up $50 million of my own money and went out and started buying up half-empty buildings. And after about a year of this I looked over my shoulder and I realized that I was the only one. It's lonely. You look and you say, 'Well, maybe I'm wrong—in which case I'm taking enormous risk.'"

What did he do? His answer is a classic illustration of how to apply the "forward focus" Success Promoter: "I went to bed and got up the next morning. I thought I was right, and I thought it would turn out right, so I just kept going. . . . I've done some deals that were horrible, and that I have regret over. But you can't have any regret over missed opportunities—because there are always more. The entrepreneur's attitude is that there are an unlimited number of opportunities. He always believes that he can re-create it again."

Here are some ways to help yourself stay on forward focus:

Build Confidence wth Your Personal Brand

Fear of the unknown is really a fear of your inability to survive the changes it will bring. *One of the most important instincts you can have is the knowledge that your own resources will let you overcome whatever obstacles will come.* As I said earlier, entrepreneurs are confident that their idea is good. But what they're really confident of is that regardless of whether the idea pans out, they'll survive and even thrive. It's that understanding of and confidence in themselves, even more than their belief in an idea, that lets them constantly move forward.

One of the reasons I was able to transform myself from research scientist into entrepreneur and corporate executive was that I knew my capacity for hard work. As I said earlier, I believe my mild ADHD is part of the reason I'm always looking for new challenges. (I wouldn't be writing this book otherwise!) However, it also made studying tough for me. I always had to read something five or six times to really get it. I took endless notes in the margins of my textbooks, went over them again and again, stayed up late reviewing them. I knew that there might be other people who would be smarter than I was. But I also knew there wasn't going to be anybody who put in more effort.

Knowing that really paid off, not only at school but when I went to work at a local A&P to help pay my way through college. I had a tough boss, and I swear he worked me harder than anybody else there; I can still hear him calling over the loudspeaker, "Harrison, aisle three, clean up the ketchup." Eventually I was promoted from stock boy to cashier, and I always wanted to be the fastest one to get customers through the line. Friday nights were our busiest, and I used to race one of the other cashiers to see who could ring out the most sales and handle more customers. One night I was ringing up items so fast that I literally burned out the cash register. No kidding: I could smell the machine starting to fry! Yes, my boss got mad as hell—but I won.

Being sure of my capacity for hard work is part of what gave me the confidence to get through that daunting experience with the P&L at Pfizer. It's been part of *my personal brand*—the way I view myself, and the way I want others to view me—ever since I can remember. As Americans, the idea that anyone can get ahead if they work hard is part of our collective psychic DNA. But to me, hard work was important not just for what it produced, but for the level of confidence it brought out in me. *Hard work was—and is—the foundation.*

I'm incredibly happy heading over 150 marketing services agencies, but writing this book felt almost as daunting as starting Harrison & Star. In some ways it was almost as big a leap as the agency. If I didn't think its messages are important ones, I probably wouldn't have tried it. Even if you're born naturally confident, there are always moments of self-doubt, times that give you pause when you're faced with a challenge. Knowing what you're capable of, knowing you can rely on yourself to hang in there in the face of obstacles, is critical to success. You have to be certain you can count on yourself to come through. Understanding your personal brand is critical to that. I'll talk more about personal branding in Chapter 10, "The Challenge of Being a Nice Guy." Right now, just remember that understanding your personal brand can be a confidence-builder that helps you take on risk.

Don't Go It Alone

The most successful entrepreneurs I know aren't loners—quite the contrary. Most have a solid network of people who help them test their thinking. My wife, Pam, is a great touchstone for me; as I said, her advice when I was trying to decide about starting my own agency was invaluable. Her saying "What's the worst that can happen? With your reputation, you'll always be able to get another job somewhere else" reinforced my own feelings.

When I talk about having a panel of consulting experts, I don't mean relying on a consensus of opinion. That kind of research homogenizes your decisions. As Zell says, "If you have to take a vote, you've lost." But confidence benefits from knowing that you've tested your intuition with some research. That research should include the perspective of people whose judgment you trust—successful people. And if you're paralyzed by anxiety, getting the view of people who are lower on the Neuroticism scale may help you see positive aspects you might have overlooked.

When putting together a panel of advisers, look for people who know you well and are frank and open about your weaknesses as well as your strengths. They're the ones who can substantiate how your genetic pros and cons might play out in a given situation. The last thing you need is someone who simply wants to make you feel good about yourself. Any false confidence they give you will disappear quickly if there's a bad fit between you and the challenge you've undertaken.

Use Commitment as a Confidence-Builder

There are times when you just have to commit yourself. Sometimes being between a rock and a hard place brings out commitment. And committing yourself to something can actually make you more confident. It forces you to keep your head down, focus, and forge ahead no matter what. It leaves little room for neurotic waffling. It's like the line from *Apollo 13*: "Gentlemen, failure is not an option."

When Al Neuharth proposed creating a newspaper that would be available nationwide and present the news in short, easy-to-read stories with colorful graphics, he knew it was an all-or-nothing proposition. He bet his career at Gannett Co., Inc., that *USA Today* would be a success.

"It was the biggest single risk [of my career] because of the size of the investment and the odds," he explains. "There weren't many new newspapers being started in the 1980s. It would either make me a hero or I'd be the officeboy. But I took care of that by agreeing with the board that if the venture that I was recommending failed, that they had my resignation in their hip pocket in advance. I had to recognize that on something like that, if you take a risk that size, you have to have total commitment and you have to be willing to either be the hero or the villain. What happens is, if one of those things catches on there are a lot of people who think they were among the architects of it. If it doesn't catch on, you're the only one."

Some people work best when they give themselves no way out. If you're one of those, make a commitment—and make it big enough that you have to stick to it.

Give Yourself Room for Risk

When John Bogle Jr. was trying to convince his partners to come with him to start Bogle Funds, he took much the same tack with them that Pam did with me about starting my agency.

> "All of my original three partners came from more established companies—the bluest of the blue-chip companies, where you could work the rest of your life and earn a good living. I wanted them to feel comfortable with the risks of joining this hugely risky start-up. I told them, 'The bottom line is, you should feel entirely comfortable doing this. Number one, collectively I think we can all make this thing work. Look at the other three people in this group; do you think they have the ability to make it work? But moreover, if it doesn't work, if this thing blows up, you guys are incredibly accomplished with terrific careers. And now you would have something even more interesting on your résumés, that you tried to start up this entrepreneurial venture.' I told them that even if the economy soured or the market soured, they are eminently hirable individuals who shouldn't have to worry about failure at all. There might be a little embarrassment that something failed. But if that's all it is, they've got nothing to worry about, because they can easily find another job and put bread on the table. I think I got them to believe, as I believe myself, that there was no downside to the business."

Bogle used not only his own confidence but his inborn analytical, logical bent to analyze why risk wasn't really risk—and to sell his prospective partners a certain comfort level as well.

One of the best ways to switch on risk blindness is to have a game plan for dealing with disaster. Having some idea of what you'll do if the worst happens can paradoxically give you greater confidence. It lets you quit worrying about it. You can simply lock it away under "Plan B" with a mental note that says DO NOT OPEN EXCEPT IN AN EMERGENCY. That frees up mental bandwidth. Instead of having vague fears kicking around in the back of your mind, draining your energy, you can concentrate fully on making Plan A work. Remember, confidence comes from trusting that you'll come out okay, no matter what. In this case, you're simply mapping a different route to coming out okay.

This may sound like the exact opposite of what I just said about committing yourself. It's not. It's simply another way of putting a floor under whatever risk you're taking. If Al Neuharth hadn't had confidence that he would survive personally somehow, even if *USA Today* failed and he had to resign, he probably wouldn't have been able to make the total commitment the launch required. Plan B is a landing pad. Plan A is a rocket ship. You need to pick whichever one makes you most comfortable with risk.

Being Wrong Isn't Wrong

Okay, it's not great, but it's not *wrong*. Great leaders aren't always right. They're not immune to being shown to be wrong. They just don't personalize it. They learn from it. If you're afraid of being wrong, you won't do anything new, different, or entrepreneurial; you'll certainly never be lead dog. You'll just follow all your life. How boring!

Let Risk Narrow the Competition

To David Gardner, who co-founded the Motley Fool online investment site with his brother Tom, *risk can actually improve your chances of success.* How? By reducing the competition for what you're trying to achieve.

"If you're surrounded by lemmings who are completely unwilling to take any risk, that actually reduces the amount of competition for those who do want to take it on, and likely increases their rewards," he says. "I think because there is such an obvious reward to taking risk and succeeding—whether you're starting a business or doing any one of a number of things we can do as adults—it still does incent people to take risks, and to take risks that benefit many others."

An avid gamer, Gardner thinks strategy competitions such as Settlers of Catan have encouraged his appetite for risk taking: "What you're forced to do in those games is take risks to try to win. It's a little microcosm of what we do in life. You're able to test your mind out against other people, and you're able to fail and not have it hurt too much. I think many adults give away games or think they're childish, but I think that contributed to the comfort I felt starting something, and that I felt all the way through—running something, hiring other people to help run it. I'm willing to take the risk even if I don't feel I can see the future in my industry."

After watching my own twin sons play online games, I wonder whether the online world may contribute to developing kids who see risk simply as part of the path to a goal. Playing in ways that help them see themselves as natural risk takers may help switch on the entrepreneurial thinking of a new generation. They're learning the strategy of winning.

Confidence in taking on change means knowing what's in you that fits each new picture you envision for yourself and your career. In my case it was my knowledge of science and medicine. Even though I had never been a salesman, I knew what parts of my background and personality would let me fit into that picture of a salesman I had created for myself.

I'm blessed to have been born with a high level of confidence, so let me tell you one more thing I'm confident about. Even if you feel you don't have swing-for-the-fences genes, experiment with some of the strategies I've suggested. I'd be willing to bet they'll at least improve your ability to step up to the plate.

CHAPTER 5

The Challenge of Seeing Around Corners: Tap Your Intuition to Spot and Seize Opportunity

One Christmas holiday when I was home from graduate school at West Virginia University, I dropped into a florist's shop in Hagerstown, Maryland. I wanted to send a dozen roses to a girl I liked at the time. When I filled out the card on the roses, I gave my address as Morgantown, West Virginia, where WVU was located. The salesgirl asked if I went to school there. When I said yes, she told me she also was going to WVU, as an undergraduate. She introduced herself and told me she was working in her dad's flower shop while she was on her holiday.

I liked Pam from that moment. As I left the store, I thought to myself, "She's really beautiful. I'm coming back here tomorrow." I did, and she waited on me again. (I spent the last of my available money on a candle for my mother so the visit would look legit.) I was broke financially, but not emotionally; that candle turned out to be one of the best investments I ever made. After talking with Pam more, I realized I really wanted to get to know her. She hadn't been in her dorm room five minutes after she got back from that Christmas holiday before she got a phone call from me. We started dating. We've now been married for more than thirty years.

One of the most important aspects of entrepreneurial thinking is the ability to recognize opportunity—and not only to recognize it, but to take advantage of it. Capitalize on it. Turn opportunity into a positive reality. Meeting Pam was one of the best opportunities of my life, and I thank my stars every day that I not only recognized it but acted on it. In fact, that was probably my first real sales job. For a few years, on Easter, Christmas, and other holidays, Pam and I would go back to the shop to help out her father, and to earn ourselves some extra spending money for pizza and salads *with* olives. Pam's dad and I both noticed I had a real ease and style in selling to the public.

And of course, if I hadn't recognized the potential in starting an ad agency focused on health care, I would never be where I am today. As I've said, my career path may seem surprising. One of the main reasons I've been able to go from the lab to the corner office is that I've been able to recognize an opportunity when it presented itself, even if that opportunity wasn't obvious to anyone else.

Intuition is vital to living like an entrepreneur. Why? Because your brain can process information your conscious mind may not even realize it's getting. That lets you spot what others can't, helps you sort out which information is most vital, and allows you to make decisions faster. They may not always be the right decisions, but a decision at least will move you in a particular direction—usually forward.

People often think intuition precedes information. I think it's the other way around. I believe intuition occurs when whatever data, information, and experience I might have about a market seem to be aligned in such a way that my gut says, "How can this possibly be a mistake?" It's almost like being able to recognize a constellation in a vast array of stars. Not only are the stars in the right place to form a pattern, but you have to be able to pick out that pattern from all the other possible combinations of stars. That particular alignment of stars seems to come into focus all at once. Intuition is really just a mechanism for making patterns—integrated series of data points—out of information and then aligning that information with opportunity. I might be looking at two or three or four opportunities at a time, but generally there will only be one that produces that feeling that everything connects up and works together, that makes me comfortable it's the right choice. It's the ability to make a decision and then be able to sleep at night knowing that you properly assessed the data available to you.

There's another reason I think information-based intuitive decisions are so important to thinking like an entrepreneur, and this one is on a more personal level. They're usually a better fit with your understanding of yourself, your genetic personality assets, and the picture you've painted for the next step of your evolutionary vision for your life. We'll talk more about this in Chapter 9, "The Challenge of Punctuation Points." For right now, I'd like to focus on how inborn traits help us make those calls, and what you can do to make the most of whatever intuitive ability you've been given.

ORDERING WHAT'S NOT ON THE MENU

Cars are one of my passions, and I always like to check out the latest innovations. There's a snazzy new feature that's beginning to show up on some high-end models. The headlights swivel, allowing the driver to "see around corners." When I first heard about them, it reminded me of how a born entrepreneur is able to synthesize information from a variety of sources and understand not only what it means today but the impact it will have several years from now. As Sam Zell says, *"Entrepreneurs not only see around corners; they believe what they see."*

"Seeing around corners"—and acting on what you see—involves a lot of the other qualities we've discussed, such as believing in yourself, your ideas, and your analytical skills, as well as being able to embrace rejection. But spotting opportunities also takes an instinctive ability to understand how events are most likely to unfold. It's like hockey legend Wayne Gretzky saying he skates to where the puck will be—not to where it is at the moment. That's as true for corporations as it is for individuals. In fact, it's perhaps even more important, since it's notoriously much harder to shift the course of a corporate tanker than an entrepreneurial sailboat. I'm sure it was an entrepreneurial thinker at IBM who first began prodding the company to launch "computing on demand." By giving companies the ability to outsource their IT operations, the concept is transforming a traditional hardware manufacturer into a services company. In pushing that idea, that entrepreneurial thinker was focusing not only on how the shift would help the company now but whether long-term trends would even let the company survive without it. He understood where the market was going to be.

Logic would say that former American Airlines CEO Robert Crandall is the exact opposite of an entrepreneur, since his career was built in the corporate world. However, he clearly encouraged entrepreneurial thinking in the company. On his watch, the company launched AAdvantage, the first frequent-flyer program; deep-discount airline tickets; the industry's first yield-management system; and transformed itself into a leading international carrier. Identifying an opportunity and then realizing anything from that opportunity are two very different things, he says:

> "You can divide business management into two parts: the conceptual part and the execution. You have to ask yourself, 'What is the business going to look like five years, ten years, twenty-five years from now? How am I going to put this company on a track to be in the right place ten or fifteen years from now?' Intuition in the absence of analysis is another word for stupidity, but good intuition combined with good data is a recipe for success. In the end a decision is based on how you interpret information. Take the guy who just took over Procter & Gamble [CEO A. G. Lafley]. He's done a terrific job of returning that company to its roots. You can be sure there's a lot of intuition in what he's doing, which is very different from what analysis led his predecessor to do. Lafley's intuition is that P&G is going to continue to make its money the way it's traditionally made it: grinding out incremental product changes to suit an ever-changing consumer and modestly changing consumer want lists. His predecessor had the idea that [the company] had to radically change what it was doing. Both men had access to the same group of analysts, the same data sets, but they came to very different conclusions."

What lets entrepreneurial thinkers see opportunities that others don't? Two things: being a MythManager, and practicing "two-steps-ahead" thinking.

BEING A MYTHMANAGER

When I was a kid, my first-grade teacher used to get angry at me. When we were all playing with building blocks, she wanted each of us to assemble the blocks in the same way. When we read about Spot running, she wanted everyone paying attention. However, I didn't conform; I was usually off thinking about something else. She would always pull my left ear to try to keep me in line; at one point, the constant pulling made my earlobe not only bleed but actually split away from the side of my head! I just didn't want to do the same thing everyone else was doing.

If you're going to think like an entrepreneur, you can't be bound by existing myths—and there are a lot of them. If Bill Gates had listened to the myth that no one except hobbyists and nerds would ever want a computer of their own, think what the world would be like today. The bigger the idea, the more it may fly in the face of conventional wisdom. Entrepreneurs are good at asking "What if?" about things that no one else has taken seriously. John Patrick was a key player in getting IBM to recognize the power of personal computing and the Internet; he now is president of his own consulting company, Attitude LLC. He believes that you can tell whether a new Internet technology is going to be successful by the degree of skepticism about its value: the more skepticism, the greater the potential impact. He cites blogging—online individual journals—as an example. What if blogs, which are sometimes conducted surreptitiously within corporations, became the de facto method of communication and knowledge-sharing for the company? What if customer blogs had more sway over consumer opinion than corporate communications did? What if blogs provided a cost-effective way for the company to communicate to its customers or clients? What-ifs are the starting point for innovation.

Conventional wisdom is sort of like those building blocks that I used to organize in my own way. Just because you think you have a better way to organize the blocks doesn't mean you have to get rid of the blocks altogether. I think you have to respect conventional wisdom, learn from it, build on it, and move on. If you put yourself or your company in a picture and "the norm" suggests you can't get there from here—say, if you're a cell biologist facing the myth that only biz school graduates can become CEOs—you need to be able to see what the building blocks are and how you can begin to organize them to fit the picture you've created. You need to be rational enough to know how to take advantage of what already exists—and then begin to fill in the gaps between today's reality and the picture you've developed. Sometimes the steps you take toward your picture are small, but their incremental impact moves you in the direction you want to go. A series of well-planned infinitesimal steps will get you to your goal.

For example, let's think about the current health trend. People want to eat, or snack, healthier. Companies know this and want to capitalize on this trend. PepsiCo and Coca-Cola market bottled water as well as colas that have the taste of their parent drinks with only a fraction of the calories. PepsiCo also took transfats out of Fritos®. Fast-food chains such as Wendy's have responded by offering consumers the choice of a side salad or French fries, and McDonald's is revamping its menu. In all cases, the concepts are perfect, the marketing is brilliant, and the timing couldn't be better. These companies knew where they needed to be in order to increase their market shares and fill a huge— and growing—gap in their offerings.

Truly revolutionary ideas are scarce, but you can also make an enormously successful career or company by being a MythManager. Plenty of successful entrepreneurs have questioned existing myths just enough to create a new, more successful way of doing things. They've assembled the blocks in their own way, not by ignoring myths but by managing them.

Two-Steps-Ahead Thinking

But asking "What if?" only gets you so far. Entrepreneurial thinkers also are good at what I call "two-steps-ahead" thinking. They don't just ask themselves "What if?"; they also ask "What then?" If your what-if scenario actually comes to pass, what happens then? Two-steps-ahead thinking started for me at a very early age. There was an insurance broker who used to come to my parents' house every year. When I was sixteen, I bought a life insurance policy from him on myself, naming my mother as the beneficiary. I was very protective of my mother, and I remember thinking that if anything ever happened to me, I wanted her to have a little extra financial cushion. Although my mother has been gone for two decades now, that insurance policy is still in force today; I think I pay $300 a year on it. It's that "always save for a rainy day" mentality.

Opportunity isn't always going to slap you in the face and say "Here

I am!" Often, you have to create the opportunity by looking at what people's needs are going to be in five, ten, or fifteen years (asking "What if?"). and apply creative thinking to that ("What then?"). That's what happened with Kay Koplovitz. She was pulled into entrepreneurship by her belief in her idea: original programming to be delivered via cable network. "I didn't always know I wanted to be an entrepreneur. It took some time after graduate school for me to realize that I really liked business and that there was a creative aspect to business that was attractive to me." At the time, cable programming was a pretty creative idea. "When we started out, people were like, 'You gotta be crazy if you think we're going to pay for TV.' People thought it was nuts. 'We're going to pay somebody to watch TV? I don't think so.' It's completely different now; the marketplace has a totally different mind-set. Now they have to have their TV, and every kind of TV."

Intuition may have lit a spark, but her idea was developed and refined by thorough analysis:

"It wasn't an idea that was hatched overnight. I had written a master's thesis in communications nine years earlier on the satellite network. I began working toward getting myself in a position to do that, which was really not conceived of in the industry at the time. I really liked my idea. I continued to refine it and worked in businesses that were essential to do what I wanted to do. I worked in satellite communications; I was a television producer; I went to the cable industry because I thought that was the industry that would be most likely to need the product. I sort of looked at the landscape and said, 'If I want to do this, who's gonna want some kid from Milwaukee who doesn't have any background in doing it?' I looked at myself and said, 'I've gotta learn about these different businesses because these are the businesses that are necessary to know in order to launch this kind of product.' Each step along the way I just became more and more convinced that it was the right thing to do."

Koplovitz asked herself "what if" cable systems continued to be solely a distribution mechanism; her "what then" answer was to create programming that could generate additional revenues.

The automobile-manufacturing industry continues to reinvent itself. Look at the Chrysler Group, now part of DaimlerChrysler. It asked, "What if moms and dads continue to spend more and more time in their cars transporting their children and all their stuff?" The company's What-then was the minivan—and a new era of vehicles was born. That era gave way to SUVs, more macho versions of the minivan that appealed to the market that wanted bulkier, higher, heavier, safer transportation for their families. Now the automobile industry has created the crossover vehicle, a smaller SUV that is today's version of the old station wagon. People are tiring of SUVs and want something smaller but still roomy.

Two-steps-ahead thinking applies on an individual level with careers, too. Successful careers involve creating a sequential series of visions for yourself—visions that match up with your genetic strengths and weaknesses—seeing yourself in the picture you've painted for yourself, and taking whatever steps are needed to make the picture a reality. Each picture that you develop for your evolving career becomes a personal marketing plan. You see yourself in a particular professional situation, then you determine the steps you need to take to get you there. It's a bit like a personal chess game. You know the rules of the game and what you need to do to win; you just need to figure out your personal moves to get you to where you need to be.

GENES, INTUITION, AND OPPORTUNITY

If you're a woman, you may have rolled your eyes when your guy shows up dressed in wildly inappropriate colors. Don't blame him too much; it may be in his genes. The way we see color is determined in part by tiny cone-shaped structures in the back of our eyeballs. The gene that determines the development of the cones that let us tell red from green is found on the X (male) chromosome. Sometimes that gene is defective. That's why more men than women are likely to match up a lime-green sweater with a pair of flame-red pants. They literally see colors in a different way than the rest of us.

The genes of born entrepreneurs also let them see things differently from others. In this case, though, they see *more*, not less. Just how our genes might affect that ability is difficult to measure precisely at this point. After all, spotting opportunity is one thing. Seizing it may also depend on many external factors, such as financial resources and whether you've got some of the other traits we've talked about. But both management and scientific studies present a tantalizing constellation of evidence that suggests they certainly play a role.

Twin studies give us some clues about genetic influences that may affect our ability and—just as important—our desire to pursue new opportunities. One study compared the similarities in work values between identical twins and fraternal twins. It measured six aspects of work values: the needs for Achievement, Comfort, Status, Altruism, Safety, and Autonomy. The highest correlation between genes and attitudes was in the area of Achievement: 56 percent of the differences between individuals seemed to be linked to their genes. That was followed closely by Status (43 percent), Safety (41 percent), and Autonomy (34 percent). All four are precisely the areas that are most likely to affect whether someone has an entrepreneurial personality.[1]

Intuition is critical too. Nearly everyone interviewed for this book said intuition plays a key role in their decision making. Recognizing whether all variables are in the right alignment depends largely on how you process information. Intuition is all about how we absorb, process, and interpret information. Identical twins often report having a special intuitive bond with each other; it's possible that at least part of that intuition may be related to their close genetic connection.

I haven't seen any research formally measuring the heritability of intuition. One problem is that it's not formally part of the Big 5 aspects of personality. However, there's a lot of overlap between four of the Big 5 traits and those measured by the Myers-Briggs Type Indicator test, which corporations often use to assess personalities. If you've ever heard someone say "I'm an INTJ" (or some other combination of four letters), they're talking about one of the sixteen Myers-Briggs types. Myers-Briggs *does* measure intuition, and what it calls "Intuition-Sensing" corresponds closely to the Big 5 trait of Openness to Experience.

One study of 100 sets of twins found that about 40 percent of the difference between people's levels of Intuition-Sensing is genetic.[2] That corresponds roughly with the heritability of Openness, estimated at anywhere from 45 to 61 percent (Openness ranks just behind Extroversion in terms of genetic influence). And as we discussed in earlier chapters, having a healthy dose of Openness to Experience can help keep conventional wisdom from putting blinders on you.

MARKERS FOR THE "SEEING AROUND CORNERS" GENE

- You cultivate a wide intuition network that can help you spot opportunities.
- You not only recognize opportunities, you act on them.
- You see conventional wisdom as a building block instead of a box.
- You practice two-steps-ahead thinking to see how trends may play out.
- You look for patterns in data, events, conversations, and everyday life.
- You look for simple ideas that have been overlooked.
- You live where the opportunities are.
- You scan a lot of information to spot trends.
- You focus intently on any potential opportunity to see things you might otherwise miss.
- You don't assume that an opportunity will be around forever.
- You take time to recharge your brain.

Another study of genetic effects on intuition has been questioned because of a relatively limited sample size and population. However, researchers believe it does demonstrate at least some genetic component to intuition. Women have two X chromosomes; men have only one. A gene on that extra chromosome, inherited from the father, seems to be linked to the ability to understand a social situation intuitively based on nonverbal cues such as facial expressions and body language. Researchers say this may be a genetic clue to so-called feminine intuition.[3] As with most genetic links to behavior, researchers say one gene can't explain everything, but it does hint that intuitive abilities may get their start at the cellular level.

When I was CEO of Harrison & Star just before it was acquired, I tended to hire female creative directors and account executives more often than males. I felt that women listened to clients better, were more service oriented than their male counterparts, and tended to interact better with clients. While my experience does not constitute a study, I certainly saw real-world differences in my agency's performance.

The concept of intuition being a feminine characteristic has to be taken with a grain of salt, though. A study using the Cognitive Style Index, a test designed to measure intuitive thinking, found little difference between female and male managers in terms of their intuitive orientation. It did find, however, that female non-managers were more analytical and less intuitive than their male non-manager counterparts or female managers.[4]

ATTITUDE AND FOCUS: ARE THEY IN YOUR GENES?

There's another way genes may help a born entrepreneur spot opportunity, though it's more indirect. It involves staying on forward focus and having an optimistic outlook. I think being blessed with a generally happy perspective on life makes it easier to focus on future possibilities. It's a lot tougher to see potential if your energy is being diverted into nonproductive regret over the past, which you can neither re-create nor relive. A more positive outlook frees up more mental bandwidth for spotting a potentially lucky break. Not many base runners spot a way to steal home if they're concentrating on the guy who tried to tag them out on the last play.

Researchers studying levels of happiness in 2,000 pairs of twins found that one twin's level of happiness was a better predictor of the other twin's happiness than was either twin's IQ level or social, financial, or marital status. Identical twins raised together reported almost identical levels of well-being, even if their circumstances were very different. That indicates a strong genetic component. And those levels of feeling good tended to come back to a set point that seemed to remain relatively stable for each individual. Circumstances—disaster or good fortune—might push someone's level of happiness up or down temporarily. However, that level tended to return to that individual's happiness set point after about six months (although recent findings indicate that a strong reaction to major life events such as widowhood or unemployment did tend to lower that set point a bit).[5] The twin study mentioned above found that that set point determines about half of a person's sense of well-being.[6]

Finally, there's an interesting study that I think sheds some light on an entrepreneur's ability to pursue a goal even though the outcome is highly uncertain. Researchers at the National Institute of Mental Health turned ordinary monkeys from procrastinators into workaholics simply by switching off a gene that helped them know when they would be rewarded for completing their work. In the experiment, the monkeys were given juice after they finished a series of tasks. They could tell how close they were to getting rewarded by watching a bar grow on their monitor (reminds me of humans waiting while downloading a piece of software!). The closer the monkeys were to getting their reward, the better they worked and the fewer errors they made. Researchers say they behaved like humans who procrastinate about doing anything to get a reward that's a long way away (such as saving for retirement, for example).

Then the researchers shut off the function of a gene called D2, which affects a chemical involved in how our brain processes rewards and learning. The monkeys could no longer tell just how close they were to getting their juice. They began working more efficiently and making fewer errors, as if the reward were constantly just around the corner.[7]

In the same way, entrepreneurs are able to attack an opportunity and pursue it relentlessly, even though they may not know precisely when it will pay off. As I've noted elsewhere, one of the facets of Extroversion is a high energy level, the desire to be active constantly. I think this contributes to the entrepreneurial sense of urgency that leads someone to grab opportunities rather than simply dream about them. "Once you've got that idea, you've got to execute," says American's Crandall. "We certainly thought of ideas earlier than our competitors did, but we also executed on those ideas better. Before we ever announced AAdvantage, we had all the computers programmed to handle it, and we announced the recordkeeping system the same day we announced the program. Our competitors simply couldn't catch up for a long time, and we sustained a huge competitive difference for ten years as a result. You've got to pay a lot of attention to execution."

MULTIPLY YOUR LISTENING WITH AN INTUITION NETWORK

Entrepreneurs have a reputation for being loners. It probably comes from the ability to persevere in pursuing one's idea despite the people who say "That will never work." But determination doesn't automatically make you a loner. In fact, the most successful entrepreneurial thinkers I know are people who create networks of support for themselves and their ideas. Just as important, they recognize that other people can play a big part in helping them spot opportunities. An "intuition network" can be one of the most powerful tools in helping you do that.

I've talked about information-based intuition. But where do you get the information in the first place? Sure, you read newspapers, magazines, books, and memos, and all of that is useful. But I think your intuition network can be just as important if you know how to use it.

Everyone knows that listening to customers is important. I'd argue that a born entrepreneur excels at listening for the Big Idea in everyone. You never know who is going to have a comment, a quote, a piece of data, a story, a statistic—something that might turn on that lightbulb over your head. I'm not saying that someone told Michael Dell, "Hey, you ought to start a business producing made-to-order computers." I'm saying that listening to what people are saying with an eye to how it might create an opportunity is a characteristic of entrepreneurial thinking. This book is an example. It was prompted by interest from business acquaintances who were intrigued with the non-linearity of my evolution from scientist to CEO, with the idea of my being an entrepreneurial CEO managing entrepreneurs, and with the similarities I saw between myself and those I managed.

"Listening gives you the ability to control the conversation," says Pat Croce. "The only way I learn is by listening. There's an old Italian saying: 'Listening brings wisdom; speaking brings repentance.' That's been key to my success: listening, observing, and reading. It gives you new ideas, new ways of looking at things."

There's another reason an intuition network is so important: It has a multiplier effect. Think about it for a moment. When you listen to a client or customer, you're not just listening to that individual. You're able to explore the knowledge of that client's clients and colleagues, indirectly tapping the forecasts, observations, and knowledge of far more people than you could hope to reach on your own. That doesn't mean you necessarily have to use that aggregated indirect wisdom, but it can create a baseline or foundation of input that you can act on. It also can give you a broader sense of the opportunities out there waiting to be explored.

The flip side of listening to your intuition network is knowing how to use the information you get. Often information still boils down to intuition. "Certainly in my case and I think perhaps with other entrepreneurs I've known, even if you say you're going to be objective, your instincts and your intuition or your wishes are a factor," says Al Neuharth. "I know there are many times when I attached greater weight to certain research findings, if you will, because they told me some of what I believed going into it. And then it became a matter of trying to figure out how to achieve what those goals were, rather than debating interminably whether to try to achieve it. *USA Today* was a major example for us. I had four young geniuses who were in their late twenties, early thirties, research all aspects of that—and this was over a two-year period before the decision to go with it was made. They all confided in me afterward, first individually and then collectively, that they knew I wanted the decision to be a go rather than a no-go. And there were ways—even though a lot of fact went into their fact-finding—there were ways that those facts were tilted. I think that's one thing you have to look out for, including your own inclination to tilt them in the direction that your instincts want you to go."

SPOTTING PATTERNS

Seeing opportunities isn't strictly intuition, of course. Another way to spot business opportunities is to be good at recognizing patterns: behavior patterns, buying patterns, patterns in reported customer problems, patterns in connections between short-term events and long-term trends. It involves subconsciously matching existing circumstances against something in the past that has either worked or not worked. Scott Cook credits his experience with consumer-testing products at Procter & Gamble with helping him create Quicken as user-friendly personal-finance software, even though Intuit and its products were not remotely like Crisco.

It's not so much that an entrepreneur sits down and says, "I think I'll look for some patterns today." Patterns just seem to emerge. Anyone who saw the movie *A Beautiful Mind* probably remembers the scene in which the lead character looks at a wall of numbers. Suddenly some of the numbers seem to emerge from the rest, highlighted in boldface, forming a pattern apparent only to the scientist. Okay, I'll grant you that the character was genuinely delusional. Still, it's a terrific visual metaphor for the way entrepreneurs seem to make connections that others don't. And besides, plenty of entrepreneurs have been considered delusional by people who didn't see the patterns they did.

SEEING MEANING IN CHAOS

Try reading this paragraph:

Aoccdrnig to a rseearechr at Cmabrigde Uinervtisy, it deosn't mttaer in waht oredr the ltteers in a wrod are agnrared; the olny iprmoetnt tihng is taht the frist and lsat ltteer be at the rghit pclae. The rset can be a total mses and you can sitll raed it wouthit porbemls. Tihs is bcuseae the huamn mnid deos not raed ervey lteter by istlef, but the wrod as a wlohe and the biran fguiers it out aynawy.

I'll bet you didn't have much trouble. The reason why is in the text itself. Our brains are wired to create meaning from what we observe. We see a familiar pattern—a word—within each chunk of scrambled letters. We don't rearrange the text logically; we intuitively "see" the correct pattern and its proper meaning.

Our brains are geared to see patterns. They can be as mundane and negative as "My boss always keeps me later than everyone else" or "Any stock I buy always goes down right after I buy it." Or they can be as profound and useful as realizing that many important biological objects are paired, which led James Watson to conceptualize the structure of DNA as many sets of base pairs—a double helix. *Entrepreneurs may simply be better at spotting useful patterns than other people.*

In my case, a key pattern was created by multiple clients who kept saying over and over, "If you ever start your own agency, we want you to represent us." Clients were unhappy with some of their agencies because their people just didn't seem to care or think about innovative ways to communicate brand messages. I would have had to be pretty dense not to recognize that that pattern clearly indicated an opportunity for an agency that specialized in health-care marketing, and that addressed that market in a way that respected clients' and customers' intelligence.

Patterns can be spotted in even the most casual incident. When I went out to lunch with the president of Mercedes-Benz, I reached into my pocket just as I was starting my meal and said, "I hope you don't mind but I'd like to take my vitamins." I had about five or six that I threw in my mouth. He said, "My God, I'm so glad you did that." He reached in his pocket and brought out a handful of his own vitamins. He said, "I'm kind of generally embarrassed to do it, but since you're doing it, I'm going to do it." We talked for the next hour about maintaining health. The same thing happened with a small-business entrepreneur who said she and her husband take many vitamins and minerals daily. When I'm participating in a forum, I often ask, "How many people take vitamins?" Consistently, about half the people raise their hands.

To anyone but the blind and closed-minded, this would strongly suggest that there is enormous potential in Eastern modalities of managing health. These anecdotes tell me something about the opportunities in what I call the "phood industry": neutraceuticals, vitamins, minerals, all the things aimed at maintaining health rather than treating illness. This will absolutely affect our Western health-care delivery. After all, what would you rather do, maintain health or treat illness? It's that simple.

Pattern recognition is important on a personal level as well. Recognizing patterns in your interests, in your relationships with people, in your successes, and in your failures can help you paint the next picture in your evolutionary vision for yourself—one that's based on a profound understanding of your own innate strengths and weaknesses. And as we discussed in Chapter 2, "Imprinting Pleasure: Creating an Addiction to Success," recognizing patterns successfully improves our ability to recognize more of them in the future.

"It's almost subconscious," says John Bogle Jr. "I think that's strongly a part of genetic makeup. I don't consciously do it. Over time the patterns just start to make sense in your mind. You start to think to yourself, 'Gosh, I've seen this before.'"

SUCCESS PROMOTER: THE "SEEING AROUND CORNERS" GENE

Nobel Prize–winning scientist Linus Pauling is said to have told a student that the way he arrived at his great ideas was to have a lot of them and throw away the bad ones. Even if you don't feel you're naturally intuitive, there are things you can do to help yourself get better at spotting opportunities and taking advantage of them. Remember, thinking like an entrepreneur doesn't demand that you actually be one. Tapping the power of intuition can help you in making even day-to-day decisions.

Borrow Other People's Brains

In addition to developing and using your intuition network, you can team up and work with someone whose intuitive radar is more finely tuned than yours. If you can find someone like that, a partnership can be the best of both worlds for both of you. Of course, we're talking partnership, not idea theft.

Look for the Obvious

Sometimes the best ideas are so simple that they're overlooked. Customer self-service has changed the way most companies do business. Ebay has built a business on the idea of facilitating individuals selling to one another. Market by hiring college students to go to student hangouts and talk to other students about how cool a certain product is. Slice the bread. Manufacture computers one customer at a time, as Dell does. Create software and hardware that let people download and play the music they want to hear. Ideas like these can transform entire industries.

I do some volunteer work for the New York Academy of Medicine, whose Manhattan offices are on Fifth Avenue in the 120s. Not long ago I was sitting in the office of the president. We were talking about specific opportunities and needs in urban health care. His office has large windows on two sides. At one point, he swiveled his chair to look out the window that overlooks Fifth Avenue. He said, "Tom, why is it when I look out this window, I see people who have great health care, great quality of life, and live generally longer"—he swiveled his chair just ninety degrees to face the window that looks out on Harlem—"than the people I see out of this window?"

In a single sentence this person had crystallized a situation—urban health care—with potentially huge opportunities for anyone who can begin to tackle them. Big ideas to address big problems are scarce, but they hold the ability to shape the future. They empower entrepreneurs. That creates opportunity. And opportunity creates industries.

Live Where the Opportunities Are

The reason John Patrick evolved into IBM's Internet evangelist, both internally and to the company's customers, was because he was a lifelong computer hobbyist. "You've got to live in that world. Innovation comes from living where these things happen. You can't be on top of Internet technology unless you use it. You have to play and work and live in the space where those things happen. You need to be in the thick of things. Especially in big corporations, you can think sometimes that the outside world is down there in one of the divisions. A field trip means visiting a division. It's essential to be out where the people are. You've got to think like the Internet is, get down to the real grass roots. You've got to put your idea out there, get feedback on it, get more feedback, change it. You need to think big, act bold, start simple, and iterate like crazy."

The same is true of other areas. You can't start a new agency by replicating past or even current models. Innovation isn't about "me-too's." Imitation may be the best form of flattery, but it doesn't create industries; it only genericizes them. You can't design a minivan without being with mothers and understanding their needs. You can't invent the iPod without knowing how teenagers want to get their music. You need to be on the playing field to see openings to score.

Scan the Horizon

Backing off from details regularly lets you absorb a bigger picture. I think of it as "seeing horizontally." Sam Zell reads five newspapers a day and six magazines a week; he says he can't remember individual stories but that broad-based reading allows him to spot trends. Seeing horizontally across a wide range of subjects and sources as well as vertically—focusing intensely on a specific niche—gives intuition more information from which to generate ideas. Again, intuition follows information.

Focus

It may seem contradictory to scanning, but it's not. Having an intense focus on a potential opportunity can help you see things you otherwise wouldn't. The entertainment industry is changing rapidly. I'm not precisely sure what the next evolutionary step is for media companies, but I'll bet it incorporates other industries, which will affect consumer demand, brand awareness, and client spending.

Start to Swing Before the Pitch Is Over the Plate

As I've said, entrepreneurial thinking involves a sense of urgency about pursuing an opportunity rather than wasting time endlessly refining it—or, worse, simply dreaming about it without doing anything. I met a woman a few years ago whom I wanted to hire. I tried arranging interviews through her assistant, but they always got canceled. When I contacted her personally to set up an interview, she told me she couldn't do it for a couple of weeks because of her travel schedule. I asked her what she was doing after work that day. "Going to the gym," she said. "Great!" I said. "I'll pick you up at work and drive you to your gym in Connecticut." So that's what we did. I hired her before we ever got to the gym. She still works for me today. She's terrific, and that trip was a good opportunity for us both.

Once David Neeleman of JetBlue was convinced that a route to the Dominican Republic made sense, he wanted to move immediately. "He had a gut about it from talking to customers on planes who said, 'Why don't you fly there?'" says Ann Rhoades. "He consistently kept getting it, and his gut told him the numbers would be great, so he said, 'Let's just announce it. Let's apply for international status.' Then he had his team look at it. And thank God the numbers supported it. I think if your gut's an educated gut, it's usually backed with a lot of data. It's reinforced by having been successful."

In baseball, you can't wait to swing until the pitch is directly over the plate. You have to anticipate, move—and move fast.

Take Time Off

The part of your brain that intuition works from needs time and space occasionally to refresh itself. You've got to make sure you take breaks to let it do that. I'm constantly amazed at the thoughts that my brain can generate just staring at a sunset. You need to find what relaxes you, and what gives your mind the peaceful setting to think BIG.

AND IF YOU MISS AN OPPORTUNITY?

Very few of the people interviewed for this book could recall any opportunities they had missed, though they all said there probably were some. Entrepreneurs don't look back. They simply have a sense that there are always more possibilities out there, and that looking back is useful only if it can teach them something about the future. Looking back is generally not an option for them.

Remember, things go in cycles. This may not be the right time for a particular opportunity, and the next turn of the wheel may bring others. And even if you do feel that entrepreneurial urgency, don't be afraid to sleep on a decision.

This doesn't displace entrepreneurial urgency. Intuiting—or sleeping on—decisions and instinct are not mutually exclusive. In fact, they're quite complementary. Every entrepreneur must strategically wrestle with his BIG idea and get very comfortable with it before reacting. Entrepreneurs are more proactive planners than reflexive actors. That gives them the luxury of being able to think their instincts through. They plan for and generally reach success.

The Challenge of Fighting Fear, Part II: Understanding and Believing in Your Product

When I see elaborate ads for antidepressants and erectile dysfunction in the middle of the Super Bowl, I have to laugh. When I became an ad man, you didn't advertise medicines to consumers, only to doctors or other health-care professionals. Drug-company ads were in the medical journals and were loaded down with type. Most general ad agencies saw pharmaceuticals as boring and not at all creative. They wanted nothing to do with drug advertising. But at Harrison & Star, we really *liked* what we were doing—and our enthusiasm showed. We tried and succeeded at injecting creativity into what could have been boring ads. Boy, did we have a good time.

My partner had a better brain for understanding the science than anyone with whom I had worked. And I had always been able to let the science make my case for me. During my days as a professional sales rep at Pfizer, I had almost never used the sales materials that were shipped to us; I would sit in the cafeteria with doctors and diagram how and why a particular drug worked better than our competitors'. Sometimes I would use a clinical-study reprint pulled from the hospital library. However, my most effective visual aids were always the cafeteria's white paper napkins on which I'd draw my diagrams.

That rich familiarity with the science behind the medicine and the "DNA" of doctors helped set us apart for the pharmaceutical companies who were our clients. We also knew we were in the right place at the right time. Our growth was jet-propelled by a steady stream of new and important drugs being developed, and an aging population with greater demand for advanced medicines. We weren't selling advertising; when I talked to prospects, I was selling our understanding of our clients' industry, their particular brands, and their customers: the docs who wrote the prescriptions. Knowing that—and knowing how valuable that was—gave me a profound belief in what we were offering. That belief made winning business—a lot of business—a piece of cake.

It's hard to think like an entrepreneur without having that belief in your product, whether the product is a thing, a service, or yourself. As I've said, successful entrepreneurs understand the risk of what they're doing conceptually. But often, it just doesn't *feel* like risk to them. And part of the reason why is that they not only believe in themselves, they believe in what they're selling—and understand why they believe in it.

One of the best sales pitches I ever got was from a BMW salesman. This guy knew absolutely everything about the car. He was able to answer every question off the top of his head, and in a very entertaining way explain some of its unique features. For example, he told me that when you shift into reverse, the right outside mirror tilts down twelve degrees. I asked him, "Why twelve degrees?" He explained that eleven degrees wouldn't let me see the curb. I'm a detail-oriented, analytical kind of guy; I was sold by his profound understanding of why the car was engineered the way it was—and by his realization that I was the right customer for that sort of information.

When I talk about understanding your product, I'm not just talking about the product itself. Understanding your product—whether it's a product, a service, an idea, or yourself—means understanding what the market is for what you want to sell, and what it takes to get it sold. That means knowing who and what your competition is. More important, it means understanding what your market will need in a year or two or three, so that you're always relevant to your market. Finally, it means analyzing your own limitations, and knowing how to make up for them. You may not be genetically wired for confidence, but working through all of those issues and constantly reminding yourself of the answers can improve your ability to believe in success—your success.

When John Bogle Sr. launched the Vanguard family of mutual funds, investing was by and large done through brokers—when it was done at all. The idea of marketing directly to consumers, so common today, was practically unheard of. And yet Bogle makes clear that for him, the idea of increasing investor returns by reducing the costs of running a mutual fund was so simple and obvious that success was, well, just a sure thing.

"To be honest, I never thought there was any risk whatsoever in starting Vanguard. I knew being the low-cost provider in a field where low cost is, over the long run, almost everything, was a guaranteed formula for success. The only question was how quickly would we get big," he says. "It seems kind of nutty that we were the first ones to eliminate the whole broker-dealer distribution system and go no-load; to create the first three-tiered bond fund, which changed the nature of bond investing; to create the first stock index fund. How could those things happen? The answer is easy. Any idiot knew they would work. . . . I don't think most people are really risk takers. A lot of risk takers are oblivious to the notion that there's even a risk going on."

Debbi Fields Rose was a bit different. She definitely knew she was taking a risk when she opened a store to sell cookies. Her parents had told her she was crazy to think about building a business out of her longtime baking hobby. Her husband had said, "I bet you can't do even fifty dollars' worth of business in one day." But she was determined to show the world she could be more than they expected. That determination had been "switched on" when she was twenty-one and a dinner guest in the home of one of her husband's wealthy clients. Still in junior college, she was both terrified and anxious to impress her hosts. At one point, the man asked her, "What are you trying to do with your life?" Hoping to sound smart, she replied, "I'm trying to get myself orientated." Her host picked up a heavy dictionary, threw it at her, and snapped, "Listen, if you can't speak the English language, don't speak at all. The word is 'oriented.'" The humiliation and tears reinforced her desire to do something big—*really* big.

So there she was, on her first day, her heart in her throat. At twenty-five cents a cookie, she would have to sell more than 200 cookies to beat her husband's fifty-dollar challenge. Hours passed without a single sale. "I realized I was failing big time. I said to myself, 'I can either stand here in the store feeling this way, or I can do something about it. If they taste them, they'll buy.'" Determined to prove her husband wrong, she went out onto the sidewalk and started giving away her cookies. Customers followed her back to the store. She went home that night having sold seventy-five dollars' worth of cookies, and customers kept coming back for more. Her little store eventually became Mrs. Fields Cookies—talk about getting herself "oriented." What kept her going on that first day was her belief in the value of her product, a belief that became the foundation of her entire business model.

I don't think anyone can truly be successful at thinking like an entrepreneur unless he believes in what he (or she) is doing. No entrepreneur is going to take the kind of risks that starting a business involves unless he knows at a gut level that what he's offering is valuable. And if it's important for an entrepreneur, why should anyone else settle for less? After all, even if you're working in a corporation, you're taking on risk. You're risking your time, your energy, your career, your company's money. It should be for something worthwhile. And if it's worthwhile to you, it will be easier to make the effort to figure out why it's worthwhile to others and convince them of that.

Thinking like an entrepreneur means being able to sell—your product, your ideas, or yourself. If you don't or can't believe in your product, you're better off doing something else. And if you're going to be convincing, the first person you have to convince is yourself. Either you need to find a reason to believe in your product or you need to find something else to sell. Unless you understand your product and know exactly why your customer should too, you won't be successful. You may be able to list pros and cons. You may find ways to talk around problems. But you won't have the kind of success that comes with a profound understanding of the value of your product for each individual customer you approach.

If you do your homework on that, you won't have to worry about whether you'll succeed. Passionate understanding creates confidence.

NEUROTICISM: BEING A "SAMURAI WORRIER"

Can you inherit the ability to believe in something so strongly that you're able to convince others of its value? Maybe. It's no accident that entrepreneurs are sometimes described as having an "almost religious" belief in their product. Studies about religious belief in twins may hold some clues as to how our genes may affect our attitudes. Identical twins tend to share similar attitudes about religion even if they were reared separately.[1] One study looked at the influence of genetics on the attitudes of 336 pairs of adult twins about what the study called "Organized Religion." The study estimated the genetic influence was .45; by contrast, the influence of a shared environment, such as family, was .00.[2] The choice of religion wasn't linked to genes—only the *capacity* for belief.

Another possible link is a gene called VMAT2; Gary Hamer, chief of the gene structure and regulation section at the National Cancer Institute, has dubbed it the "God Gene." In Hamer's research, it seems to be linked to a quality labeled "self-transcendence."[3] Psychiatrists describe self-transcendence as including a sense of being connected to something larger than oneself and a willingness to accept some things on faith without demonstrable proof. *I think that any genetic capacity for having faith in something may simply get expressed in a somewhat different way in entrepreneurs—in their belief in their ideas or products.*

The other genetic advantage is a lack of anxiety. *Successful entrepreneurs just don't tend to get overwhelmed by life's dark side;* if anything, they can be too optimistic. Inheriting a high level of Neuroticism imposes a double jinx for thinking like an entrepreneur. It predisposes you to experience life generally more negatively than others. Even worse, you tend to react more strongly and emotionally to that perceived negativity. For example, if a venture capitalist treats you badly, you'll experience that as a major blow instead of just another step in the process. On top of that, you'll tend to let that negativity spiral out of control: "This must mean I'm a failure." "I'll never get funding." "What was I thinking?" Or it may prevent you from even approaching VCs in the first place. It turns you into what I call a "Samurai Worrier."

Doesn't sound like any successful entrepreneur I know.

Researchers have made some progress identifying genes that may contribute to making you a Samurai Worrier. We talk about people "tearing their hair out" when they're worried or anxious about something. An experiment with mice at the University of Utah shows just how apt that phrase is. Researchers knocked out a specific gene called Hoxb8—that is, they prevented it from functioning. The mice began to groom themselves and their cage mates so much and so hard that they wound up with bald patches and skin wounds. The behavior is similar to what in humans would be called obsessive-compulsive disorder, which in humans is often linked to anxiety.[4]

Other intriguing research has been done with a certain variation of a gene that helps regulate the levels of serotonin in the brain. (Prozac works by helping the brain use serotonin more effectively.) That variation of the 5-HT gene seems to stimulate chronic anxiety, depression, and a tendency toward what psychologists call "Harm Avoidance." Some studies have begun linking their functions to Neuroticism, a highly heritable personality trait that can really get in the way of believing in yourself and your product.[5]

Most entrepreneurs exhibit qualities that indicate that they're low on inherited Neuroticism. If you've inherited a full cup of Neuroticism, you probably know it instinctively even without taking the Entrepreneurial Personality Quiz. By contrast, people with a low genetic level of Neuroticism are relatively stable emotionally:

• They're not worriers. People who are highly neurotic tend to be chronically anxious. They not only see a lot of potential threats, but they react strongly to their fear of them.

• They don't fly off the handle. Either they don't get angry easily, or they treat anger like any other passing emotion.

• They're depression-resistant. Instead of letting obstacles throw them into an emotional tailspin, they're resilient in the face of problems that leave others discouraged and depressed. It's true that some successful people have had to combat severe clinical depression. However, they likely have other qualities such as Conscientiousness, that when coupled with professional treatment, enabled them to persevere despite their depression.

• They're not self-conscious about or overly sensitive to what others think of them.

• They're able to control their impulses. Even if they crave risk, they don't act impulsively on those cravings.

• They cope well with stress and don't tend to be overwhelmed emotionally by pressure.

As with any of the heritable personality traits, people can have some of these factors and not others; for example, someone may get angry easily but lack other Neurotic characteristics and be able to function quite well.

THE VOICES OF NEUROTICISM

	LOW NEUROTICISM	HIGH NEUROTICISM
Chronic anxiety	"Risk? What risk?"	"It's too risky. I'd probably fail, and then I'd probably have to declare bankruptcy, and my whole family would starve."
Chronic hostility	"Hey, that's life."	"Every boss I've ever had has played favorites and been a complete jerk."
Tendency toward depression	"Tomorrow is another day."	"I hate my life. I'm a complete failure and I always will be."
Self-consciousness	"Who cares if they think I'm crazy?"	"What will people think?"
Difficulty handling stress	"When the going gets tough, the tough get going."	"Oh no! This is a disaster! I can't handle this! What am I going to do?"
Impulsiveness	"No, thank you. I'd love a piece of chocolate, but I want to lose ten pounds and I've got four more to go."	"I can't believe I ate all that chocolate. Another piece? Oh well, I've already blown my diet. Why not?"

Neuroticism in smokers has been tied to having greater trouble with quitting.[6] In my experience, it also leads to problems with making and sticking to decisions—especially when those decisions involve taking risks. Being a Samurai Worrier about everything equally is a *big* problem for thinking like an entrepreneur.

Being chronically angry or hostile alienates the network of people you need to help you accomplish your goals. If you're easily discouraged, you'll likely see only the obstacles, not how to get around them. That can not only sink an enterprise but keep it from being launched in the first place. Being self-conscious can impede risk taking by making you anxious about looking foolish or being thought wrong. Vulnerability under stress can leave people unable to make a decision at all, or cause them to make decisions on a purely emotional basis rather than tactical or strategic.

"Employees who score high for Neuroticism are probably going to find something to complain about no matter how enlightened the management," says Robert McCrae,[7] one of the researchers who has worked extensively with the Big 5 personality factors. I know people like that, and I'll bet you do, too.

Being low on Neuroticism doesn't automatically make you a risk taker, and it certainly doesn't guarantee a belief in what you're selling. Indeed, people with a high level of Neuroticism may develop risky behavior, such as drug experimentation, to help themselves deal with the inner demons brought on by a chronically negative outlook. But anyone who knows that they're chronically anxious, hostile, self-conscious, or depressed should seriously think twice about trying to be an entrepreneur. A description of Neuroticism certainly doesn't fit someone who's going to be good at dealing with risk, even assuming they could convince themselves to take a risk in the first place. It's tough to believe in your product when your inner Samurai Worrier is interpreting everything in the worst possible way.

THE RISKS OF NOT UNDERSTANDING WHAT YOU'RE SELLING

We talked earlier about the value of Openness to Experience. If you didn't inherit much of that, take heart; that lack of Openness might actually help you be more comfortable with taking risks. Research with people at risk of contracting HIV has shown that people who deny the risks of contracting HIV through unsafe sex have a lower Openness score than those who recognize the dangers they run. Openness involves the ability to imagine and conceptualize. It helps give your brain the raw data it needs to analyze a situation. Researchers speculate that having a low level of Openness leaves those people in denial. They simply have trouble imagining that the life-threatening consequences of unsafe sex could actually happen to them. Lacking imagination seems to give them a certain feeling of invulnerability.[8]

In a way, it reminds me of so many dot-com companies. The brand was everything. Many of them forgot to get real about understanding what they were selling and what (if anything) made it valuable. Amazon isn't selling things; it's selling comprehensiveness and convenience. Too many dot-coms were simply selling ether. Most dot-com "entrepreneurs" didn't realize the Internet was just another communication medium. Those who made it understood what the Internet really is, and had a way to monetize their business model.

Being in denial isn't smart risk taking, though. I knew a person who had a phenomenally successful, lucrative niche medical-communications business. He was smart enough to have big ideas about how to morph his business, and he tacked on a bunch of other businesses. He siphoned off executives from the core and put them in charge of operations they knew nothing about. A supersized ego somehow blinded him to the consequences of what he was doing. He couldn't imagine the core business getting sick. Well, not only did it get sick, but the disease turned out to be fatal. When the core business died, so did everything else. Like someone who knows he has a genetic risk of heart disease but eats a steak every night for dinner, this person wasn't "open" to the potential impact of bad judgment.

The Openness that lets entrepreneurs recognize a great idea also should help them recognize that others have great ideas, too. Maybe they're ideas that might improve their product—or maybe they're ideas that might displace their product. Openness allows you to assess your product and your market constantly, understand competition, and stay ahead of those who may try to erode your market.

"There's this incredible tradeoff between persistence and belief and all that, and a willingness to listen to what the world's saying back to you," says the University of Michigan's Tom Kinnear. "If the market-place is telling you something, if customers are saying the same thing over and over again, and you don't listen, you've got a problem."

The trick is having enough confidence in your idea to be willing to expose it to testing, to listen to feedback that can make it better or tell you to go in another direction altogether. Understanding your product well enough to be able to assess information accurately about what's involved in developing and using it means being open enough to analyze out the risks.

SUCCESS PROMOTER: THE "COLD CALL" GENE

I've seen a lot of books that talk about risk taking, but I've never seen one that links it to sales skills. Show me something that forces you to take a risk—starting a business or project—and I'll bet you that being successful at it involves being able to sell. You have to be able to convince other people to believe what you see in something. You can have the greatest idea in the world, but if you can't persuade other people of the value of what you're doing—your idea, yourself—you won't get very far.

A creative director at one of my agencies today used to work for an agency that was launched at roughly the same time Harrison & Star was. It too focused on health care, and it was headed by four incredibly talented people. When it was launched just after we started our agency, it made a huge splash. At the time, my partner and I were worried. Here we had risked everything on our new business, and already somebody was trying to take over our little niche. I knew I couldn't let the challenge overwhelm me. Instead of spending energy on worrying about the competition, I made up my mind to let it refocus and re-energize me. We told ourselves that the fact that they were there and in business reaffirmed that we should be doing this, that there was a solid market here. I had never had any problem making cold calls, but having to look over my shoulder gave me a little extra motivation to get out there and reach every client I could before they did.

Actually, that proved to be a snap. None of those four talented people really felt comfortable with cold calls. Me—I loved them! Cold calls were a chance not only to recruit new clients but also to find out things that would help me make the next sale after that. The other agency never managed to position itself with potential customers and eventually closed its doors. It takes more than talent; they were all incredibly talented. It takes the entrepreneurial gene, the gene that says, "I'm going to succeed on my own and not wait for someone to 'make me successful.'" Remember, people will just naturally make *themselves* successful before they take a chance to make you successful.

MARKERS FOR THE "COLD CALL" GENE

- You understand what you're really selling and why it's valuable.
- You understand what makes you uniquely valuable in promoting your idea or product.
- You have enough confidence in your product or idea to listen to feedback.
- Your product or service offers values-based value.
- You really listen to the customer.

The Cold Call Gene Success Promoter requires you to understand thoroughly what makes your idea or product valuable. After I left Pfizer, I went to work for an ad agency. When I was introduced to my first client—another large pharmaceutical company—I got a quick lesson in what my personal product was for these folks. The guy at the other end of a big boardroom table sat me down and said, "We just want to know what you did for Pfizer." I wasn't selling advertising. I was selling my experiences in sales and marketing for Pfizer. I was selling strategy. I realized I was a brand that stood for intelligence and strategic thinking. That was what this client wanted, not another ad campaign. And that's what they got. I actually strategized the most successful brand launch that that client had ever had till that time. It was the same when I ran my own agency: I was selling my brand of thinking. I took that task away from my clients so they could focus on all the other tasks of brand management.

In my current role, my team and I are responsible for assessing not only companies but the people in them. When we think about acquiring talent, one of the most important things we want to know is their approach to thinking and to creating value. If we don't understand it, neither will anyone else.

Brightstar's Marcelo Claure probably wouldn't have been successful if he hadn't had a profound understanding of what his business was all about. In fact, he probably would never have gotten past selling cell phones out of the trunk of his car. People said he was crazy to try to become a major distributor of cell phones in the Latin American market. "When we came into this industry, we were competing with a company called Cellstar and a company called Brightpoint. Both were publicly traded companies with a billion dollars in market cap with $300 million to $400 million in the bank. We had $100,000 to start. Everybody told us, 'Look, it's a crowded space, it's low margins, there's no room for you, it's a business that takes a lot of cash.'" Other companies didn't want to operate in a region with frequent political and economic turmoil. And Claure was trying to enter the market by distributing phones that not only cost more than their competitors' but were, in his words, "a piece of junk . . . God, they were ugly!"

Claure's strategy: Concentrate on making it easier to do business with him than with his competitors. The company not only delivered new phones to retailers, it bought back their excess inventory of the old ones (and oh, by the way, resold those older models elsewhere at a profit where phones—any kind—were harder to come by). And Claure made Brightstar indispensable by taking over chores such as forecasting inventory and handling the logistics of shipping, warehousing, and customs.

"People are lazy by nature. If you make [a buyer] pay for gas, manage his own shipping, figure out how many phones he needs, if you make him do all that—sure, they'll do it. But if you suddenly show them, 'Hey, you don't have to think when you do business with me. I'll do the thinking for you'—that's pretty attractive. It didn't matter that my phones were more expensive and uglier. Eventually it became a matter of people saying, 'Hey, you know, this isn't a focus for me. They can deliver the phones in my own country, they can bill me locally, they can handle payment and do forecasting. I'll just buy more and more phones from these guys regardless of the phones.'"

Claure understood exactly what he was selling, and it wasn't phones. It was convenience and ideas.

If you aren't a born salesman, here are some Cold Call Gene techniques that can help you be more persuasive:

Create Values-Based Value

Entrepreneurs succeed when what they're selling is in tune with their own values. Even better, some have managed to create what I call "values-based value." Their core values become a focal point of what they're selling.

Perhaps the best way to explain this is by example. John Bogle based Vanguard's low-cost approach to running mutual funds on his belief that it was the best way to deliver maximum return to shareholders. Because of that core value—maximum shareholder return—he made index funds the foundation of Vanguard's approach to investing. "Any idiot had the knowledge and the opportunity to do what I did. These weren't new ideas; they were just things that hadn't been done before. . . . I had created a company that depended on low costs, so I needed to create funds where we can deliver those low costs in the most obvious manner. It all seemed obvious to me then; it seems equally obvious and logical to me now." Vanguard's 500 Index Fund is now the largest mutual fund in the United States.

At Harrison & Star, one of our core values has always been integrity. We wanted to run an agency that relied on substance as much as, if not more than, style. We didn't sell ads. We sold peace of mind. Because we were always thinking about and driving our clients' businesses, they knew that someone other than themselves had the responsibility for their success and the success of their brands.

JetBlue's core value is a positive customer experience and satisfaction that goes beyond low airfares. The company hires employees based on their willingness to take risks to satisfy a customer. Harley-Davidson's turnaround in the 1980s came because they understood that they were selling not just motorcycles; they were—are—selling exhilaration to the community of people who rode Harleys. They nurtured Harley clubs, sponsored Harley events, and facilitated communication among Harley owners. The concept of "customer community" was values-based value. Starbucks isn't just selling coffee; it's selling an experience, a third space complete with a WiFi connection where you can go to relax, meet a friend, listen to music, conduct business, and, oh yes, buy a great cup of coffee.

David and Tom Gardner believe that going where others aren't and challenging conventional wisdom is the best way to produce above-average investing results. That's one of the reasons their Motley Fool Web site adopts an unassuming, relaxed, optimistic atmosphere, complete with their famous court jester caps. In seeking out unrecognized bargains and trying to make people comfortable with taking risks, they're creating values-based value.

Perhaps the most obvious example of all is Google, whose founders incorporated into its IPO filing documents an "owner's manual for shareholders." Among other things, the statement promised to establish a Google foundation to help "make the world a better place," focus on long-term opportunities, and take risks in pursuit of innovation. By making these idealistic promises part of its IPO, founders Sergey Brin and Larry Page are making public their belief that their values are an intrinsic part of their company's value.

Make your values part of the value of your product or service. If you do this, your customers will believe in you, in your brand, and in what you're selling. And their belief gives you the edge of an insider, a selling partner inside each of your selling targets. Values-based value lets you be natural, more comfortable selling. It complements your genetic makeup and lets you be more successful.

Remember That You Are Your Best Sales Tool

At Pfizer, one of the drugs I represented was a very expensive oral antibiotic. During one of my cafeteria meetings, a doctor hit me with a competitor's argument—a competitor I knew was not only a very seasoned rep but a longtime friend of his. The doc said my competitor's antibiotic was just as good but lots cheaper. I got out my trusty napkin and talked about my drug's scientific mode of action. I diagrammed how it actually blew up and killed the bacteria instead of just hindering their growth. That doctor was one of the reasons I became Rep of the Year; he became one of the most prolific writers of prescriptions for that antibiotic.

Being able to sell effectively means knowing what makes you uniquely valuable. If I hadn't understood how to use my cell biology background as a sales tool, I probably would never have considered switching careers. From the very beginning, I knew that if I could just get an appointment with a doctor, I could speak to him *in his language*. Doctors have even less patience than most people with anything they perceive as merely a sales pitch. I could answer their questions about the science behind why and how a certain drug would work for their patients. I even told doctors which patients weren't suited for a particular drug. How novel: honesty.

Understanding the value to others of that ability let me constantly overcome fear, even though I knew I was selling against more seasoned sales reps who had long-standing relationships with the same docs. A well-grounded belief in what you personally have to offer—your own unique selling proposition—makes it easier to understand how to use those qualities with others. It lets you work who you are to create a personal brand. What Tom Peters has so aptly named "Brand You" makes you memorable in others' eyes. Just as important, understanding your personal brand and why it makes you valuable to others can give you the confidence to do a better job of selling.

Think About What You're Giving

One of the reasons I was good at selling to doctors was that I always knew that a patient somewhere was going to feel better if a doctor prescribed my products. Sure, I wanted something from him for myself: a sale. But I also knew that I was offering something that would benefit people.

Entrepreneurs who are successful genuinely believe they are offering a way to do things better—a better product, a better service, a better talent. One of the quickest ways to get over being a Samurai Worrier is to think not in terms of what you want to get, but what you're giving. Offering something to the world that's going to make it better not only takes your focus away from yourself; it's also more inspiring to whomever you're trying to sell. After all, your customer doesn't care whether your company succeeds. He cares that it will make his life, his company, his work, his world, better (and so does she).

Listen to the Customer

Dell Computers is a great example of a company that understands what it's selling. Its business is built around tailoring a computer to your precise needs. When you call them, there's not a question the rep can't answer to help you figure out exactly what kind of computer is going to suit you best. What a model: mass specialization!

Okay, so "listen to your customer" is the oldest advice in the book. It's also the single most important thing you can do to bolster your belief in your product. If confidence is a problem for you, focus on letting your customer tell you what he needs. Then look for ways to anticipate those needs. It's the quickest way to a customer's heart. If you can consistently, accurately assess those and match them up with a profound understanding of your idea or product, you'll know you're selling the right thing to the right person in the right way. That will bring the kind of success that conveys confidence—the kind you can get addicted to.

When my friend who worked at the electronics company consulted with me on buying a home sound system, he wanted to know what kind of music I liked. I asked him why he did that. "If you listen to what you like and not what I might want to play, you're more likely to enjoy the experience," he said. "It will sound like what you're actually going to hear if you buy it, and you won't get turned off by the music itself." I always thought that was a great example of anticipating and aligning with a customer's needs and desires.

You need to ask yourself three basic questions:

- What do I need to know about this customer that will help me sell most effectively?
- What's the best way to get the information?
- How do I present my case, build my story, in the most non-obtrusive, most acceptable manner possible?

Be smart about whom you're listening to, though. You're not going to sell a mobile home to someone who's in the market for a $10 million mansion. When I was a pharmaceutical detail rep, I spent a lot of time just going around to doctors and learning about their practices: what kind of patients they treated, how they treated diabetic or hypertensive or depressed patients, how they felt about treating patients with a particular class of drugs. I knew their likes and dislikes, what they were comfortable prescribing and why. The information I gained told me which features and clinical data from my understanding of the drugs I represented was right for each doctor. Even though there were thousands of doctors in my territory, I sold to one doctor at a time.

In some ways, thinking like an entrepreneur basically comes down to common sense. And common sense is often tied to—you guessed it—really listening to people. It helped me take a lead in transforming pharmaceutical advertising from an industry that spoke only to people in white lab coats to one that spends billions of dollars talking to the guy on the street in a bomber jacket—the patient. Our understanding of communicating about our products had to shift. Providing healthcare information for patients was a dramatically different task than educating doctors. We had to become very smart very quickly about how you communicate with the consumer, and in a lot of cases the changes involved simple common sense. For instance, who better to learn from about communicating with consumers than the major general packaged-goods agencies? Their understanding of the consumer came from talking to them every day.

WHEN YOU'VE GOT A PRODUCT YOU CAN BELIEVE IN . . .

- Clients say, "If you go out on your own, we want you to represent us."
- The product sells itself.
- People voluntarily refer business to you.
- Price isn't an issue.
- Clients actually look forward to getting information from you (being sold).

But What if I Just Don't Believe in What I'm Doing?

What if you're stuck with promoting an idea you know is a dog? I know this sounds harsh, but if you're serious about being successful, find something else—a different product, a different company, anything. You don't have to, of course. Lots of people have earned a living by simply taking the money and checking out at the end of the day. But I promise you this: If you don't believe in what you're doing, you won't have the energy it takes to find out what you need to understand your customers and the value of your product to them. You won't want to do whatever it takes to make your idea succeed. And if you're a Samurai Worrier, you probably need a strong belief in your product just to drag yourself into work each day, let alone be successful at promoting it.

Remember: You stand the best chance of believing in your product, your project, your idea, or yourself if what you're doing aligns with your values and with who you are. I enjoyed my scientific training and research, but I realized I didn't love it. It was a means to an end—getting a graduate degree—but I didn't really like the confinement of the laboratory or the repetitive, routine nature of lab work. I wanted to relate to, talk to, sell to *people*. My adviser in grad school made me aware of that. Becoming a sales rep switched on those genes so that they got expressed every day. I could never have had as much fun or done as well in the lab, but God, could I sell!

When you do what your genes direct you to do, you're more comfortable, happier, more energized, more focused. And those qualities bring success—whatever success means for you.

CHAPTER 7

The Challenge of Embracing Rejection: Learning to Love Hearing "No"

When I was in high school, I knew I would have to find a job if I wanted to be able to afford going to college. Being a stockboy at the local A&P may not sound like much, but it paid better than any other starting job in our rural area in Highfield, Maryland, and there was a lot of competition for each slot. I knew I had an uphill battle; as a Maryland boy, I was competing for a job just across the state line with local guys who typically were given preference. You can't imagine how hard I worked to get that job. Starting in the spring of my junior year, I went to see the manager of that A&P at least once a week. Every Friday night I'd walk up to the little office where cashiers deposited their money and I'd stand in front of its iron bars. And every Friday night the manager would say in his booming voice, "Nothing yet." "Nothing yet."

I'd ask, "When do you think?" "Not sure. Check back," he'd say. Our routine went on for a year. But I had never really been intimidated by the word no. I knew if I kept at it, that A&P job would be mine. Finally I told him, "I'm graduating next week." He said, "Come back next Monday at 2 P.M. and you start."

Rejection wasn't pleasant, but it got me to college. For four years, I stocked shelves and unloaded tractor-trailer delivery trucks. I'd drive back and forth to college; I couldn't afford to live in the dorms. Often I'd work the night shift, come home, take a shower, study, then head out to classes the next morning. I probably appreciated the job more and worked harder because it had been such a tough sell to begin with.

And I lasted. After that, hearing a lot of no's on sales calls later would be a piece of cake.

One of the biggest challenges for any entrepreneur is dealing with rejection and setbacks. It takes something a little different from being determined to launch things in the first place. Many people have the smarts to start a business (like those four talented people who started a competing ad agency around the same time I did). *Sticking with it takes not just smarts but guts.* You may be crazy about your idea, but if you're thrown by obstacles that inevitably come up, you won't get very far. Maybe you'll face VCs or other people who don't want you to succeed and who pooh-pooh your idea (they're out there, believe me!). Maybe you'll discover that you're not immune to competition from a start-up similar to yours. Maybe you'll get a cold shoulder on cold calls. Maybe you'll come up against people who don't have time to think about change or listen to what you have to say. Most likely, you'll be faced with all of them—and more.

Successful entrepreneurs are like Hummers: they're unstoppable. Unlike people who seem to crumple at the first discouraging sign, they simply continue to roll. They keep moving forward, even if that motion is in small increments each day. Keeping it together and succeeding takes being totally sure of yourself, your talent, your sales ability, and what you're selling. Some people have to struggle every day to acquire and remind themselves of those attributes. Born entrepreneurs seem to come by them naturally. They use rejection in the way a track runner uses a starting block: as something to push against to move forward.

Peter Ueberroth became an entrepreneur because of a rejection—specifically, getting fired:

> "I was wrong, but I didn't think so at the time. I was performing very well, but I had a difference in judgment on an important decision involving a bunch of people who reported to me. I was twenty-one, twenty-two. I was told to give these people on a certain day their two weeks' notice, period. I said, 'Look, on the day I let them go, they go home without a job. They don't have a chance to get ready. Let's at least give them four weeks' notice, because they've worked huge amounts of overtime and we've not been charged for that. They've done an incredible job under difficult circumstances.' My employer

argued with me. And then I went back to him. We had gone to Vegas one weekend—he and his wife, my wife and I. I had watched him gamble with one roll of the dice more money than we were talking about for some forty people. Brashly, I said, 'Okay, we're only talking about one roll of the dice last weekend.' That broke the camel's back. He said, 'I took you along as part of my personal life and you know we always understood that personal life and business life are two different things. And now you're starting to judge my personal life, and you've crossed the line. You can join the forty people that you're letting off.' When you lose your job and you get fired on the spot, you start to think it would be really a bit better if you could make those decisions yourself.

"Rejection always hurts, but you know it's coming. Maybe it's like a good martini: seven to one. You get seven rejections for every acceptance. But you know that can happen. You know it's part of the game and it doesn't stop you and knock you out. You don't have to consciously say I'm going to recover from this rejection. You just keep going."

REJECTION ISN'T OPTIONAL—YOUR ATTITUDE IS

Most people think of entrepreneurs as being good at battling rejection. Actually, it's more complicated than that. If you think of rejection as an enemy you have to fight, you've already lost half the battle. You have to have a very different mind-set—one that transforms obstacles into opportunities.

If you go into a situation saying "I'm going to battle rejection"—well, it's like trying to walk through a brick wall. Why? Because your skin can get only so thick. You have to do more than be able to fight off being discouraged. You have to *embrace* the fact that you're going to have rejections—probably more than you expect—and use them to make you more passionate about what you're doing. Embracing rejection means anticipating it, appreciating it, respecting it, and being passionate about it. You almost *want* it to surface because you're ready to overcome it.

Being smart about how you prepare for rejection can help you convince yourself of the value of your product, of your abilities. For example, if you're facing a tough presentation, arming yourself against rejection means you're going to anticipate resistance. You're going to figure out how to answer any objections. And in figuring out those answers, you're reinforcing in your own mind what makes your product or idea valuable. When rejections happen, you have to be able to say to yourself, "I want to figure out how to turn No into Now, or No into Yes, or minimize the 'No's, or prevent them from occurring in the first place."

I actually looked forward to my Friday night "No"s from the A&P manager. I knew that with each rejection, the manager and I were developing a closer relationship. We liked each other; he looked forward to my coming in. At a minimum, I knew he knew who I was!

I've already told you that I got nothing but rejection for most of the first year after we launched Harrison & Star. Every potential client I called either didn't return my phone calls or said they were happy with their current agency and would call if they became disenchanted. I knew not to hold my breath; I would have died from lack of oxygen! Instead, I'd call back with ideas—ideas I thought would grow their brands. During all that time, our only business was a $35,000 job. We lost money on it because I overserviced and overproduced the program, but we were proud of it. It was our firstborn.

Then after fourteen months, the phone rang! On the other end was Mary. I had never met her, and until she introduced herself had no idea who she was or who she worked for. But I'll never forget what she said: "I've been told you know something about anti-infectives." A medical publisher I had known from my Pfizer days had stuck his neck out for me and recommended my agency.

My heart sank into my socks at Mary's next question: "How many people in your agency?" I knew my answer could mean a quick end to the conversation. But I also knew I had to be honest. "Four people," I said, as proudly as I could. "Well, we do business with large agencies, not little shops like yours," Mary said. "I'll call you back at 2 P.M. if we're interested."

I was so excited that I never went to lunch that day. A sandwich wasn't worth the risk of missing an early call back—if it came at all. To my surprise, at exactly 2 P.M., the phone rang. It was Mary, who seemed as surprised as I was. "I don't understand this, but they want you to come in and make a capabilities presentation," she said. "Let me tell you, you have *some* reputation." We were asked back after our presentation (in which we talked about how we thought, how we branded products, our successes) and won our first million-dollar-plus piece of business, competing against larger, well-established agencies. Harrison & Star was on the map! If we could build that client's brand, we knew we'd build our agency. We did both. The sales for that client's brand grew more than ten times. And our agency became the fastest-growing new health-care agency in the industry.

Thinking like an entrepreneur means expecting and even welcoming rejection, using it to fuel your vision and make you even more determined to succeed. The agency we beat out for that million-dollar assignment was an agency that had rejected me about a year earlier. The principals of that agency had planned to hire me; because of my track record, they knew I could bring them more business. But they had a change of heart at the last minute. And I do mean last minute: they dumped me when I arrived at their offices to sign my contract.

I wasn't angry—they explained that it was purely a business decision—*but it was a "punctuation point" that helped me see that I shouldn't work for or rely on anyone else.* I should just start my own agency and do it my way. I wouldn't have to answer to anyone except my clients. I can't say I welcomed that last-minute rejection, but it definitely fueled my vision of what I wanted.

Cold calls were a challenge for Rich Teerlink, who shepherded the turnaround of Harley-Davidson in the 1980s; he considers himself an introvert. And yet he was faced with the challenge of arranging financing that would save it from bankruptcy, and, eventually, of taking the company public. "I cold-called everybody on Wall Street—I would venture to say probably a hundred organizations—looking for financing. I just kept the faith that we had a good story and finally found someone who would listen to it."

How do entrepreneurs deal with constant rejection? "They get rid of it," says Teerlink. "[They say] 'I'm rejected. Okay, that's fine. Where's the next one?' If you dwell on failures or you dwell on shortcomings, I'll guarantee you you're not going to get to where you want to go, because you're wasting good energy." Just learn quickly from it and move on!

If success is part of your vision, you'd better welcome obstacles. They're the steppingstones to success—and the higher you go, the harder they are to climb over. Instead of steppingstones they become boulders. The bigger you dream, the more people there are in line waiting to tell you you're nuts. As we saw in Chapter 2, learning to handle problems early can be an advantage. Your genetic ability to overcome resistance only gets honed if you actually have to overcome it. The earlier that starts happening, the more practice you get. It's kind of like evolution. The more your body needs to do something, such as walk upright, to survive, the more your body's genes will evolve to make that action easier. We learn more from screwing up than from getting it right. After all, we don't question why we got something right. But if something blows up on us, we sure as heck try to figure out what happened so we can try to prevent it the next time—at least we do if we're smart.

Remember, entrepreneurial attitude isn't just confidence that something will work. That's certainly important. *But it's not as important as the knowledge that when there's a problem, you'll be okay, that ultimately you'll survive and thrive.* After all, there are only three things you can do about a problem (at least there are only three things that are any help): You can solve it, eliminate it, or survive it. Knowing you'll be able to do any or all of those gives you the resilience you need to embrace and be passionate about rejection.

REJECTIONS ARE OPPORTUNITIES TO CREATE TRUST

Smart entrepreneurs train themselves to want to hear more objections, not fewer. Why in the world would you want to hear *more* rejections? Seems counterintuitive, doesn't it? And yet every objection is valuable. Here's why. Every answer to a sales pitch or proposal contains two types of information:

- Yes/No information
- Why or Why Not information

Yes/No information is the answer to your sales pitch. In conventional thinking, Yes means success, No means failure. Yes/No information is what most people focus on.

Asking questions that lead to Why or Why Not information is key to embracing rejection. They're what allow you to use each objection, each point of resistance, as a learning opportunity. Yes/No information may or may not give you a sale. Why or Why Not information allows you to craft an ongoing strategy that produces recurring sales. It gives you information about your product and your customer that you can apply to understanding all your products or customers more intimately. It's what lets an advertising guy like me help a CEO or his marketing department develop innovative marketing strategy to build their corporation and brands, instead of simply selling another TV spot or direct mail campaign.

Yes/No Information	How to Get Why or Why Not Information
"I've tried that and I'd never do it again."	"Could you tell me about the problems you had?"
"I don't need your idea/product."	"Do you have a minute to talk about this other idea that might address the needs you expressed?"
"I'm too busy."	"When would be a better time for you?"
"Forget it."	"Is that your final answer?"
"It's not a priority for me."	"What are your competitors doing about this?"

That's why you're better off hearing more objections instead of fewer. Not only does it give you the chance to answer this customer's objections, it gives you more Why or Why Not information that can help you figure out how to deal with the same problem on the next visit, or for the next customer. Studies of consumer psychology have shown that if you can satisfy an unhappy customer, that person tends to be more loyal than a customer who has never had a complaint. If your customer feels you genuinely listen to his or her objections and address them honestly, you're more likely to win that customer's trust. That trust can create a more powerful bond than an easy sale does.

As a detail guy (pharma-speak for "sales rep"), I never promoted any product for patients whom I didn't feel would benefit from that product. *Sometimes I even promoted other products for certain patient types if I felt they would work better.* Boy, did that raise my selling credibility! That enhanced credibility reduced the number of rejections I had to overcome later. It all has to do with integrity—and I think we've all learned a lot about the impact of individual integrity or lack thereof over the past few years.

I had a powerful demonstration of the power of trust. My district manager had come along with me to call on a doctor—not the most comfortable situation for a rookie sales rep. There we were, sitting in the doc's office, discussing the merits of a particular drug. The doctor, never known for his patience, suddenly snapped at me, "I'll never prescribe that drug." He told me in no uncertain terms that my drug was too expensive compared to the other products he prescribed. Talk about rejection—and in front of my boss.

I reached across the desk, laid out a clinical reprint I had pulled from a medical library. I pointed to the figure indicating the rate of success with each drug. "That's your bottom line," I said. "It's not just per-pill cost. These could be your patients. How many times do your patients return with the same recurring problem? How cost effective is it to treat the same condition more than once?" That doctor eventually became one of the biggest writers of prescriptions for that drug in my Baltimore sales territory.

EXTROVERSION: THE WILL TO WIN

Carlos and Jorge de Cespedes came to the United States from Cuba when Carlos was eleven and Jorge was eight. The brothers lived without their parents for five years in a camp for Cuban exile children, nicknamed the "Pedro Pan" program. "You were on your own, and you had no other choice than to be entrepreneurial at a very early age," Carlos recalls. Boys at the camp got $1.40 a week allowance, but only if they handed in a letter to their parents in Cuba—not a top priority for pre-teen boys. "People wanted to get their $1.40, so Jorge started writing letters on behalf of other people. He'd sell those letters for twenty-five cents. He got so busy that he outsourced the writing of those letters to a bunch of girls at another camp. He would give the girls fifteen cents and he would keep ten cents.

"At the end of every summer, the priest who ran Monsignor Pace High School would ask me to empty all the lockers. Back then there were an awful lot of well-to-do children who went to school there who wouldn't pick up their books. We'd take those books home. I'd get myself ten or twelve big erasers, erase all the markings on the books, and come late August or September I would sell them as used books. You can imagine being in the ninth or tenth grade and making $500 or $600 in one week. In the mid-sixties, that was all the money in the world to a fourteen-, fifteen-year-old."

The same entrepreneurial spirit helped when the brothers later went to work for SmithKline Beecham and it became clear there was a limit to how much they could earn as sales reps. "I felt I was wasting my life," de Cespedes says. "Both Jorge and I were only working about fifteen to twenty hours a week, and we were first and second in the country out of 400 people. It wasn't rewarding enough. I had a very good relationship with my bosses, but I knew a Carlos de Cespedes would never be president of an English company based out of Bristol, Tennessee. Simple as that. They were never going to let a Cuban run the company. At that age, you're very, very fast in your tracks; you want to be president by the time you're thirty-five. My boss took me aside and said, 'Listen, it's not gonna happen. We've never had a thirty-five-year-old president. You're Cuban; you're not English, et cetera, et cetera.' I immediately realized that although it had been a wonderful eight, nine, ten years I had spent with them, that it was time to look at other possibilities."

The two brothers decided to start their own company. Pharmed Group is now a $600 million company, the largest independent full-service distributor of pharmaceutical and medical supplies to hospitals and other health-care organizations; they also own parts of twenty-two other companies. Does entrepreneurial spirit run in their family? "It always has," says de Cespedes. "It's one of those things that's innate."

That attitude illustrates a key leadership attribute: Extroversion. In psychological terms, Extroversion is more than simply being outgoing. In many ways, it's the mirror image of the Neuroticism that represents such a problem for entrepreneurial thinking. People who inherited a lot of Extroversion in their personalities like to dominate their environment. They prefer groups and excitement to solitude and tranquility; they have high energy levels; they're very assertive. Extroversion is more than just the absence of the negative outlook and chronic emotionality associated with Neuroticism. It's a tendency to experience life actively in a *positive* way, to be focused on the external world and believe in one's ability to have an impact on it. It also seems to be one of the aspects of our personalities that's most influenced by our individual genes.[1]

A huge genetic advantage for an entrepreneur, right? Absolutely. Embracing rejection is all about being determined to win—so determined that you are able to see over and around obstacles to get what you want. The desire to dominate is a fundamental aspect of Extroversion. You probably inherited a good dose of it if you like to take charge, make decisions, and be noticed. Those traits are among the qualities that make someone a born leader.

At least one study has found that genes account for roughly 30 percent of the differences in leadership. Researchers tested 646 pairs of twins and found that the individuals who had demonstrated leadership—being a business executive, or taking charge of projects or events—shared certain personality qualities: achievement orientation; being forceful, decisive, and persuasive; enjoying leadership; and taking charge. All of those qualities correlate with being highly Extroverted.

So far, no surprises—at least not for those of us who deal with entrepreneurs every day. But the study also found that both leadership and personality profiles tended to be shared between twins. If one twin demonstrated these qualities and had a track record of leadership, the other tended to do the same. Identical twins, who have the same DNA, were more similar in their leadership records and personality traits than fraternal twins, whose DNA is similar but not exactly the same. The study's conclusion: The same genetic factors explain both leadership and the personality traits that contribute to it. That connection between demonstrated leadership and genes is largely the result of personality traits that are inherited.[2] In another study, leaders demonstrated Extroversion more consistently than any of the other Big 5 aspects of personality.[3]

But couldn't those similarities in personality traits or leadership patterns also be the influence of growing up in the same family? The researchers say no. They found that shared environment played almost no role in whether someone became a leader or had certain personality traits. Other studies have found the same thing: that family influence accounts for less than either genes or the influence of peers and experience outside the home when it comes to the Big 5 personality traits. In fact, one study found that the biggest impact of family influence had to do with the amount of autonomy a child has—whether he or she learns early to operate independent of the family.[4]

The results seem to confirm a Canadian study of "leadership personality" in twins. It found that Extroversion and Conscientiousness were not only highly influenced by genes; they also were good predictors of a person's leadership style. Traditional "command-and-control" leaders seemed to have inherited significantly less genetic Conscientiousness and Extroversion than leaders who facilitated creating trust, concern, and empowerment in others.[5]

The ability to embrace criticism also showed up in a survey of fifty start-up executives. The study found that they have a higher tolerance for criticism than typical large-company executives.[6]

Tom Kinnear recalls a legendary joke about fund-raising that also illustrates the concept of embracing rejection: "There was this guy in college who always had a date. His friends could never figure out why, so finally they asked him. He said that he asked ten people for a date, and usually one out of ten said yes. He didn't care about the nine no's. That makes a good fund-raiser, and that probably makes a good entrepreneur. Every good idea I've been successful or unsuccessful with, some venture fund turned down, and probably turned down adamantly with some backhanded dismissing of it as a dumb idea."

People who score high on the inherited trait of Extroversion are natural salesmen. Others aren't. If you're not, you need to understand that instead of kidding yourself or simply trying to tough it out. Understanding makes it easier to think about techniques that can improve whatever ability you have instead of thinking of yourself as some kind of loser. People who score high on Neuroticism may have a lot of trouble embracing rejection. They need to find ways to depersonalize it. For example, they can remind themselves to think of a rejection as an information-gathering opportunity that can help them next time. Embracing it may always be more of an uphill battle for them than for Extroverts, but they can improve their ability to manage it.

Still, some rejections are tougher than others. If I hadn't been born with a good dose of Extroversion, I could easily have been flattened by something that happened shortly after we launched Harrison & Star. I had left Pfizer on good terms, and, naturally, I thought we'd be able to get some of their advertising business. At one point, when I was talking to some of my former associates, I decided to go see a guy I had worked with for five years. As far as I knew, we had had a good relationship. I had called him repeatedly after I left, but he had never returned my calls. When I dropped by his office and mentioned I'd been trying to reach him, he said, "Yeah, I heard you started an agency. I don't think you're going to be successful; I don't think you have it in you to be successful. That's why I didn't bother to call you back."

I was stunned, but I learned a lesson from it: Never confuse acquaintances with real business. Everyone in this book has had similar setbacks, if not worse. What lets them keep going is their understanding that rejection has nothing to do with them personally.

SUCCESS PROMOTER: THE "WHAC-A-MOLE" GENE

I guess it was inevitable that there would be an online version of the old "Whac-A-Mole" game. If you haven't seen one on the midway at a county fair, "Whac-A-Mole" basically involves grabbing a large mallet, watching a platform that's covered with holes, and whacking moles on their little mechanical heads as they pop out of the holes one by one. The longer you play, the faster the moles emerge. Those little suckers just keep coming back for more.

An entrepreneur is a human Whac-A-Mole. Resilience is one of the most important Success Promoters for thinking like an entrepreneur. Even if you've got a personality that's unstoppable, there are still things you can do to nurture it, to keep it switched on. And if you're not naturally extroverted, if you're short on the will to win, you need even more practice at bullet-proofing yourself against the slings and arrows of life. You also need to find an occupation that minimizes them—if you can.

I'll bet every person interviewed for this book has heard something similar to what a friend of mine said recently. We were talking about some of the ideas in this chapter, and she said, "When I get discouraged about a project, I think to myself, 'How would Tom approach this?' It helps me stay focused and keep moving." I'm fortunate that unstoppability comes naturally to me. But everyone can get better at being resilient. You might not ever be as good at bouncing back from rejection as someone who's got it in their genes, but you can probably improve your batting average. After all, just because someone's a natural risk taker doesn't mean those risks will always work out. Everyone, even a natural risk taker, needs to be able to welcome whatever lies on the other side of taking the risk and keep on going. They need to embrace rejection for what it can teach them.

Take One Step Back, Two Steps Forward

People who start their own businesses know there will be obstacles. They're just not always prepared to be hit with them right off the bat. You may not be able to get up a head of steam before having to deal with the unexpected.

I don't believe in the idea of taking two steps forward and one step back. I think it's usually just the other way around: You're darn lucky if you get to take those first two steps before hitting a roadblock. The difference between born entrepreneurs and everyone else is that the entrepreneurs are prepared to get knocked down even before they see any results, yet they bounce back and get closer to their goals.

An entrepreneur with whom I've become good friends had an idea—actually, his idea was his *big* ideas. He would come up with the most well-thought-out, simple, yet significant brand-building ideas. His company was part of another company that either did not understand his business or didn't want his ideas to overshadow theirs. He eventually bought his company back, built it, and is incredibly successful today. His continued belief in what he was doing—and how he was doing it—was strengthened (yes, strengthened) by rejection. Being pushed back and held down actually ended up getting him closer to his entrepreneurial dream. I'm convinced his company is about to make its mark on a national stage.

Taking those forward steps is even more gratifying when you've overcome obstacles to take them. Winning the World Series for the first time in eighty-six years is great, but any Boston Red Sox fan will tell you that the team's historic 2004 win in the American League playoffs after being down 0–3 against the Yankees made it that much sweeter. "One guy naysayed me on buying the Sixers, and on another project before that," says Pat Croce. "When I finally mentioned to him recently that I was going to be doing a TV show, he said, 'Okay, I believe you. I'm in.'"

Let Rejection Build Your Confidence

The consulting report's conclusion was not good news for Canon. In the 1960s, the company was trying to figure out how it could create a product with better profit margins than the cameras on which the company had been founded. Copiers seemed like a logical choice, but the report said that Xerox had essentially cornered the market on patents for copier technology. But Keizo Yamaji of the company's R&D department took that as a challenge, an opportunity. Xerox copiers were designed for heavy use and many copies. If Canon could somehow figure out a way to develop original technology for small, inexpensive, reliable machines for the low end of the market, the company could dominate that market as Xerox did the higher end. Yamaji's determination not to be cowed by an apparently impregnable competitor eventually led to Canon's market leadership in copier/printers.[7]

Everyone says, "Learn from experience." I say when it comes to facing rejection, learning from the past is only valuable if you think of it in terms of what it can do for your future, for your evolutionary vision, for the end result that you want. Each rejection, each setback, can be a guidepost to what to do in the future that can bring success. Think about it this way: You can't do anything about what's already happened. On the other hand, your vision offers opportunities for action. Creating something new from what you've learned—a new product line, a better sales pitch—can benefit from hindsight, but only if you view rejection as one more step in doing what you want to do. Action gives you new opportunities to succeed and build your confidence. Giving up doesn't. There are only so many "No"s in the No bank. Sooner or later, you'll get a Yes.

MARKERS FOR THE "WHAC-A-MOLE" GENE

- You embrace rejection rather than fighting it.
- You use rejection as an opportunity to create trust.
- You listen for Why or Why Not information.
- You are prepared to take one step back and two steps forward.
- You think of rejection in terms of how it can help you do things differently in the future.
- You never ask "Why me?"
- You do your homework to help yourself forestall rejection next time.
- You stay linked to your vision.
- You remind yourself of your victories.
- You keep going.

Being unstoppable is not the same as ignoring feedback. You have to be able to recognize when being unstoppable requires shifting gears. I remember one of my first sales calls for Pfizer. It was on a very busy doctor (is there any other kind?) with little patience for wasted words. I was about two sentences into my presentation on a specific obstetrical drug when his face turned bright red. "Don't *ever* talk to me about that drug," he said. A rookie, I never asked why; all I knew was that he meant it! I casually put my reprint away, apologized, and asked if I could return to talk about another product that had great applicability in his gynecology practice. My respecting his gut reaction to drug number one calmed him down. He invited me back and ultimately prescribed boatloads of the other product. We actually became friends.

Shifting gears still keeps you moving forward.

Eliminate Two Words from Your Vocabulary

Two words are guaranteed to keep you from embracing rejection. Don't say them. Don't even let yourself think them. The two words: "Why me?"

Got it? Now forget them! Rejection seems to come as a big surprise to many people, and that puzzles me. I'm tempted to say, "Why not you?" Do you really think you should be immune to setbacks? Are you so special that you will be the first person in the world simply to sail through life, getting whatever you want whenever you want it? Saying "Why me?" puts your brain on a track to nowhere. Why? Because you'll never get an answer to "Why me?" Regardless of whether you're highly Extroverted or not, all you generate with it is negative emotion. Trust me: no matter how much energy you have, you don't have enough to spend any of it on asking "Why me?"

"Leadership in business is a bit like the Pilgrim fathers," says Barry Gibbons. "Every day they woke up and they faced challenges that nobody on the planet had faced before: 'What the hell do we do with this? How do we . . . ?' And what they did is, they woke up and they got through the day. They drew on their limited resources, on what the hell they could get their hands on, and they got through the day. And the next day they woke up and did it again. And that's really what business is about. It's making it happen, getting through the challenge. Sometimes you can draw on a piece of literature, sometimes you might be influenced by a guru, sometimes you might think, 'What the hell did my father do?' Some days you just sit at your desk and you think, 'What the bloody hell would the Lone Ranger do here? I've run out of ideas.' But you draw on all of them and you get through the day."

Always be prepared for the possibility of rejection; that way it won't knock you flat. Embracing rejection empowers you to take action to eliminate it or prevent it in the future.

Get More Information

When does "No" really mean "Not now"? Almost always. For a born entrepreneur, "No" is never final. It simply means there's some piece of information that you haven't yet found that would change it to a Yes.

Pat Croce experienced setbacks in launching his chain of sports-medicine clinics. Naysayers, he says, are one of the biggest obstacles to success that any entrepreneurial thinker faces. "You're going to be excited about talking about this new dream or vision. If people who know you don't believe in it, that's a hurt. They may not be right, but it still hurts, even if you really believe in your idea."

His biggest setback happened during his rookie season as president of the Sixers: "The first year was painful. My optimism blinded me. I really believed we would be winners overnight. I hired a rookie manager, who hired a rookie coach; the problems just multiplied exponentially. It's one thing to be optimistic and positive, but I learned it could also get me in trouble. I learned I needed to balance it with more input, more homework."

When he faces rejection now, he has learned to say to himself, "Maybe I didn't ask the right questions." Rejection, he says, is nothing but a learning system. "We all have self-doubts, but as entrepreneurs we bounce off the obstacle. But during that little bounce, we've done more homework. We don't come right back at it. You gotta come back at it with more information."

Stay Linked to Your Vision

I saw Matt Lauer on NBC's *Today Show* one morning when he was interviewing Eric Clapton. He introduced the segment by saying, "I love my job, I love my job, I love my job!" As a huge Clapton fan, Lauer was thrilled at getting to interview him. As I recall, on the same show, there was a clip of Lauer as a reporter early in his career, doing a stand-up segment with a chimpanzee. I'm guessing that when he was doing the chimp segment, he may not have been saying "I love my job!" But I'm also guessing he didn't see himself as a chimp co-star; he saw himself as someone who was ultimately going to be able to interview Eric Clapton.

One reason why putting yourself in the picture you've created for yourself is so important is that it gives you a model for how to behave when the chips are not only down but disappearing. If the next step in your evolutionary vision for yourself is to make your restaurant into a worldwide franchise operation, you have to see yourself as the head of a franchise operation. How would the head of Starbucks convince people to become franchisees? Persuade investors to put money into your idea?

Keep Your Heart in the Future, Keep Your Head in the Present

John Bogle Sr. knows something about setbacks. He launched Vanguard only after a very public humiliation: being fired from Wellington Management, by people he had brought into the company by engineering a merger. He's battled heart trouble all his life; at thirty-one, after a massive heart attack, he was told he probably wouldn't live to be forty. Even at Vanguard he had to fight a pitched battle with the board of directors over being forced to abide by the company's mandatory retirement age of seventy. Since then, he's become even more outspoken about the scandals that have rocked the fund industry.

How did he deal with the pain of being publicly jettisoned at Wellington? "It's all about attitude," he says. *Life is not about what happens to you. It's about dealing with whatever happens to you.* You can get beaten down, you can get humbled, you can get humiliated, you can get excoriated, you can get laughed at, you can get people talking about you tongue-in-cheek, you can get disrespect. I'm not sure any of that matters."

Bogle says he has two rules for dealing with setbacks and rejections. "One rule is, live the day. First get out of bed in the morning. If you don't get out of bed in the morning, nothing much is going to happen. Then live your day. Try to enrich your own life, your family's life, the lives of the colleagues around you. Learn something. Teach something. If you have an opportunity, do a good deed. If you do those things during the day, then you're entitled to a good night's sleep.

"Rule Number Two is: Repeat Rule One the next day."

Staying linked to your vision doesn't get you off the hook for having to actually *do* things to make it real. If you weren't born to embrace rejection, you have to do the same thing entrepreneurs do with risk: set it aside and simply take action. As long as you're taking informed action and it fits with your vision, it will move you forward.

"I take a step back and say, 'Let me look at all the positives,'" says Herman Cain. "When we were doing the LBO of Godfather's Pizza, we put together this nice dog-and-pony presentation for financiers. Nobody wanted to do it. We got rejected eighteen times. On the nineteenth try we got the financing.

"It's sheer determination. Some people would have given up on the sixth or seventh try. If you strongly, strongly believe in it, that you can make it work, you keep on going. If you don't believe in yourself, don't try. You've got to believe in yourself, but realistically. I've talked to people who have great dreams, but their dreams are not matched with their natural capabilities. You've got to be honest with yourself."

Remember: Taking action—keeping on—allows you to get more information that can help you learn to embrace rejection—and overcome it.

Reboot Your Memory

Find a way of reminding yourself of what you've accomplished. Born entrepreneurs learn from their mistakes, but they don't dwell on them. Their accomplishments are just as real to them as anything they've done wrong. By contrast, if you inherited a big dose of Neuroticism, you may have a tendency to dwell on what's missing and what went wrong. Any progress that's been made gets overwhelmed by a focus on the gap between where you are and where you want to be. Entrepreneurs examine that gap, too—but only so they can figure out what needs to happen to fill it.

If you're prone to a negative outlook, figure out a mechanism for reminding yourself of your victories. Pat Croce suggests a journal, but a bulletin board with reminders of successes works just as well.

Rejection? Learn to welcome it for what it can do for you. What does it have to teach you about your picture of success, and how you can develop it? As Barry Gibbons says, "What's the alternative? Sit down? Sleep? No. You just say, 'Okay, I'm not going there, I'm not doing that. Right. What's next? What's next on my list? Where are we going? Let's go. Go. Go. Go. Go. Go. Go. Go.'"

CHAPTER 8

The Operational Challenges: Breaking Things Down

You're probably hardwired in the way you approach problems like obtaining financing, acquiring capabilities you don't have, deciding the best way to use limited resources, or delegating tasks. There are a lot of people who can very quickly let their gut take over, and they come up with the right solutions. Other people have to say, "Well, this is the problem; there's the opportunity," and then the intuition comes in. Whether you start with the intuitive response or a more analytical approach depends on how your genes are wired and where your zone of comfort lies.

I was born with an analytical brain. In English class, the part I liked was diagramming sentences, breaking them down into their component parts. Even if I hadn't spent all those years working in a lab with the scientific method, it just seems to be the way I tackle things. That training has served me well in everything else I've done. It also has helped me understand that once I've analyzed a problem or opportunity and arrived at a conclusion, I still should retest my conclusion from time to time to make certain that the conclusion is still relevant to today's circumstances. It was a big part of the reason I've always been driven to think of innovative ways my organization—whether it was Pfizer, my own health-care agency, or my current company—could stay ahead of and apart from our competitors. I constantly analyze what we do better than other agencies—and I promote the hell out of it.

But even if you start from a gut reaction, at some point you're going to have to apply a little analysis to that instinctive call. Having a template for working through that process can speed and clarify what needs to be done. In grad school, I liked to use an acronym to remind myself of how to define and tackle a scientific research project. Even though I'm now responsible for decisions that will affect hundreds of companies as well as thousands of people and clients instead of a few cells under a microscope, it still comes in handy.

The acronym is **POHEC**. Each letter stands for a stage of the scientific method: **Problem, Observation, Hypothesis, Experimentation, Conclusion/Recapitulation.** Does it still work under today's circumstances? Let's take each one and explore what it means:

P: Problem The first step in any experiment is to clarify just what you're trying to accomplish. What's the problem I'm trying to solve? What's the opportunity I'm thinking about pursuing? For a researcher, it might be finding out if and how genes affect an individual's likelihood of developing a specific disease. For an entrepreneur, it might be, say, trying to figure out what business makes the most sense given important demographic, cultural, and purchasing trends projected for the next decade.

In tackling this step, remember to focus not just on what you think the specific problem is based upon gained insight, but on what outcome you think might be best. In our entrepreneurial example, the outcome might be "a successful business that can define a new market opportunity and have staying power over the next decade."

O: Observation Once you're clear about what you want to accomplish, the next step is to examine the data that can help you understand the existing situation and what it means for the outcome you want. This is the reconnaissance phase: scouting out information that assists you in making informed decisions and taking action. You want information that leads to insight. For a scientist, that involves finding and reviewing any existing research that seems relevant. In our hypothetical example, a researcher might find out which genes have already been tested for linkage to a disease, what testing methods were used, and what that research showed. For an entrepreneur, it means learning about a market, understanding the strengths and weaknesses of existing players in that market, analyzing your own strengths and weaknesses in addressing it, and looking at how others have tried to solve the problem. In our entrepreneurial example, it might involve learning about the demographics of working women over the next decade, or learning what baby boomer needs, wants, and trends will be as they age. Essentially, this involves defining what you need to know, figuring out how to get it, and understanding its significance.

H: Hypothesis Having reviewed the information, a researcher develops a hypothesis about how the problem might be solved. Our hypothetical researcher has to target a specific gene to research and figure out how to set up an experiment that will give useful information and confer impact on a specific disease process. And our hypothetical entrepreneur? Reviewing the data should suggest market opportunities in helping women cope with balancing career opportunities and families, or appealing to boomer desires to live and age well. The entrepreneur's hypothesis is a marketing or business plan—a logical, innovative way to define or redefine a market, improve market share, or both.

E: Experimentation Now the hypothesis is put to the test as the experimenter collects data. What happens when the experiment is run? What happens when the product or service is put on the market, tested with its target audience or sources of financing? What happens when the company enters a new target market? A key part of either a scientific or an entrepreneurial experiment is deciding what information is necessary either to prove or to disprove the hypothesis or business plan assumptions. In business, that means choosing the metrics by which you'll measure success.

C: Conclusion Once data collection is completed, the researcher or entrepreneur has to decide just what it shows. In some cases, the information totally validates or disproves the hypothesis. Deciding just what the experiment reveals can be one of the most challenging parts of the process. In either case, it usually leads back to the first step of the POHEC process. If the hypothesis is right, the next step is to look at whether the experiment has implications in other cases—in other words, generating a new hypothesis about how the gene works. If the hypothesis is flawed based on the data, the researcher has to try to figure out what happened and why. That means creating a new hypothesis and setting up an experiment to test that new hypothesis.

For an entrepreneur, the conclusion may not be clear-cut. Is the hypothesis wrong, or is it simply undergoing the normal challenges and tests of any market or entrepreneurial venture? I talked earlier about the born entrepreneur's ability to keep the faith in spite of discouraging circumstances. I think it's much like a scientific researcher simply going back and retesting his hypothesis based on new information. The problem or opportunity hasn't necessarily changed (assuming the information-gathering process was done well in the first place). However, it may need a new hypothesis, a new way of tackling the same problem, based on the new data. This is part of what's called "recapitulation": constantly retesting or challenging the conclusion to make sure it's still valid in the face of change or new information.

THE POHEC PROCESS IN A NUTSHELL

Define the **P**roblem

Observe the data

Develop a **H**ypothesis

Experiment to see what happens

Draw **C**onclusions, and revisit them periodically to see if they still hold

---

This sounds more complicated than it really is, and it shouldn't lead to "analysis paralysis." Let me walk you through how POHEC would apply to a specific example from my own agency: our launch of a medical-education company in 1988.

Problem: When we started Harrison & Star, the biz was health-care advertising. In the late eighties, it became clear to me that ad budgets were going to be dwindling for traditional health-care advertising, our core business. We would need to be able to replace revenue as ad budgets were redeployed to reach our sophisticated audience of physicians in other ways.

Observation: The more I talked to our clients, the more I realized that a lot of money was beginning to be spent on medical education: ongoing communication with doctors about scientific discoveries that led to development of a drug or changes in the ways a particular drug could be prescribed based on its label.

Hypothesis: One day as my partner and I were coming back from lunch, I said, "We're going to start a medical-education company. What are we going to call it?" We started figuring out what the name could be. I said, "Well, our agency name is Harrison & Star . . . H&S. Let's play on that." Literally, in the middle of the block near Thirty-sixth Street and Park Avenue, I said, "HS . . . Health Science." We went back that afternoon and incorporated a new business, Health Science Communications.

Experimentation: We linked Health Science Communications directly to Harrison and Star at first, serving the same clients. It grew, but not phenomenally fast. Then we tried distancing it from Harrison & Star so it could serve other clients as well as the agency's. That's when it took off. Health Science Communications doubled in size, then doubled again, and, yes, doubled again.

Conclusion: We were absolutely delighted with the results of that experiment. Health Science Communications today is one of the largest, most successful, and fastest-growing companies of its kind. Clearly it had made sense to extend our business. We did the same thing later when we started another new company, this one focused on direct-to-consumer health-care advertising. Same dynamic! What started as a few ad dollars being diverted to "talk to consumers" is today a multibillion-dollar segment of the health-care advertising industry, one that continues to evolve and create entrepreneurial opportunities. The direct-to-consumer agency we started as part of Harrison & Star is now part of a national consumer ad agency in New York City and a major contender for many of the largest, most significant DTC drug-ad budgets. And so far, the recapitulation process has suggested that the original conclusion is still valid. The problem of diverted ad dollars, through observation, hypothesis, and experimentation, created one of the industry's most notable direct-to-consumer agencies.

Sometimes the POHEC steps get collapsed. Sometimes observation leads to defining the problem instead of the other way around. But the steps are all there every time.

FILLING GAPS BETWEEN WHERE YOU ARE AND WHERE YOU WANT TO BE

Thinking entrepreneurially is all about filling gaps. Gaps in the market. Gaps between the resources you have and the resources you need. Gaps between your current skills and the next step in your evolutionary picture of yourself. Basically, you want to turn things you need into things you no longer need because you've either gotten them, found a substitute, or made them unnecessary.

There are several ways to fill gaps between where you are and where you want to be. Which you choose will depend on your own genetic makeup, your resources, the competitive situation, and the market.

Create

This one's obvious, so I won't spend a lot of time on it. You thought about it when you realized there was a gap in the market that needed filling. Innovating may not be the easiest way to fill a gap, but it's the most durable if you get it right.

Some health-care manufacturers are addressing a gap between the cost of medications and Medicare patients' ability to pay for them. Some are coming up with Medicare card discounts. I think it's a brilliant creative approach to getting their products to patients in a cost-effective way, especially since many elderly patients take multiple drugs consistently. The cards get the brands used by the people who need them. The companies have positioned both brand and company in a socially conscious manner. It's an incredible way of identifying with a real issue. These marketers have analyzed their way into multiple benefits.

Entrepreneurial creating isn't just about product development or marketing strategy. One of the most important things you can create to help you fill gaps is a network of trusted information sources. If you don't create and maintain that network, your ability to analyze how to fill a gap won't be as robust. You'll be short on valuable information and the ability to test your hypotheses with people whose opinions you trust. Your circle of trusted resources should be large enough to be meaningful statistically but not so large that it's unwieldy. That creates inertia, thought without action—thinking and rethinking and, yes, rethinking.

Integrate

When you launch a business, think big but conceive small. What do I mean by that? If you're going to start a business, you need to think about how big the business can legitimately be. Just how large is the market for whatever you're proposing? Even if you decide you want a small operation, you need to think big to ensure that you've identified not only a market but a way to reach it. It seems obvious, but if the market is too small or there's no way to reach it, you may want to rethink your idea. You'll be creating a niche business with little future. And if you're not thinking big but others are, you leave yourself open to the first competitive threat that comes along. Someone else may capitalize more than you on your idea. What a shame that would be.

However, to get your idea off the ground in a way that lets you retain control, you need to conceive small. John Bogle Sr. said that he knew from the beginning that "the key to Vanguard's success would be in how slowly it could grow." Starting a business means an entrepreneur usually is doing many, many things that are outside his or her usual comfort zone. There are just not a lot of people to do it all. You take care of everything until you can afford to bring the people in to do the operations or do the finances or be the traffic manager or whatever. Until then, don't try to give birth to an elephant.

Even once you reach the point of being able to bring in additional skills and talent, you're still integrating people, talent, resources, and ideas. You're just doing it at a higher level. Even though you're no longer doing it all, being an integrator is essential for an entrepreneur to know just what pieces still need to be filled and how to fill them. Whatever the vision of the company, the core business you're in, everything needs to come back to that hub. Diversity brings new ideas, new talents, new capabilities into any organization. The adoption of new ideas that work—innovation—has kept mankind evolving and surviving for thousands of years. It works for companies, too.

TiTi McNeill has grown her company, TranTech, by being very disciplined in how the company pursues business. She applies a stringent set of criteria to determine whether a particular job is something the company can deliver on. Unless it meets those criteria, the company doesn't go after the business. "It's really just bid smart and bid right. Any small company like mine has limited resources. If you just throw darts to see where they stick, you're going to be really tired. We try to do smart things. We review all the RFPs out there, all the opportunities, and then match each one with our capabilities to see if we have the right resources, the experience to do it, whether we know the client and their requirements. Then we rate ourselves on a scale to see where we stand in terms of the risk, the performance, what are they looking for, what kind of people do we have to produce if we win this. We try to focus more on what it will take to win, instead of just bid, bid, bid. That way we save a lot of agony, because if we bid things that we can't qualify for, we are going to lose every time."

MARKERS FOR THE "POHEC" GENE

- You develop your problem-solving skills by taking on problems to solve.
- You fill resource and skills gaps by creating, integrating, co-operating, delegating, or eliminating.
- You protect your ideas from yourself.
- You use POHEC analyses to help combat negative thinking.
- You constantly test your conclusions to make sure they're still valid.
- You exercise to prevent memory problems associated with stress.

Co-Operate

I don't mean this in the sense of getting along with people, although Nice Guys definitely do that. That is "cooperating"—no hyphen. By "co-operating," *I mean that you benefit when you can fill gaps by partnering with someone who can benefit in turn from working with you.* It can be especially important for entrepreneurs who are trying to figure out how to finance their business idea. The minute you get a venture-capital firm or investors, they're going to want to take a portion of your business. Depending on the nature of the VC firm or the financial backer, they might want a small portion or they might want a majority. That means you're not really running the business; either you're answering to someone else or you're just employed in your business. If you can find a way to co-operate with someone else who stands to make money or benefit in some other way, you'll have a lot more flexibility and freedom to run your operation. I always felt I was co-operating with my clients. Our business grew if we did a good job at helping them strategize how to grow their business.

In a sense, co-operating applies to filling the gaps in your own skill set, too. I'm a pretty good idea person. I'm not sure I'm the best operations guy, and I know I'm not the best financial guy. If you're going to be a success, you're probably going to have to co-operate within your own organization, identifying and assessing your partners based on whatever shortcomings you have that they can complement or make up for.

Co-operating is a good way to avoid the most obvious way of filling a gap: buying what you need. Filling each other's mutual needs not only can solve an operational problem, but it can also create a bond that can be valuable in other ways. Many entrepreneurial tech companies benefited during the late 1990s from vendors' willingness to lend them money to buy their equipment. Even though many of those loans went south when the companies themselves went bankrupt, it's an example of resourceful co-operating by those entrepreneurs. It's the business definition of symbiosis.

When you're co-operating, you need to make sure the DNA of the partners or companies is compatible. The last thing you need is a mismatch of culture or personalities. Compatible doesn't necessarily mean identical. I've seen very successful individuals who were so similar in their thinking and deliberation that as partners, they couldn't get things done. (They had a tendency to argue in front of clients. Talk about a formula for failure!) What's needed is not cloning. It's a similarity in understanding and respect for complementary capabilities. Culture is the underpinning of the enterprise; personality is the talent. These are not just part of the game—they are the game.

Delegate

As I said, at some point you move from being a one-person integrator to being a multiperson integrator. In other words, you become a delegator. Doing that allows you as an entrepreneur to get back to what you need to do and like best, which is to think about the big ideas. Delegating can be a challenge. The same determination that leads you to believe you see something in an idea that no one else does can create problems when it comes time to evolve from integrator to delegator. Some people tend to feel that no one can do it as well as they can because "it's my baby."

I think to succeed at anything other than a mom-and-pop enterprise, you have to have an innate ability to delegate, to give things away, to empower people to do things. As I said earlier, when you're starting out, you're it. But as you grow, you either get mired down in the operational issues and get taken away from what you're really good at, or you begin hiring people who are complementary to you. Then you push these responsibilities out so you can stay in your comfort zone. You often hear about the need to hire people who are better at certain things than you are. I would phrase it a different way, one that's especially useful if you're high on the Neuroticism scale: Think instead about hiring people whose skills complement yours. You not only eliminate the value judgment, you also remind yourself that you need to focus on the next big idea.

Entrepreneurs are good at thinking and taking risks. You need to say to yourself, "What I need to do is spend my time on the things that are going to make us the most successful and make us the most money." Generally, that's not focusing on operations. It's focusing outward on the clients' needs, the markets, and the trends that will affect them. It's listening to your circle of resources. It's revisiting POHEC to make absolutely certain you are staying ahead of your competitors, that you're not simply analyzing "best practices" to imitate but setting your own strategy for being the best.

Here's a suggestion for making sure you're putting your energies in the right place. I like to think of it as a rolling forecast for your career.

As you grow, constantly try to shift 20 percent of your time from less productive, operational issues to tasks that will move the business—or your career—forward. It might be identifying new opportunities or clients, developing the kind of co-operation partnerships I just mentioned, or developing a new product. You should constantly be thinking about delegating the least growth-oriented 20 percent of your time and effort and spend it figuring out ways that you can grow the business—or your career—so you can delegate even more.

Imagine that your business is a train. The caboose is the necessary stuff that has to get done; the engine moves the train forward. You want to figure out a way to spend more of your time in the engine room and less in the caboose. The percentage that you shift is less important than the concept.

All aboard!

Eliminate

Another key task in entrepreneurial problem-solving is to eliminate what's not necessary. Rule of thumb: *If you can do without it, you're probably better off.* It goes back to the "think big, conceive small" idea. Many entrepreneurs forget that it's easy to figure what your expenses will be; it's forecasting how much money you'll take in that's tough. They take on fixed costs that feel good, such as expensive offices, but that don't really add anything substantial to the business except overhead. Those fixed costs are what put the company under if revenues don't pan out.

Believe in your idea enough not to pamper it to death. The gap between where your company is and where you want it to be is a lot narrower if you're not having to pay for things that don't drive the business forward. Keep it simple. Perhaps the most absurd example I ever heard was the small publishing entrepreneur who had trouble paying the company's share of its employees' health-insurance premiums on time yet had a rock band on salary.

I've seen entrepreneurs who got so caught up with consultants—and their power to hire a stable full of them—that they became paralyzed. The consultants were providing more and more information, both valuable and unusable; however, ideas couldn't hatch and activity was hindered. Remember: Adopting the habit of thinking things through before turning to outside "experts" is key to expressing whatever natural analytical ability you have. If that's not switched on, you may become addicted not to success but to consultants.

Filling gaps requires an entrepreneur to eliminate what's irrelevant. Focus what you react to and act on based on what's involved in getting to the next picture that you've painted for yourself or your company. That includes information. What's urgent often tends to push aside what's important. Your first screen should be, "What am I being asked to act on now versus what's important?" That at least lets you acknowledge that the two aren't necessarily the same thing (in fact, they're often mutually exclusive). Then you can figure out the mechanism that works best for you in keeping the important from working its way to the bottom of the slush pile. Delegate the urgent; ruminate and act on the important.

Even great ideas go nowhere without flawless execution. Some people are lucky enough to have both inspiration and execution in them. More often, they need to fill in the gaps between what they've got—in skills, in personality traits, in resources, in information—and what they need to get their business and career to the next step of their evolutionary vision. They need to be absolutely clear about what those gaps are, and create a personal marketing plan and gap analysis to work around or fill them.

Even if you were born with the entrepreneurial spirit, at some point you'll need to operate on something other than instinct. The University of Michigan's Tom Kinnear, who has helped coach dozens of budding entrepreneurs, says that a common mistake he sees is the belief that being an entrepreneur is easy: "You think that because your idea's good that you'll get the money and it will work. [People] underestimate the people problem, and how many hundreds of hours you have to put in to make it work. There's a bit of a misconception, especially among those who have done it, that it might be an easier path than some other paths. I think it's probably a harder path, because there's nothing to fall back on, no big corporation to catch you."

GENES AND THE SCIENCE OF BREAKING THINGS DOWN

Trying to figure out just how our genes affect our ability to solve problems, analyze a market, create a business, or acquire resources is complicated. For one thing, scientists don't even agree on just what constitutes "intelligence" and how best to measure it. Also, because cognitive skills are so complex, it's even more difficult to link them with individual genes. Researchers have targeted roughly 150 genes that seem likely candidates because of how they affect human cognition or even the learning and memory of fruit flies or mice,[1] but thousands of genes could be involved. Estimates of the likely genetic influence on problem solving have ranged anywhere from 40 to 80 percent; the most recent seem to settle in somewhere around 50 percent.[2] When you overlay the ways in which personality traits affect complex cognitive functions such as memory, logic, and how quickly we process information, it's no wonder that scientists have their work cut out for them when it comes to trying to isolate just how our genes might or might not endow us with the ability to solve problems. And even that doesn't begin to explain how learning, experience, and even nutrition affect what is broadly labeled as "intelligence."

However, here are some of the clues that scientists are beginning to uncover about how our genes help shape our problem-solving skills:

• The more genetically similar we are, the more our IQ scores tend to be alike. Identical twins (i.e., identical genes) reared in different families are only slightly less similar in their IQ scores than those reared together. Fraternal twins are the next most closely matched. Siblings reared together have less correlation than twins, and parent and child are even less alike than brothers and sisters.[3] That descending similarity in both genes and IQ points to at least some genetic influence.

• Our genes also seem to affect our analytical abilities by influencing how our brains develop. Some people literally have more "gray matter" (a technical term, by the way). Comparing magnetic resonance imaging scans (MRIs) to IQ scores, recent studies have found that the more gray matter in brain regions associated with general intelligence, the higher the IQ scores.[4] And according to another study that also used MRIs and IQ scores, the closer the genetic connection—between identical twins, for example—the closer the correlation between how densely the brain is wired and IQ scores.[5]

• Solving problems and analyzing information also involves applying your experience to help you figure out the future. Scientists are developing memory-enhancing drugs based on research that shows that a specific gene helps create long-term memories. New experiences trigger that gene to help make connections between brain cells.[6] And MRIs have shown that one variation of another gene important in helping neurons grow and survive also seems to affect people's ability to remember events.[7]

• In the last several years, scientists have identified specific genes associated with diseases such as schizophrenia, which can impair memory and rational thought processes. Because those genes are linked to mental impairment, researchers believe they may also affect normal intelligence levels.[8]

• Our genes gradually seem to become more influential as we age. In older people, the impact of family environment on IQ scores seems to have dropped to practically nothing, but the influence of genes seems to increase. By middle age, as much as 80 percent of the differences in IQ scores may be linked to genes.[9]

If something gets you what you want, your brain makes connections that let you retain that information to use the next time you have to solve a problem. A gene somewhere jump-starts that process. If we couldn't remember the fact that fire burns or that tigers are dangerous, we wouldn't have made it to the Neanderthal stage, much less the era of wireless communication. Our brains are geared to encode what works. Every time we have to do sophisticated marketing analysis or figure out what will convince a sales prospect to buy, our genes help lay down circuits in our brains that in turn may help us solve a similar problem next time.

As with personality, it's important to remember that just because intelligence may have a genetic component doesn't mean those genetic influences can't be changed or improved. Even the researchers who found a close connection between genes, IQ scores, and brain volume also admit they don't know precisely how it works. Having more gray matter might cause higher intelligence. Or it could work the other way around; people with higher intelligence levels may do things that prod their brains to create new connections—and more gray matter. Maybe increasingly complex tasks in everyday life—multitasking or even having to do our own computer tech support—are helping our brains develop new circuitry. (At least maybe we're getting some benefit from it!)

Also, there seem to be two different types of intelligence. One kind, called "fluid intelligence," seems to increase during childhood, level off at maturity, and then decline in old age. This is our "on-the-spot" reasoning and problem-solving ability. It seems to have a higher genetic component than the other kind, called "crystallized intelligence," which involves learned skills and knowledge[10] and which tends to go up as we get older and gain experience. Even if you were born with a fixed amount of one, you can compensate by exercising and increasing the other.

There's an old tongue-in-cheek saying that goes something like "Old age and treachery will overcome youth and skill." Personally, I'd substitute "experience" for "treachery," but you get the idea: imprinting success with problem-solving can help compensate for deficits in whatever you inherited. But it's a double-edged sword. That "crystallized intelligence" can lead people to become stuck in a rut, increasingly unwilling to take chances even if they might have done so at an earlier age. It's speculation on my part, but I wonder if that inborn "fluid intelligence" is what allows innate risk taking at a young age that might not happen at an older age, when "crystallized intelligence" takes over.

Don't Confuse . . .		
Good idea		Good product
Good idea		Good timing
Good idea		Good business
I can do it	**With . . .**	I have to do it
It has to be done		It's the right thing to do
Activity		Accomplishment
Rejection		Failure
Getting funding		A real business
Luck		Skill
Well-meaning friends		Genuine customers
Big idea		Big need for your idea

Even if genes play a role in our cognitive abilities, success in school isn't necessarily a predictor of success and wealth-building in the real world. In my experience, problem-solving skills develop if you've got problems. Guys I know who were born with a silver (or platinum) spoon in their mouths and who were given every opportunity often fail to see new opportunities and just keep going back to the same old well for life. Believe me, if IQ scores had been my only genetic legacy, I might still be spending all my time socializing with lab rats. This is an area where Success Promoters have enormous impact.

The combination of Big 5 traits we inherit also plays a role in our ability to apply analytical skills to problem solving. If you're high on Neuroticism and prone to depression, it may be harder for you to pull yourself out of your emotions enough to think things through. And Conscientiousness deals with our ability to plan and organize our behavior to pursue and achieve a goal. If you've got a strong dose of it, you're naturally wired to keep plugging away at a problem until you've solved it. My Conscientiousness has always been off the scale. My father always said, "Tom, don't start anything you can't finish and finish well." I think it was hardwired in us both, and it was certainly a great lesson.

I'm not trying to resolve the debate over just how much of our smarts are inherited and how much we develop after we're born. I'm simply saying that the ability to apply thoughtful analysis to problem solving is a valuable skill for any entrepreneur, and our genes may affect whether we're naturally inclined to do that. But whatever problem-solving skills we've got are useless unless we put them to the test repeatedly to improve them. Like the saying goes, if you don't use it, you lose it.

Home Depot's Bernie Marcus puts it perfectly:

> "My mother used to say if you use your mind a lot, it gets better over time. I developed a theory that the mind is like a muscle of the body. There are a lot of people who don't use it. They go to business school, they learn theory in a case study, and somebody else has figured out the solutions for them on the case study. They don't get the ability to think the solution through themselves. When you think it through yourself, you can come to the same solution, but you've now developed it through your thought process. You're developing that muscle—those muscles that think things through. As an entrepreneur,

you are always challenged with things that are not planned. In the retail business, things happened that had never happened before to me. There's no book that gives you where you can look it up in a glossary and find that situation. Things just happen that have never happened before. You speak to other retailers and they say, "No, that never happened to me." But you have to be able to adjust your mind to it and solve the problem, because you can't go back to Harvard Business School and find it written up somewhere. The ability to use your own common sense and to understand the problem, to think it through, think through the various solutions and what the ramifications are—that's very, very important for an entrepreneur."

It's not just the *ability* to think through a problem that's crucial; it's that *desire* to do so. And I think that comes from somewhere in your genes.

SUCCESS PROMOTER: THE "POHEC" GENE

The more practice you get at problem solving, the better you get at it. If you've got a natural analytical bent, you're ahead of the game. If not, you'll need to find ways to supplement your natural intuition.

Know Thyself

Understanding the unique combination of assets you bring to the table—your own combination of "success genes"—is the most important analytical ability of all. Doing that analysis shows you what you've really got and what you lack. Review where you stand on each of the Big 5 aspects of personality. Think about what each one means for your ability to improve either your capabilities or your company's, no matter how you scored. Think also about what gaps in personality traits you need to fill by partnering with someone else. Even if you're not naturally analytical, you need to apply at least enough analysis to know what you don't know.

Protect Your Ideas from Yourself

Related to the analysis above is the ability to analyze when to keep your mouth shut. All the research in the world won't help if you get in your own way. Part of the data in any problem are the personalities involved in what you're trying to do. Al Neuharth recalls an agreement to buy CBS slipping through his fingers because he hadn't completely thought through that aspect of the deal:

> "You must dream and dare and do big things, but you have to keep your ego under control if you want competitors or potential acquisitions to buy your deal. At one point when I had been chairman and CEO of Gannett for some time, CBS was in trouble. This was when Tom Wyman was running it, and Ted Turner had made an unsolicited offer and put it into play. CBS really didn't want to be acquired, but they were looking for somebody who would be a better partner than Ted Turner. I thought there was an opportunity for Gannett to acquire the company, which by most measures was a little smaller than CBS, although the stock market attached a greater value to our stock float than to CBS's. We spent several months laying the groundwork for it and came right up to the brink, where both Tom Wyman and I were prepared to call our boards together and ask them to approve the deal. And my ego got in the way. In front of the key executives of CBS and our executives, I made the mistake of telling that group that I would be running the merged company. Wyman and I had agreed that that would be the case; I'd be chairman and CEO, he'd be president and chief operating officer. I made the mistake of not letting *him* tell them. When I told his associates that I'd be running the merged company, he realized what a shock that was. He went back and they thought about it, and they went out and raised a lot of money to try to fend off Ted Turner.
>
> "That was my mistake. My ego blew the deal. I was still pretty young then; I was only in my fifties. I just thought that I was such a hotshot that everybody, including the boss of Big CBS, should recognize that not only did I have a bigger ego but I was better than he was. It would have worked if I'd let him come to that conclusion without my trying to shove an unwanted object down an unwilling throat."

Use Analysis to Stay Focused

A formal problem-solving methodology, such as POHEC, can help prevent you from being distracted by negative thinking. Applying logical, rigorous analysis can help keep you focused on moving forward and on what you can do about a problem rather than getting mired in blame or nightmare what-if scenarios. That can be especially helpful if you think you're high on the Neuroticism scale.

Constantly Reexamine Your Data

In science you constantly go back over your data to make sure it's assessed correctly. You recapitulate. You also assess new available data. If you put blinders on, you're not going to be able to react to internal stimuli and be flexible. Businesses are not static enterprises, and neither are marketplaces. You have to be smart enough to analyze what market trends will demand in two to three years or more, and how to morph your business to capitalize on them.

Recognize gaps between what you anticipated and what is actually happening. Kinnear says one of the most common problems for entrepreneurs is underestimating the speed at which their idea will get adopted:

> "There's more than one entrepreneur still scratching his head around this area, who had an idea to save millions and millions and millions of dollars for the auto companies and never got it past the beta test in some obscure part [of the auto companies]. Even though it proved out perfectly, they never implemented it because they are so risk-averse at implementing newness. It just takes forever. [Take] bill payment on the Internet. You say, 'That's a great idea, it makes perfect sense, it's so much simpler.' And yet you have to ask, 'How fast will people adopt that strategy? What percentage of the population at what pace will accept that idea?'
>
> "Most entrepreneurs overestimate the pace at which those kinds of things will happen. What I always say to them is, 'Supposing that your sales in the first year are one-tenth of what you said they were going to be, and the pattern of acceptance and sales follows an two-month, two-year lag based upon what you've looked at because of this consumer who may not be quite as receptive, who even if he says

your idea's wonderful may not buy it for a long time. How does your business model work in those circumstances?' "

Exercise

If you're under a lot of stress, the brain releases cortisol, which affects cognitive functions such as memory. Chronically high cortisol levels also can cause permanent changes in the brain. Nerve cells shrink. Production of new cells in the hippocampus, which is involved in memory, screeches to a halt.[11] That makes it even more difficult for the brain to handle stress-induced floods of cortisol in the future. Exercise seems to help control cortisol levels as well as carry oxygen to the brain. If you want to think better, get out there and move.

This is one of the shortest chapters in this book because, in my view, if you're a born entrepreneur, operational challenges are in some ways the least difficult to deal with. Why? Because all the other qualities of the born entrepreneur help you meet them or delegate them. If you're not operationally gifted yourself—and many entrepreneurs aren't—you have the ability to recognize that and do what's needed to fill that gap so that you're able to focus on what you're genetically wired to do in the first place. That's thinking like an entrepreneur.

CHAPTER 9

The Challenge of Punctuation Points: Making Better Decisions

Sam Wyly didn't set out to launch an entrepreneurial career by founding a computer company. But his football career was over at age seventeen: "There was simply no college market for a hundred-and-fifty-five-pound nose guard. I was out of work." Then he had a summer job as a clerk for the state legislature, which moved him to decide he wanted to become governor of Louisiana. "That was my mission when I went to college, but you can't be governor until you're thirty-five. I was getting my people network teed up in different towns around the state so that when I got to be thirty-five I would have a shot at it."

In the meantime, his innate curiosity led him into journalism, and then into accounting. He took an investment course in which students had to put together an imaginary five-stock portfolio. "One that I picked was IBM. The reason I picked IBM was because I was impressed with this very smart, well-dressed IBM salesman who called on my parents. Hey, nobody in town had a Cadillac, and this IBM salesman drove a Cadillac. I did research. I went to the library and studied the numbers all the way back to 1919. I became hugely intrigued with this leadership character named Thomas J. Watson Sr. who was building a great institution. I had this good feeling about IBM. I didn't decide to get into what was then the electric accounting machine world, which became the electronic and then the computer world. I just kind of got into it, and one thing led to the other." He went on to start University Computing Corporation, the first of what would be his many ventures as a serial entrepreneur.

Sound familiar? It did to me, too. It's almost exactly the same experience as my seeing the pharmaceutical rep in the medical center. If I hadn't seen doctors listening to that well-dressed guy and decided that pharmaceutical sales might be an appropriate picture to paint myself into, I'm pretty sure I wouldn't be where I am today. After all, you don't get a lot of experience with P&Ls when you're torturing lab rats. It was the first of a series of major career decisions that might seem pretty counterintuitive. But each was a crucial step in my evolution from research scientist to sales rep to marketing exec to agency owner to CEO.

For entrepreneurs, I'm not sure that there's such a thing as "career pathing." Maybe in large corporations you can plan a route to the top— unless, of course, the company merges and your nice little "career path" is suddenly crowded with people from the other company you're being merged into. Even in corporations, career paths these days are much less clear-cut. And entrepreneurship has always been less about following a path than about trying to create a map of uncharted territory. As both of these stories illustrate, *entrepreneurs are open to circuitous, serpentine career moves dictated by opportunities—ones that appear to them as well as opportunities they make for themselves.*

"But I Don't Have a Vision for My Life!"

If you've known what you wanted to be ever since you were nine, congratulations on being part of a select minority. For most of us, having a vision isn't quite that simple. But even if you don't have an overarching vision for your life, the unique combination of personality traits that can help you be successful is already part of you, like the DNA in each cell. Developing a vision can mean focusing those traits one vision at a time instead of knowing the precise long-term outcome they'll produce.

In a rapidly changing world, you may even be better off with what I call an evolutionary vision—especially if a high degree of Openness to Experience is part of your personality. Being attracted to novelty and excitement, without a vision to guide your desires, can leave you scattered and unfocused. The key to unlocking the power of Openness is to channel that ability instead of letting it simply lead you by the nose from one unfinished project to another.

There's a theory of evolution called *punctuated equilibrium*. It says that evolution doesn't happen gradually but in dramatic bursts. There may be long periods of small, incremental changes, but the creation of a new species happens relatively quickly. It's a bit like opening a jar lid that's stuck. You twist and twist and twist while the lid moves slowly. Then suddenly the vacuum seal breaks and the jar is open. Something changes gradually, and then suddenly it takes on a very different form.

I think entrepreneurial careers happen in much the same way. There are key points in everyone's lives that can cause dramatic change or even create entirely new careers. At those moments, we either recognize and go after opportunity or we don't. Making a career change, starting a business, launching a product—each has the potential to shape everything that comes after it, just as punctuated equilibrium has the ability to create an entirely new species and shape all life that succeeds it.

These decisions and opportunities are what I call "punctuation points." Punctuation points create the next picture you compose for yourself, the picture that guides how your career or business evolves. They can help create the addiction to success that we discussed in Chapter 2. Seeing the pharmaceutical rep was a punctuation point for me, just as seeing the IBM salesman was for Sam Wyly. It led me into an entirely different career than the one I had studied for. Launching my agency was another punctuation point. Selling my agency and becoming intrapreneurial within a large corporate arena was still another.

In some ways, a career is simply a series of decisions, some more critical than others. Successful decisions at punctuation points call on not only our skills and experiences but on whatever genetic abilities we have, and they test all three to their limits. We need to make sure our decisions at those punctuation points align with our genes, our experience, and our picture of ourselves. The Success Promoters can help us switch on our genetic abilities at punctuation points.

In fact, you might say a successful decision at a career punctuation point is really just applying the Success Promoter habits to find whatever course suits your genetic makeup. That's the course that will give you the best chance at success. And punctuation points are all about the success of what comes after them. They can either confer success or block it. How do we recognize punctuation points before they pass us by? How do we deal with them when they occur? And how do we reproduce success from decision to decision?

RECOGNIZING PUNCTUATION POINTS

Remember our earlier discussion of your evolutionary vision being like a series of pictures? You move from one picture to the next, imagining yourself in each one. Punctuation points don't just involve painting a new picture. Sometimes the new picture is in an entirely different style or different setting.

You can recognize a punctuation point by three things: (1) the degree of change it involves; (2) the level of discomfort it creates; and (3) the consistency between external and internal inputs about the decision.

Just how different is the new picture you're painting from the one you're in now? Would you be leaving a tranquil Impressionist seascape for an angular, abstract Picasso? Changing careers into a completely new field—going from, say, information technology to owning a garden store—might be just that dramatic. Or are you simply going from, say, a seascape to a landscape, the way you might if you leave a corporate IT job to do consulting or launch a new company—or, in my case, a scientific research post to a pharmaceutical sales representative?

The bigger the change, the more different the new picture is from your existing picture, the more critical it is to make sure they both have some common elements. In the case of a painting, the artist might use the same colors, or paint the same subject. In the case of a career, it might involve skills or personality. Some common elements for me in moving from molecular biologist into pharmaceutical sales were my understanding of cell biology and biochemistry, their underpinnings of medical or pharmaceutical therapy, and my people skills. Fortunately, they were already in my genetic makeup (although the people skills weren't terribly valuable in my relationships with lab rats!). A punctuation point is easy to spot if you think about how different the situation will be after you allow it to happen.

The second way to recognize a punctuation point is to think about how easily you will be able to deal with that change. How comfortable are you going to be in that new picture? How well does it suit your genetic makeup? To what extent does it move you out of your comfort zone? Does the new picture use many of the same colors as the previous ones, or will you need an entirely new color palette? In my case, I needed a new "color" in my palette when I moved from sales rep to marketing executive: a better understanding of finances. Any punctuation point is likely to involve at least some discomfort initially. If it doesn't, it's not a career-expanding period. The best ways to make the transition easier is to envision yourself as fully as possible in that new picture. The more you've painted yourself into that new picture before acting on the punctuation point, the fewer surprises you'll have to deal with and the more comfortable you'll be taking action. Again, it's aligning that picture with a critical analysis (POHEC) of the opportunity that lies before you—what the upside is and what the downside may be.

Finally, if external inputs match your own inner urges, that's a signal that you may be facing a punctuation point. When my adviser suggested I think about dealing with the public instead of killing rats, that was a mind shift, and it caused me a bit of discomfort. But a couple of days later, when I saw that well-dressed pharmaceutical rep in the medical center, all the building blocks started being put into place. It all seemed to make sense—so much sense that I acted on it and never returned to the lab.

QUESTIONS THAT HELP YOU SPOT A PUNCTUATION POINT

- How dramatic is the change?
- How much discomfort does the change create?
- Are your analysis and gut reaction aligned with external feedback?

THE GENE/GROWTH ALIGNMENT

A little discomfort isn't a bad thing. It can help us evolve and grow. Stretching yourself by putting yourself in a new environment can actually trigger your innate abilities. There's a great example of this in nature. There are certain fish whose genes trigger changes in their appearance and behavior, depending on their environment. When the fish are moved from an environment where they're submissive to one in which they're dominant—when they become a big fish in a small pond, so to speak—the change immediately begins to affect their genetic messages. They develop an eye stripe. They begin to sport brighter colors. They become more sexually active. It's as if the fish's genes are toggling back and forth between two genetic codes: the "wimpy fish" code and the "winner fish" code.[1] All of these changes that cascade from a change in the genetic instructions and turn on certain genes happen only after they've emerged as a dominant fish. (Remind you of any corporate executives you've known?)

Remember my story about facing competition immediately after starting Harrison & Star? That new, talent-driven agency altered the environment I was operating within. The challenge really switched on my Cold Call Gene! I became ultra-aggressive at trying to get meetings with prospective clients so we could preempt that newer agency. I'm glad to say I succeeded.

I think much the same thing happens with humans. Putting ourselves in a new picture can trigger the use and development of our genetic abilities. Unlike fish, we as humans have the advantage of being able to choose our environments, to "switch on" certain aspects of our genetic makeup by painting a new, challenging picture for ourselves. That's what happens at punctuation points. If we're smart, we choose environments that bring out our own inborn "winner fish" genes.

There's one rule of thumb you need to remember at a punctuation point. I call it the "Gene/Growth Alignment": The bigger the change, the more closely it needs to reflect your genetic makeup. Change produces discomfort and growth. You need to understand what you've got that can help you meet the challenge. If the new picture doesn't "switch on" the right combination of your genetic personality traits and help you express your own psychic DNA to deal with that discomfort, it's not likely to produce dramatic or long-lasting success—if indeed you can achieve any success at all. Can you adapt? Probably, if your genetic backbone is consistent with change. Can you learn? Of course. Can you succeed? Maybe. But unless you use a punctuation point to put yourself in a situation that stretches you and yet is aligned with the way your genes have endowed you, you're facing an uphill battle. Change should naturally align with who you are innately and can ultimately become.

WHAT'S "ESSENTIAL TO YOU" INFORMATION?

At a punctuation point, it's important to understand the difference between "essential data" and "essential to you" data. You need both. "Essential to you" data is whatever lets you be more comfortable with a decision. "Essential to you" data may also be essential data, but sometimes it isn't. It could be a particular statistic, another person's opinion, a worst-case-scenario strategy. It may not be relevant for someone else, but it's absolutely necessary for you to live with your choice. Pam's opinion about my starting my agency was "essential to me" data. Without it, I wouldn't have felt comfortable making that call.

"Essential to you" data can be just as important for you as all the other information combined. And what is "essential to you" data will probably be influenced by your genetic personality. If you're a Samurai Worrier, you may find that you tend to want more "essential to you" data than others. In that case, put an arbitrary limit on the time you'll spend poring over it. Punctuation points don't last indefinitely. Jobs aren't open forever. New markets won't remain untended long.

PAINTING YOUR VISION WITH PUNCTUATION POINTS

Instead of worrying about a grand life plan, pick a vision that works for you now. Focus on painting a picture that's linked to your answer to that first question: why you want what you want. Then go for it. Really pour yourself into achieving that short-term vision, knowing all the while that a new version of that vision—or even a different vision—will emerge from pursuing this one. If it's truly linked to why you want what you want, it will pull you in the direction your personality naturally leads you. More important, it will help crystallize your longer-term vision.

Pat Croce's original vision was launched when he was working in the basement of Haverford Community Hospital near Philadelphia as a sports therapist. The room had no windows, and he found himself wondering, "Why does this have to be down here? Why can't it be in a sunlit room the way a sports-team training facility would be?" That initial vision expanded to launching his own private physical-therapy practice. That evolved into a chain of sports-medicine clinics called Sports Physical Therapists. The next evolutionary vision was his purchase of the Philadelphia 76ers; later came his career as a writer, speaker, and sports commentator for NBC. His latest vision: a pirate museum in Key West.

As Croce's example demonstrates, vision doesn't have to be a linear path; in fact, most often it is anything *but* linear. Give each stage of your vision your best, even if you think it may change later. An evolutionary vision doesn't lock you in—just the opposite. It's enormously freeing, because it can actually make it easier to switch visions later on. By encouraging immediate success, it may give you a more solid financial base from which to build. For example, succeeding on Wall Street may give you greater resources to start your own business later. Being successful at this stage of your evolutionary vision may put you in contact with other high-achieving people, creating a network that can help you switch to the next stage of your vision. It develops habits that let you succeed in whatever you do. Finally, playing with everything you've got even though your vision may not be as clear as you like can refine your sense of what you don't want. Being halfhearted will be far more costly in the long run.

DON'T AVOID PUNCTUATION POINTS—SEEK THEM OUT

Punctuation points are where the opportunities lie. The more you tackle, the more they help train your decision-making instincts and make you comfortable with the kind of discomfort we just talked about. Brain-imaging research shows that new experiences cause more brain activity than familiar ones. Things that surprise us make a deeper impact than the "same old same old." They stimulate our genes to lay down new connections in our brains.

There are several reasons why a vision created by punctuation points works just as well as any vision that comes to you early and guides your entire life:

• *It lends itself to your own evolution.* Keeping yourself open to experience—whether that comes to you naturally or not—helps you evolve. You may find yourself drawn to things that haven't yet produced an addiction to success but that use your personality traits in a new way. If you're learning new skills and taking on new challenges, you'll be constantly growing out of your existing vision and into a new one. Successive visions become evolutionary building blocks.

• *Industries change.* If your vision at the turn of the twentieth century was to become the biggest manufacturer of buggy whips in the country, you were out of luck when the industry disappeared. Many people at IBM have had to adjust their career visions as the company has evolved from being strictly a computer-hardware maker to a services-focused company. A series of short-term visions permits greater flexibility over the long term at the same time that it gives you a framework for setting your priorities and goals.

• *An evolutionary vision helps you avoid "dream drift."* Really devoting yourself to your current short-term vision is the best way to set yourself up for the next opportunity, the next vision. Achieving a series of concrete goals in pursuit of your immediate vision lets you build experience and a reputation. The better those are, the greater your chances of spotting and succeeding at new opportunities that can help shape your next vision.

A series of rational short-term visions that align with who you are and why you want what you want can help prevent what I call "dream drift." When your view is focused on a thirty-year horizon instead of a five- or ten-year one, any vision can seem overwhelming to all but the most invincible of us. If I had somehow decided in 1974 as a sales rep for Pfizer that I was going to be the CEO of the largest marketing communications company in the world, I think I might have been more anxious about taking the interim steps needed to get myself there. When that happens, it's easy to forget your dream, give up on it, or postpone it while you pursue "what's really important." And gradually, over time, your dream drifts away. An evolutionary vision made up of a series of short-term visions stays present and more real for you. It responds to what's happening now while staying linked to why you want what you want. That means it can evolve without disappearing. An evolutionary vision is based on the use of new information. Dream drift is based on inattention.

If you're highly Open to Experience, this can be especially important. Because you're very receptive to new ideas and experiences, you may find yourself easily lured away from completing what you're doing by the distractions of new stuff. Having a sequence of evolutionary visions can provide both focus and the novelty you crave.

Assess where you are in your current career in terms of your level of happiness. If you're totally unhappy, you've got to make some changes to align what you do with why you want what you want. Once you realize you might be able to be happier doing something different, figure out what could make your personal situation better for you. Money? Status? A different type of work? Working with different people, or a different type of people? A different leader? How would happiness or success in a new role be different from whatever happiness or success you experience now? Once you figure that out, the next step is to use the POHEC Success Promoter to figure out the building blocks that can get you there.

TRAIN YOUR INSTINCTS

Test your instincts in small, lower-risk decisions. That can help refine them as decision-making tools. This is especially important if your genetic inventory shows you're low on Extroversion. Playing with low stakes builds confidence you can draw on later when a true punctuation point comes along.

However, as you're evolving, don't allow others to change you behaviorally, because it will fight your DNA constitution. You are who you are. If you're genetically low-key, don't let others, such as a boss, try to turn you into a maniacal leader. If you try to please, you'll eventually realize the disconnect between your acted-out character and who, genetically, you really are. Be who you are.

What is your evolutionary vision for yourself?

USING SUCCESS PROMOTERS AT PUNCTUATION POINTS

• Use your strengths in collecting and processing information. For example, if you're low on analytical ability but highly Extroverted, use your natural Extroversion to gather other people's perspectives.

• Use the Picture-Painting Gene to assess the impact of your decision. Remember that a punctuation point is going to involve discomfort at some point, regardless of whether you say yes or no to an opportunity. Sure, a "go" decision is going to create some discomfort and create a lot of change; that's usually pretty obvious. And a "no-go" decision or nonaction may leave you in your zone of comfort in the short term. However, it may not produce long-term gain. If you're a born entrepreneur and consistent external input keeps trying to push you in a new and different direction but you don't do anything about it, you'll constantly churn inside, asking "What if I had done that?" There will be more second-guessing, more long-term discomfort. Do you want to spend your life looking back and saying "I could have done this"?

Think about this question: If you went as far as you could go on this path, if you were as successful as you could possibly be, how would it play out—and would that outcome make you happy? John Bogle Jr. worked at State Street Bank before joining several partners in launching a mutual fund company named Numeric Investors and, later, Bogle Funds. Despite his family's role in creating the mutual fund industry (or perhaps because of it) Bogle began his career on the banking side of the operation:

> "I remember my father and I were talking at one point about State Street and whether I would ultimately leave there when I was presented with the opportunity to start up [Numeric Investors]. He said, 'One of the things you have to think about is, what the opportunities are for running your own company or at least being a partner in running your own company versus staying at State Street. Is staying at State Street and having as an objective running the bank something you want to do?' I thought about it and at first I said, 'Yeah, I think I'd like to run a bank.' But then I thought about it some more, and I thought, 'Do I really want to run a bank?' It wasn't anything about the fact that it was a bank per se, but I had to ask myself, 'Do I want to run a huge organization like that?' My only exposure had been on the front line, whether as a banker or a money manager. Did I really want to be in management? Well, the financial rewards would have been nice; that was my first instinct. Having lots of people reporting to me would have been kind of a cool thing. But then I started thinking, 'Is that really what I want to do? I don't know what that's like. I do know what being on the front line is like, and I kind of like that. I like doing it rather than getting other people to do it.'"

In Bogle's case, even if a rise to the top of State Street Bank had played out incredibly successfully, it would not have created success *for him.* The point I want to make here is not to let discomfort be your sole deciding factor. Whichever choice you make at a punctuation point, you'll probably face discomfort at some point. As the car repairman used to say in the old TV ad, "You can pay me now or pay me later." And remember: It's never too late to make the change—as long as it aligns with your genes and you don't repeat behavior that keeps you "status quo."

• Think about what the long-term impact of your punctuation point will be on your view of yourself. With a "no-go" decision, you'll always think of yourself as someone who didn't take the risk. That what-if will always be with you. It can cloud your thinking about future punctuation points. It could make you think of yourself as someone who doesn't take risks. Or it could lead you to be so anxious to make up for missing a previous punctuation point that you reflexively jump at the next opportunity without doing the right analytics. Saying "I missed that opportunity; I'm not going to miss the next one" can lead to mistakes, too.

I once worked with a salesperson who was incredibly successful. He had been unduly restless for some time and wanted a change. He took the first "opportunity" that presented itself to him without really thinking it through. Unfortunately, it wasn't aligned with who he really was. He made a terrible mistake and never recovered. One mistake led to another. He's actually less happy today at a less influential job working for others than he was before he made the first career move.

• Use the Seeing Around Corners Gene to help you assess the scope of change that's likely to happen after a decision (punctuation points often mean dramatic, rapid change). Practice looking several years down the road at how a market is evolving, what the punctuation points are likely to be, and what your clients, customers, or company will need then. Develop a personal marketing plan that allows you to internalize the punctuation point and capitalize on all the positives around the change, all the strengths associated with it. See your picture several years out. How does it look? Is the change a natural—an aligned one—for you?

• Use the Cold Call Gene to help you think about your "immune response" to change, whether your "product" is an actual product, an idea, or yourself. What forces of resistance could lead to abandoning a punctuation point, and how can they be overcome? What can you do in advance to prevent resistance to the rapid change a punctuation point creates? What can you do to increase your understanding of how you react to change and how you can overcome potential inertia?

• Rehearse in reverse. Use the POHEC Gene to review the origins of your decision, not just its outcome. Doing so can help flag the early warning signs of inertia or disaster; it also can show you things that can promote success next time. However, when you need to look in the rearview mirror, don't focus on whatever mistakes you may have made but on what they can tell you that will help you face the next punctuation point. Ask yourself, "Am I where the picture I painted took me or not? If I'm not there, what are the differences between the reality and the picture I had in my mind of where I would be? And what have I got to do to massage the reality to the point that it gets me to my picture?"

• Use the Forward Focus Gene to keep you living into that new picture of yourself when obstacles arise. Do you ever repaint the picture? Only if you're genuinely painting a new one that still suits the genetic you. If you're not happy with the reality because it isn't what you pictured and you change the picture, you're creating a tension between that picture and the view you have of yourself based on your understanding of your genetic makeup. It's better to keep evolving your reality as it exists today by staying on forward focus and concentrating on what will put you in the picture. That way, you're always working toward something positive, up to and including the moment you find a new picture you can't wait to paint for yourself. Entrepreneurs are insatiable. Once they're living inside their picture, they realize they can still grow. They paint another and still another picture of their success.

At each punctuation point, don't forget to celebrate success. Our brains change physically when we associate success with pleasure. To encourage those changes, we need to make sure we reward ourselves when a decision turns out well. That pleasure helps keep our brains searching for ways to create new successes—new products, new business relationships, more effective processes. That's the addiction to success that thinking like an entrepreneur produces.

CHAPTER 10

The Challenge of Being a Nice Guy: Building a Reputation That Works

Among the reasons I first started thinking about launching my own agency were the conversations I kept having with clients. I kept hearing, "We really like dealing with you. If you ever decide to start your own advertising agency, I will want to continue to give you business." They made clear they weren't just talking about the quality of the work I did for them, although they seemed to appreciate that, too. Time and again, people kept telling me what a pleasure it was to work with me. My clients and I enjoyed our working relationship. Supposedly when I left to start my own agency, one of the clients I had represented at my former employer said, "There'll never be another account guy like Tom Harrison."

Those conversations made me realize that being someone people wanted to work with was more than just an integral part of my genetic makeup. It was part of the strategic value I brought to my clients—an important part. Remember in Chapter 6 when I discussed the concept of creating values-based value? Who I am is part of my own values-based value, and part of why I started my own agency. I truly believe that being what I call a Nice Guy is part of what I contribute to my company, to my clients, and, by large extension, to the way the world operates.

Up until now this book has focused largely on internal issues—how to manage yourself to promote success. But being a successful entrepreneur means being successful at dealing with other people. People used to say, "Don't do anything you wouldn't want to see on the front page of the *New York Times.*" Today it should be "Don't do anything you wouldn't want to show up on Google." Reputation has always been important, but never more so now that the Net gives it worldwide transparency. In the global village, everybody knows your name—and it had better be a good one.

NICE GUYS FINISH FIRST

When Carlos and Jorge de Cespedes started their company, each of the brothers put in $500. A friend kicked in another $500, and the three launched Pharmed to distribute pharmaceutical and medical supplies to hospitals and other health-care operations. After the first week, the friend said he had changed his mind and needed his $500 back. "I said, 'If that's the case, here's your five hundred dollars—and by the way, we made ninety-six dollars last week. Here's thirty-two dollars.' I don't need to tell you today how much he regrets not being a one-third owner of a six-hundred-million-dollar company."

The de Cespedes brothers easily could have told him to get lost for leaving them in the lurch. Or they simply could have returned his original $500. Instead, they not only chose to refund the guy's $500 but also to share equally the tiny $96 profit from their first week in business. Says Carlos de Cespedes, "Treating people with respect and treating people correctly, both inside as well as outside your company, long term pays off handsomely."

Can you be a nice guy and also be successful in business? You bet. In fact, I'd argue that if you're a Nice Guy—and I'll explain what I mean by that in a minute—you win over the long haul. It may even have immediate benefits. In my experience, businesses and America today are looking for honest, nice, collaborative leaders who embody integrity. Sure, if I hadn't created strategic value for my clients, I could be the Nicest Guy in the world—but that doesn't mean they'd want me to represent them. It's the combination of strategic value and being a Nice Guy that created "my brand."

I think it's time to defend the reputation of the word "nice" a little. "Nice" has gotten a bad rap for too long. It amazes me that people seem to think of a Nice Guy as a mealymouthed doormat, someone people can walk over or just push around. Not so! Being nice and having guts are not mutually exclusive. In fact, being nice can be one of the toughest challenges a leader has to face. When business requires you to lay off thousands of workers, or persuade investors to trust you with their money, or rally the troops to survive tough or changing times, being a Nice Guy gets you through it in a way that not only lets you sleep at night but earns the respect and trust of others who work with, alongside, or for you.

Notice that I put the term Nice Guy in capital letters. That's to make sure you understand that I'm not talking about a naive wimp or a glad-handing empty suit with an American Express card. People may tolerate and even like either of those types, but they might not want to do business with them. A Nice Guy is someone people trust, respect, *and* like. That often requires telling people things they don't want to hear, or making unpopular decisions, and always telling the truth when it would be easier to lie. Being a Nice Guy generally means you're true to yourself, to who you really are genetically.

By the way, women can be Nice Guys, too. It just sounds too patronizing to call them Nice Gals—the Nice-Guy women I know would strangle me! If you female readers will indulge me, I'll stick with using Nice Guys in the sense of "Come on, you guys!" and trust that you'll understand that I intend it to be gender inclusive.

People in business today want to deal with people they enjoy being around and trust. Businesses don't have as much margin for error to compensate for the problems created by dealing with people who lack integrity, who aren't nice, who aren't genuinely honest, and who create no value. This has always been true, of course—it certainly always has been for me—but in the wake of recent corporate scandals, I think it will be even more important in the future. Legislation can go only so far before it bumps up against human nature.

I'm starting to see this more and more as I talk with other business leaders. There's a lot of humanity in how people are picking their business partners. The relationship, the culture, the chemistry, the personal synergy—all are emerging as dominant factors in business decisions. Picking a partner, a supplier, an employee, or a manager who makes doing business easier, more enjoyable, more productive, is a way for people to regain some control over their own lives. One way to reduce

WHY NICE GUYS WILL FINISH FIRST

- **Outsourcing.** The jobs that will remain here are the higher-level ones that require a human brain, human emotion, interpersonal interaction, and hands-on service. They are the most difficult to automate or ship thousands of miles away. Listen to Federal Reserve governor Ben Bernanke's vision of the impact of overseas outsourcing: "Outsourcing abroad will be uneconomical for many types of jobs, particularly high-value jobs. Most high-value work will require creative interaction among employees—interaction that is facilitated by physical proximity, personal contact, and shared cultural experiences."[1] Jobs that can't be automated into oblivion are jobs that demand to be filled with Nice Guys.

- **Globalization.** The more successful you become, the more likely you are to have to function globally. That means bridging the inevitable cultural gaps. More than ever, entrepreneurs, CEOs, and managers need to be able to treat people with respect, dignity, and honesty. And it must come naturally, from some part of your DNA. Humanity transcends manners and boundaries. Nice Guys succeed better globally because their treatment of people is based on more than simple etiquette. People tend to recognize Nice Guys and sniff out the actors, the bullies, the insincere opportunists.

- **The need to attract talent.** People don't leave companies. People leave bosses. People leave phonies.

We all want to work with people who add to our day-to-day lives, not make them a living hell. A company attracts talent because of its leadership and what it represents about what the company stands for. Being a Nice Guy increases your ability to attract and retain talent—and in a business like mine, the talent is the core of the company. Can people survive if they have to work for a jerk? Yes, but they won't thrive. People only thrive when they work with people who are collaborative, compassionate, and inclusive. Today's knowledge workers want to be where they will be challenged without bullying, where the people they work for genuinely believe in their value and know how to help them develop that value. The difference between people just surviving and genuinely thriving can be the difference between a company's success and its stagnation—or worse.

- **Governance tests.** Companies are starting to be judged by whether they operate in the best interests of financial stakeholders. Standard & Poor's looks at a company's ownership structure, stakeholder rights and relations, information disclosure, and board structure and process. It has begun to issue a corporate governance score based on these factors. Morningstar has begun issuing a similar "Fiduciary Grade" rating for mutual funds' treatment of shareholders. The person at the top affects whether a company is a corporate Nice Guy.

stress is to work with people you like and trust. People are spending too many hours on the job to tolerate people who aren't reliable or who make life miserable for those around them.

And nowhere is being a Nice Guy more important than for an entrepreneur. Most of the qualities we've already discussed—perseverance, belief in oneself and one's product, vision, the ability to spot opportunities—come as no surprise. But most of the time you don't hear about the importance of an entrepreneur being a Nice Guy as the leader of the company he or she represents. So why am I devoting an entire chapter to it? Well, let's call it the "Martha Stewart" syndrome: For better or worse, the person at the top increasingly helps create a company's image. And that can be as true for large companies as it is for small ones. Companies must stand for something—some enduring quality or qualities that employees, society, consumers, and customers can rally around or relate to. The leader must embody those qualities. If he doesn't, there is a genetic dissonance or disconnect between the leader and the company he or she is leading.

"I honestly believe that the leadership role in a company is becoming more and more a role that evokes what the company stands for," says Barry Gibbons. "Especially when business has become so complicated, the leader is increasingly becoming a figurehead for the company, demonstrating the values of the company. Fifty percent of the top one hundred economies on the planet are now businesses. Only two of the countries are not democracies, but none of the companies are. You have to think about the people who make up the company."

Am I being unrealistic to think Nice Guys are going to finish first more and more? I don't think so. Sam Zell tells a story that illustrates why, apart from anything else, being a Nice Guy is simply more practical:

> "I once went to Detroit to buy a shopping center, and I sat down with the seller. The first thing he said to me was, 'You know, nobody's ever wanted to do a second deal with me.' And I sat there stunned. And then I found out why. This guy was just crazy; he made you nuts. And he was exactly right. I never did another deal with him.

"I do think that in any kind of a continuum, people who treat other people well will survive and prosper more often than people who bully people or who take advantage of people. That sounds like something out of the Bible, but the reality is, that's part of leadership, too. . . . I think people have always been able to survive with [bad] behavior. But is the question survival, or is the question progression and achievement? It's very difficult to succeed in today's world if you're an asshole. Unfortunately, that does not diminish the number of assholes in the world."

There's another piece to being a Nice Guy: integrity. Integrity doesn't mean the same thing as being honest, though that's part of it. The dictionary defines it as being whole, being unified. Behaving with integrity means walking the talk, making your actions match your words, doing what you say you're going to do when you say you're going to do it. Integrity involves being honest with yourself as well as others. It's looking people in the eye when you talk with them. You don't get your board to approve a huge salary increase for yourself and then tell workers they're being laid off because profits aren't high enough. You don't propose a big showy project and then quietly deny it funding because you never intended it as anything more than PR.

The business world is filled with examples of people who had the title of leader/CEO/chairman who overpromised and underdelivered—and who later got caught and fired. Being a Nice Guy is infectious. People gravitate to you. They want to be with or around you. As my graduate school adviser said, "Tom, people like to come in to talk to you. They like being in the lab when you're here doing your experiments." When I became a pharmaceutical sales representative, doctors actually liked to talk to me; they believed what I told them. They would wait for my visits; one doc actually told me once that when I went on a vacation and had failed to let him know, he had really missed my visit! That's the power of being a Nice Guy—instead of having to push your way into a prospect's office, you've generated pull for your services.

When I started my own advertising agency, I made promises that I was sure I could deliver on. If something happened that changed what I could deliver—or when I could deliver something—I always set my client's expectations immediately. People just want honesty in business.

They expect it. It's kind of the basics of business, but you'd be surprised at how many people don't pay attention to the basics.

When you're honest and have the ability to marry that honesty with talent, with value, with intellect, with standing for something important—watch out. You're an entrepreneur—a successful one.

There are "entrepreneurs" who started their agencies before me and after me. Some still have strong businesses with global clients. Some are out of business because their promise was really no promise at all. Some people who have taken over the mantle of agency leader have succeeded, some have not. Those who did not succeed did not personally represent what the agency stood for. There was an underlying disconnect, a cultural and genetic chasm. Companies, like people, have their own DNA. If the company's and the leader's DNA are not complementary, one or both will fail unless the leader is replaced before the corporation sustains too much damage.

Pat Croce puts it very succinctly: "You can be a success with no reputation. You can't be a success with a bad one. It dilutes everything you've done. How can you do business with someone you don't trust? Integrity doesn't have an on-off switch."

At least one study found that both business leaders and the general public believe it's possible for business leaders to be both ethical and successful. They don't expect business leaders to be, as the study put it, "naive pushovers or saints."[2] However, people do want to be treated fairly and honestly.

Being a Nice Guy helps give you the peace of mind that propels you to personal success, a reputation that allows you to look everyone in the eye when you talk. Being a Nice Guy allows you to exude the confidence that comes from knowing you've done your best to be honest, honorable, and humble in your dealings. Every day, some people have confidence at the expense of other people. I think the confidence that comes from not taking advantage of other people is ultimately more valuable. You don't have to worry about the baggage that comes from feeling guilty, perpetually angry, or chronically dissatisfied with what you've done to someone else.

Can you win if you're not a Nice Guy? Maybe in the past you could, and it's even possible now, I suppose. But in the wake of ever-increasing workloads and mistrust of rogue CEOs, I think your odds of personal success are dramatically better if you're a Nice Guy. And you certainly increase your odds of being content with yourself at the end of each day.

There needs to be a symbiotic relationship, a complementarity between how you genuinely feel about yourself and your business's actions, and how your clients, your customers, your colleagues, your business relationships, and those who work for you feel about you. If others feel positive toward you yet you feel empty personally, you've defrauded your public. You're an actor—and it's a difficult act to keep up for very long. If you feel good about yourself but others have a poor view of you, either you've failed to brand yourself or you are happy being a jerk.

NICE GUY GENES AND THE "SERVANT CEO" CULTURE

Is being a Nice Guy genetic? Like everything else, it's not black and white, but there's some evidence that genetics helps.

No matter how good a leader you are, your company's culture and the people who create it are what drive day-to-day decisions. When things in business and in people's personal lives change as rapidly as they do now, companies can no longer rely on the old "command and control" model of leadership. More and more companies are trying to create cultures of what's called "transformational leadership." Transformational leadership, as identified by management theorist J. M. Burns, facilitates flexibility and independent action in solving problems, quick adaptation and encouragement of change, and support for a long-term vision.

Frankly, I don't see how companies today can operate over the long term any other way. When employees think of themselves as members of a "Free Agent Nation" and companies are organized as networks rather than rigid, isolated hierarchies, can any other method really work over time? Companies and their leaders who take the short view, who don't know what their consumers will want in three to five years, who don't know who—or what—their competitors are, who are not innovating by supporting trial and error (much like the scientific method, by the way), who do not wrap themselves around a cause that they and their corporation can stand for—those companies and leaders are destined for short corporate lives.

At least one study has found that leadership styles, especially transformational leadership, tend to be highly influenced by genetics. Working with 247 sets of twins, researchers found that the closer the genetic connection between individuals, the more similar their leadership styles were. The study found that 59 percent of the difference between whether someone was a transformational leader or not seemed to be linked to genes. The genetic connection for transactional leadership (similar to the "command and control" style) was lower—just under 50 percent.[3] In other words, you can learn to become a command-and-control leader easier than you can learn to be a transformational leader. You've got it—or you don't.

And transformational leadership seems to involve being a Nice Guy. We talked in Chapter 7 about how Extroversion and the desire to dominate can confer a genetic advantage when it comes to accepting rejection and persevering. That tendency of high-Extroversion people to experience life positively and be outgoing can contribute to being seen as a Nice Guy. Other things being equal, Extroverts report having a better balance between work and home life than do people with low levels of Extroversion; they see their work as making them more interesting people to live with.[4]

In the few scientific studies that have been done so far that have tried to correlate genetics and leadership, Extroversion has been the Big 5 personality trait to show up most consistently. However, other Big 5 traits also have been found to contribute useful balance. One study found that, along with Extroversion, Conscientiousness and Openness to Experience were most closely connected with transformational leadership.[5] Most of us don't really need a study to point that out. They form one of the Power Pairs I mentioned in Chapter 1. Conscientiousness is associated with being not only hardworking and responsible, but also with being reliable. It would encourage the kind of Nice Guy integrity we discussed above: doing what you say you're going to do. Openness to Experience would promote listening to new ideas and being receptive to changing course if those ideas made sense. By contrast, the same researchers found that the traits of the so-called transactional leader—short-term, "get it today" leaders with a style based on hierarchy, structure, and control—were very different. Not only was there a negative correlation with Conscientiousness and Extroversion, but there was a clear link to the exact opposite of Agreeableness.

A study two years earlier also found a similar link between leadership and the same three traits. Extroversion was the dominant connection between leadership and personality, followed closely by Conscientiousness and Openness.[6] Still another study suggests that Agreeableness can be useful in conjunction with Extroversion to produce a transformational leader.[7] Review some of the adjectives associated with Agreeableness—trusting, candid, modest, cooperative, tender-hearted—and it's easy to see the connection. Scoring high on Agreeableness means someone puts a high value on getting along with others. They care about other people's well-being, believe people are basically trustworthy, and behave that way themselves. I don't care who you are; you cannot buy respect, at least over the long term. And respect for others begets respect for yourself.

I know these aren't the first qualities that come to mind when we think about entrepreneurs. And if Agreeableness dominates your personality, you probably aren't an entrepreneur. You may be too willing to defer to authority, too concerned about others' well-being to make tough decisions, too self-sacrificing to push your own initiatives and beliefs. Too much Agreeableness can leave you at the mercy of others. It's like having arms and legs: you need them, but having more than you need isn't necessarily an advantage.

But Extroversion and Agreeableness combined make a powerful balance; they're the second Power Pair. A little Agreeableness can help offset an Extrovert's desire to dominate—a conversation, a meeting, a transaction—and prevent him or her from flattening others in the process. And having a healthy dose of Extroversion can stiffen the spine, which is critical for an entrepreneur. Without it, an Agreeableness-dominated personality will probably surrender control too often out of a need to please others and just keep everyone happy. Even for researchers, the genetic link to transformational leadership wasn't simply a matter of adding up scores. The impact of one genetic factor seemed to affect the influence of others.[8]

Being a Nice Guy helps one become what I call a "servant CEO." Some of the most effective CEOs I've known have been people who see everything they do in terms of how it enables the people who work for them to do their jobs. When I started my own ad agency, I already had been a scientist, a pharmaceutical rep, a marketing manager, and an account guy at another agency. I knew every aspect of my clients' business and jobs because I had been in their shoes. Now, I know that anyone can be replaced, but I really understood and anticipated each client's needs so well that I became somewhat indispensable. They kept awarding our agency more business. I became a servant CEO of my own agency not only because I helped my clients do their jobs better, but also because I helped everyone who worked for me understand what it meant to "serve" the client. That meant improving their ability to do their jobs while we were doing ours—assisting them in selling their brands. In essence, we branded ourselves as the "intellectual" agency because we understood our clients' businesses so well.

"The great CEOs really believe they are no more important than the guys on the line," says Ann Rhoades, whose company, PeopleInk, works with companies to instill a customer-centric culture. "They understand that [for example, with JetBlue] without those pilots they don't have an airline. In my opinion, the companies that have historically had ethics problems had a consistent arrogance about them. . . . It's the CEO who will ask labor unions to take a cut while accepting a huge bonus. I don't get it. What's so ironic is that their stock goes down and the loss far exceeds the bonus. Even Finance 101 suggests that's not a great model."

Never have I allowed the power associated with my position to go to my head and dictate how I lead. I've always considered myself equal to the people who were helping me build my company. We come to the company with complementary skills. I just happen to be in a decision-making position, one that forces me to look into the future while others are satisfying today's needs. Superiority breeds discontent; equality breeds a culture in which people will fight for success and will do everything they can to support you. A leader whose people abandon him or her has nothing to lead.

A CASE STUDY IN BEING A NICE GUY

When I left Pfizer, I worked with a guy named Rolf Rosenthal, probably the nicest agency leader who ever existed in the health-care industry. Everyone respects him not only for how good he is at what he does but for how nice he is to everybody—consistently. At one point, the agency lost the largest piece of business in its portfolio. We were all waiting to see who would get fired so that the agency could remain profitable. The day after the loss, Rolf called the agency together, not to deliver bad news but to tell us that no one would be laid off. "We will rally and get more business to replace our losses," he said. "This loss is no one's fault." The agency got emotionally stronger, got more business, and became an example for others. Rolf is a great leader, and one of the industry's Nice Guys.

BIG EGO, BAD EGO: IS THERE A DIFFERENCE?

One of the challenges for any entrepreneur is balancing self-confidence with being a Nice Guy. Is it possible to be a Nice Guy and still have the kind of ego required to take on enormous entrepreneurial challenges and be successful at them?

Some people do seem to have that balance in their genes; I think it probably comes from that Extroversion/Agreeableness Power Pair. My wife often says that I have a huge ego, and yet, as I've said, being a Nice Guy is part of what my clients have always valued about me. *Big egos and bad egos are two different things. Your ego has to be big enough to recognize that being a Nice Guy doesn't cost you the ability to control outcomes.*

Read that sentence again; it's important. If you're smart, you recog-

nize that control comes from getting the job done, and that it's a lot easier to do that if you can recruit others to your cause. What's needed is
not so much a big ego but a smart ego. I know people who have huge
egos that are totally not in check, who can never be wrong. (I'll bet you
know a few yourself.) They might never do anything to harm a person,
but at the same time they may put undue pressure on people simply
because they can. They may be so self-involved that they literally can't
hear what anyone else is saying. And bad egos always seem to emerge
at precisely the moment when they can do the most damage. I'm telling
you, being a Nice Guy is tough. Doing it when it's easy doesn't count;
it's when the going gets rough that being a Nice Guy really makes you
extraordinary. It makes you stand tall among equals.

Ann Rhoades tells a story about someone she interviewed for an
aviation mechanic manager's position at JetBlue. The man had just gotten out of what's known as A&P (airframe and powerplant) school,
which trains airline mechanics. He was working on the line for an airline he had always wanted to work for, one that took only top-of-class
mechanics. Every airline mechanic wanted to work there. Six months
after he was hired, he was asked to sign off on a plane going overseas
that he knew shouldn't fly anywhere. He also knew that because the
airline was so well known and everyone in the field talks to everyone
else, saying no meant he probably would never get another job anywhere else as a mechanic.

"He refused to sign off on it," says Rhoades. "He didn't have a job
until we hired him. That guy said, 'I may lose my job and not get another one after going to school, but I can't sign off.' And he had a
brand-new baby, by the way."

I don't know that mechanic personally, but as someone who spends
a lot of time on airplanes, that alone qualifies him as a Nice Guy in my
book. That's integrity. That's principle. That's the ability to do what's
right even if it potentially has a negative impact on you in the short
term.

I remember once telling a prospective client that our agency
couldn't work for them for at least a year because we were too busy
with other clients. It wasn't easy; this was one of the biggest health-care
clients around. But I didn't feel I could take their business if it meant
we couldn't represent it in a way that was consistent with our culture

and style of representation. Yes, the client was disappointed. And yes, a year later they called back.

We've been through a number of very visible corporate leadership scandals in which a Teflon ego seems to have displaced integrity. The entrepreneurial desire to seek out bigger and better wasn't what was at work here. "Wanting more" basically meant "wanting more for me," not more for the genuine good of the corporation and its people. Why do leaders—entrepreneurs or intrapreneurs—want more at the expense of others? I believe it goes back to something in their genetic makeup that creates a false halo effect and causes them to act differently than they communicate. It's some sort of an inborn misalignment that allows the leader to turn the other way, pile on the lies, and attempt a cover-up when he or she knows something's dishonest. It's as though some genetic quirk allows your ego, your inner being, to convince yourself that you're really not doing something wrong, or that you're above others' pain or suffering.

It happens when one's ego has gotten so big, so out of balance, so ballooned, that the person behind the ego feels he or she *is* the corporation—not just the leader of a large body of people who together make up the corporation. "Wanting more" shouldn't be a zero-sum game between individual and company—and if you're wired right, it isn't.

PICKING YOUR BRAND OF GENES

Being a Nice Guy is part of personal branding—the "Brand You" concept that Tom Peters popularized. But as with all branding, personal branding needs to connect with reality. Your genes help shape your personal brand.

I've told you that my transition from cell biologist to corporate executive began when I saw a successful-looking sales rep talking to doctors at the medical school where I was doing my research. Actually, that guy probably wouldn't even have been on my radar screen if it hadn't been for my graduate adviser's valuable lesson about personal branding. When he told me he had noticed my people skills, it altered my view of my personal brand. I had always thought of myself as a scientist, but I learned that the personal brand that my genes had created for me—without my even realizing it—was something different than I had expected and trained for. Sure, I was a good researcher, but what differentiated me from my peers and created the personal brand that Dr. Sutter noticed was my inborn Extroversion. Without that conversation, I probably wouldn't have even noticed the rep, or thought about sales as a career. It was a great lesson in the power of your genes to shape your personal brand, and the power of that brand to shape your future. I've never forgotten it. (Thanks, Dr. Sutter!)

Your personal brand—your reputation—is a capital asset, and should be treated that way. If you invest in equipment, you have to take care of it, maintain it. Your brand is like your personal equipment, your hardware. You need to upgrade it every so often based not only on what you need it to do now but also on what you're going to need it to do in the next three to five years. It's part of what you have to offer. Certain people were willing to be interviewed for this book only because of the personal brand of the people who put me in touch with them. That means their personal brand has created an asset for them—the goodwill that comes from being able to help someone else. I owe them for that because they were able to leverage their personal brand on the book's behalf—and, believe me, I'll be happy to repay the favor by leveraging mine for them.

Your personal brand is a salesman on your behalf—often when you don't even realize it. In the early days of Harrison & Star, there was one health-care executive I must have called at least twenty-five times without a single phone call being returned. Eventually, months later, I finally heard from him. "When you first started calling, I didn't know who you were," he said. "I didn't even know what business you were in or what you were trying to sell me. But in the last six months, I've heard your name so many times associated with your new agency that I had to pick up the phone. Why don't you come visit me?" He eventually became a good friend.

MARKERS FOR THE "NICE GUY" GENE

- You understand that "Nice Guy" is not the same thing as "wimp."
- You attract talent because of your reputation.
- Your actions match your words—and vice versa.
- You do what you say you're going to do.
- You respect people enough to be honest with them.
- You respect people enough to be consistently courteous.
- You respect the humanity in everyone.
- You respect the balance between work and family.
- You know that being a Nice Guy has to be a genuine part of your DNA.
- You are willing to stand up for your ethics.
- You understand and cultivate your personal brand for the long term.
- You know that being a Nice Guy isn't always easy; being mean is.

There's another story from my Harrison & Star days that illustrates the power of personal brand as sales rep. We made a new business presentation for a "me-too" product being introduced by a major pharmaceutical company. We dug deeply into the brand, its clinical data, its positioning. We didn't get to represent the brand—but only because the client awarded us instead their number one product in the category. The decision maker was convinced that I and my agency could help grow that more important brand, the largest brand in the industry at the time. He didn't want to squander our talents on a "me-too" product.

Now that's personal branding.

All brands have cycles; you want one that will be effective for the long haul. Why? Because you shape your brand, and your brand in turn shapes your career, your success, long term. You want to be as strategic about evolving your personal brand as you are with your business. It needs to evolve without sacrificing what made it successful in the first place. You don't want to pull a "New Coke" fiasco with your personal brand.

I can hear the cynics out there saying "But Tom, it's a dog-eat-dog world out there. If I'm a Nice Guy, my competition will eat me alive. You gotta be aggressive to get anywhere." In my experience, when business feels like one big game of *Survivor*, that's precisely when opportunities are the greatest for Nice Guys to win new clients, gain market share, evolve their personal brand, and further their careers.

Think about it. Competition means there are more people out there competing for the same thing you are. In a buyer's market, it's easier than ever for a client to find someone else equally as capable, equally as experienced, equally as connected. Most of us will actively seek out people who not only excel at what they do but who make the day a little more enjoyable—or who at least don't constantly make it worse. We're all stressed out enough as it is; no one needs to exhaust their time, patience, and energy dealing with the fallout from arrogance, selfishness, and greed.

Mean is easy; we all know the pressure is there every day to go in that direction. But if you want to be extraordinary, if you want people to remember you, if you want power and support that don't disappear when the chips are down, being a Nice Guy is one of the best ways I know.

Need still another practical reason for being a Nice Guy? It lets you be more bold about risk taking. If you know that your personal brand is one that anyone would be proud to be associated with, it gives you greater freedom to take risks and make bolder decisions. The deciding factor that made me comfortable with starting my own agency was Pam's asking "What's the worst that can happen?" She reminded me that I really wasn't risking much; if the agency didn't work out, she said, my reputation would allow me to get a job anywhere I wanted. Having the security of an outstanding personal brand reduces the risk of any entrepreneurial venture.

But what if your personal brand is that you don't suffer fools gladly, that you're an egomaniac, that you're arrogant and run roughshod over people? What if your Agreeableness score is subterranean? Well, I suppose that's also a personal brand of a sort. But you need to ask yourself whether that's a brand that can carry you through an entire career, and whether you're really talented enough to survive without a network of people to help you. If that's the legacy of your genes, I wish you luck. (Actually, it's not so much luck that I wish for you, but the ability to try to be happy with yourself.) I also hope you'll take a look at some of the rules for being a Nice Guy and see if you can use them to grow and develop your personal brand so it's one that people want to be associated with. You're like any other brand: you're an experience. Harley-Davidson sells an experience, JetBlue is an experience, Rolls-Royce is an experience. So is Sam Zell. So is Jeffrey Immelt. Sam Palmisano. Bill Gates. Bill Clinton. So are you. What experience do you want your clients or customers to have with you?

And remember: Whether your genetically influenced personality profile resembles Mother Teresa's or Hitler's, integrity is one success gene everyone can have. Everyone.

What goes around comes around, and it comes around faster than ever now. Having a reputation is not optional. You can choose only whether it's one you're proud of, and your actions make that choice every day. Integrity and being a Nice Guy have always been good ideas, but now they're even more. They're sound strategies for winning—and keeping—business. And they help you build a reputation that works for the long term.

I hope this chapter didn't come off sounding too goody-goody. That's not my intent. I simply want to send you a signal, an optimistic one. Despite the spate of well-publicized executive bad behavior—or perhaps because of it—*I believe we are living in or fast approaching an era of integrity, of leadership that genuinely cares about the company being led* and *the people whose careers are being guided.* It's an era in which success is measured long term, not quarter by quarter.

This is just as true for corporations as it is for small entrepreneurial ventures. Successful corporations and successful leaders will be aligned by boards of directors who take the time to determine what the corporation stands for, and what its leader stands for. How will they do that? By selecting leadership based on the history and evolution of the individual's personal brand. Whether you practice your entrepreneurial thinking on your own or in a corporation, it is the incredibly fine-tuned, deliberate alignment of corporate and personal values that will bring both businesses and individuals unprecedented long-term success.

C H A P T E R 1 1

Decoding the DNA of Success in Leading Others

have been a company man, an entrepreneur, a leader, and an executive responsible for evaluating other entrepreneurs. In each of those roles, I've come to the same conclusion: Success for an intrapreneur today requires much of the same DNA as entrepreneurial success does. Experience is a less reliable guide to what you should do than it used to be. The world is changing just as quickly for corporations as it is for start-ups. I've never seen any statistics on this, but I'd be willing to bet that the faster things change, the more important your personality becomes as a predictor of career success. Who you are—the unique combination of personality traits you bring to bear on whatever problems you're confronted with—becomes more important than what you've already done.

This is classic entrepreneurial thinking. The people interviewed for this book generally delight in proving experience wrong, in doing things that most observers would call impossible or "too risky." It's not that experience isn't useful for them; it's just not what has created their success. Entrepreneurs aren't worried so much about whether they know what they're doing. They focus more on their inherited ability to be able to figure out just what to do when the unknown plays itself out. They embody the saying I saw on the back of a T-shirt once: "I'mpossible." In a world of rapid change, we're all challenged to do what's "I'mpossible." Entrepreneurs believe in themselves and what they do.

That means leaders who can nurture their own entrepreneurial spirit will likely do better than those who are simply happy with the status quo. How that spirit gets expressed, though, should depend on your own genetic recipe. Some people will never be happy until they pursue an opportunity on their own. Others are more comfortable with intrapreneurial opportunity in a corporate cocoon.

ARE YOU AN ENTREPRENEUR OR AN INTRAPRENEUR?

If you've got the entrepreneurial spirit, at some point you're going to have to face a key punctuation point: the decision about whether to be an entrepreneur or an intrapreneur. I've suggested elsewhere in this book that the entrepreneurial spirit can certainly be found in the context of a large corporation. Some entrepreneurs may start their careers in a corporation, but their comfort with risk taking and their belief in themselves eventually will push them out of the nest. Without those two things, even someone who tries to launch a company will almost certainly find himself either going from one halfhearted venture to another or working for someone else for much of his career.

For what I refer to as "entreprenears," the idea of being able to control their own destiny is attractive. They may think they have a great concept. They might even have speculated on what it would take to launch a company. But the ability to live with risk and uncertainty seems to be the great dividing line. These near-entrepreneurs don't seem to have the comfort with risk taking that allows them to strike out on their own. It simply isn't in their genetic makeup. They're like bungee jumpers who want to jump but also want to know that they will be pulled back to safety before they hit the ground.

Once an entrepreneur always an entrepreneur, whether you operate independently or pursue entrepreneurial ventures in the context of a corporation. You could say that I'm an intrapreneur at this point, but I still feel very much like an entrepreneur. I'm constantly thinking of new ventures, some of which I act on, some of which I don't.

Neither is better or worse, but you need to have a very good sense of which one you are. If you're an "entreprenear," you can waste a lot of time waffling about which direction you should take. If they're not careful, entreprenears can find themselves chronically dissatisfied with the corporate structure without being able to actually make the leap of faith required to start their own business. Better simply to recognize that they're intrapreneurs and operate that way while still tethered to the bungee cord.

Another type of "entreprenear" are the people who eventually try to be entrepreneurs but get distracted or discouraged too easily. They're missing the entrepreneurial genes that let them carry their plan through despite the inevitable obstacles. One problem I see for many of these people is that they view risk as a one-time challenge. They seem to think that taking that initial step and launching the business makes them risk takers. Sadly, that's only the beginning. An entrepreneur isn't a pole vaulter but a hurdler who races from one hurdle to the next. It's the ability not only to go the distance but to do it many, many times that separates the near-entrepreneurs from the true ones. And the ability to embrace that serial uncertainty, I think, is either in your genes or it's not.

If you know why you want what you want, and what you have to offer in trying to get it, the final piece is figuring out where those two things are most likely to intersect. As I hope I've made clear by now, thinking like an entrepreneur doesn't have to mean actually starting your own company.

ENTREPRENEURIAL ALTERNATIVES TO LAUNCHING A BUSINESS

- *Being an intrapreneur in a large company.* As getting ahead of change becomes more important than simply keeping pace with it, most good companies now recognize that entrepreneurial thinking is essential. They may have a variety of ways to support it.
- *Launching a one-person operation.* Entrepreneurs can start operations that grow to become the next Microsoft or Dell Computer—or they can choose to remain small. Success doesn't come just in large packages.
- *Being a facilitator of other businesses.* I still feel as

though I'm in an entrepreneurial environment because in my current role at DAS, I work with more than 150 CEOs. Even though they're part of a multibillion-dollar corporation, most of them either began as entrepreneurs and still think that way or lead their companies entrepreneurially. In many ways, I'm very lucky; I get the pleasures of the entrepreneurial life without the headaches. Being a consultant, a venture capitalist, a visionary looking into the future, a manager of a business incubator—all thrive on entrepreneurial thinking.

Knowing how big you want to dream means knowing what kind of life you want to live. Do you want to be constantly busy? In charge of a lot of other people? A world traveler? Able to take time off to go sailing whenever you want? Who would you be as a person? A polished speaker? Someone who can make sense of a financial report? Who does your vision of your future require you to be? How will you spend your time when you get there? If your idea of success means being able to spend your time however you want, that might not mean being head of a large corporation. Do you want to run a "lifestyle company"—one that simply provides you with the type of lifestyle you enjoy—or do you have a vision of transforming the world and affecting the lives of thousands of other people?

Do some research to help yourself understand this. If you want to be a CEO of a large corporation, read magazine profiles and books that talk about how they spend their days. If you want to launch a business, talk to people who have, and read about what it's like. Regardless of where you are in your career, you can do this for each step of your vision. What would that promotion mean in terms of how you'll be spending your time? Will you still be doing things, or will you now be getting other people to do things? What are the skills and—just as important—the personality traits that are needed to succeed in that role?

THE DNA OF THE INTRAPRENEURIAL LEADER

Scientists can predict a bee's occupation by looking at how its genes get expressed in its brain. Researchers were able to predict just by looking at a honey bee's individual genetic profile whether a bee was a "hive worker," responsible for nurturing the other bees in the hive, or a forager who left the hive to search for food. The difference was so clear-cut that researchers' accuracy with their predictions was 95 percent.[1]

For us humans, the differences between an intrapreneur who chooses the corporate hive and an entrepreneur who leaves to forage for new markets is not quite so clear-cut—at least not yet. As we discussed in Chapter 7, "The Challenge of Embracing Rejection," twin studies indicate that genetic factors seem to be linked to people's records of leadership. Identical twins, who have the same DNA, were more similar in their leadership records and personality traits than fraternal twins, whose DNA is similar but not exactly the same. Researchers concluded that that connection between demonstrated leadership and genes was associated with inherited personality traits.[2]

All the Success Promoter genes that we've discussed up till now— the ability to believe in yourself and your ideas, embrace rejection, spot and seize opportunity, and be a Nice Guy—in many ways apply equally to intrapreneurs who want to achieve the highest levels of success in their organizations. Genes don't operate in simple ways. Even twins may find different outlets for their genetic personality traits. As we've discussed, having an entrepreneurial personality is not the same as actually being an entrepreneur.

One study that compared corporate managers to entrepreneurs found that managers tend to have a higher degree of Conscientiousness than entrepreneurs.[3] As we've seen, there's often a tradeoff between Openness to Experience, which keeps entrepreneurs looking to the horizon for the next opportunity, and the Conscientiousness demanded by the operations side of the business. However, another study, this one of 116 German entrepreneurs, found that *successful* entrepreneurs tend to have a higher degree of Conscientiousness than less successful ones.[4] Makes sense to me. *You might be great at starting companies, but without execution—and execution is all about Conscientiousness—you're not going to get very far.* Perhaps this is why many big-idea entrepreneurs must be teamed up with operations experts in order to succeed fully in the enterprise. Carlos de Cespedes is Pharmed's forecaster and sales guy; his brother Jorge oversees day-to-day functions. Sam Wyly and his brother Charles operate in much the same way.

Perhaps the biggest differentiator between entrepreneurs and intrapreneurs is their level of comfort with risk taking. As we've seen, that involves a high degree of Openness to Experience and a lack of Neuroticism. Another difference may be how they score on the Big 5 trait of Agreeableness. We've talked about how being a Nice Guy is important for an entrepreneur. However, great ideas sometimes are so compelling that they have the ability to be successful in spite of the jerk who came up with them. At least one study has found a negative correlation between entrepreneurial behavior and both Agreeableness and Neuroticism.[5] And it's true that some entrepreneurs equate believing in their ideas with making everyone else feel stupid.

But in a corporation, Agreeableness is critical. With more and more work getting done by teams, Agreeableness is essential to being able to understand and empathize with others. A leader is responsible not only for the results the team produces, but for how they're produced. And in a corporation, it's harder to get the resources and, more important, the decision-making authority you need to implement an idea unless you have the ability to understand and motivate others. An entrepreneur is often dealing with essentially one team: his or her own. A corporate leader generally has to deal with a lot of different teams—usually all at once. A corporation multiplies the sheer number of occasions that demand Agreeableness.

One of the motivations entrepreneurs often cite for starting a company is the desire to "do things their own way." By definition, someone who is comfortable in a corporate environment is probably going to score higher on Agreeableness. They're simply more willing to go along with someone else's way of doing things. Being an intrapreneur may also be a case of a person finding the environment that suits his or her genetic nature. If people are good at empathy, buying into corporate goals and procedures, and cooperating with others, a corporate environment may nurture that nature by rewarding behavior that they're innately good at. And because they practice and get rewarded for behavior that suits them genetically, they get even better at it. It's that addiction to success that I've talked about.

Another difference in the genetic makeup of an entrepreneur and a corporate leader is the latter's greater responsibility to develop the people who work for him or her. As we've discussed earlier, an entrepreneur needs to focus on what he or she does best—think about ways to drive the business forward. Managing individuals is important, but as an enterprise grows, that personal contact is one of the tasks that sometimes gets delegated in part to others who can do just as good a job (in some cases, better). Personnel management is not necessarily the best use of an entrepreneur's time and effort. In fact, most entrepreneurs may not be good at motivating or developing the talent that works for them. In a corporation, however, managing individuals is often *the* core task. That also requires the ability to empathize that is so characteristic of Agreeableness. *Empathy is not always a core competency of entrepreneurs.* This is absolutely not an excuse to be aloof or insensitive to people; it's merely an observation that entrepreneurial skills may not be strongest in the management and motivation arena.

EXPRESSING SUCCESS AS AN INTRAPRENEUR

So how do you unlock your own DNA of success in a corporation? The Success Promoter here that allows you to express your own genetic strengths is what I call the "symbiosis" gene. It enables you to work with others to create an evolving, entrepreneurial culture within your company, large or small. That kind of culture is flexible, adaptive, and talent-centric. It's the kind of culture that encourages everyone's innate abilities to flourish. It allows people to flourish and to become their "genetic best."

In a larger corporation, you may not be able to affect the corporate culture as much as an entrepreneur who runs his or her own company. But that doesn't mean you have *no* ability to have an impact on that culture. I believe that the more entrepreneurial the culture in which you work, the greater the chance of success—for you as well as for the people who work with you. As an intrapreneur, you are a critical part of helping to establish that climate. In fact, one of your key roles as a leader is to provide a work environment that allows people to be at their optimal performance level.

Even if you're not an on-your-own entrepreneur, there's a good chance you're going to be dealing with people who are—or who at least think that way. You may be negotiating with entrepreneurs, working next to a former entrepreneur, or competing against people who think like entrepreneurs. Businesses today often find it more effective to grow by acquiring other companies. More and more, corporations find themselves overseeing a collection of independent yet integrated entrepreneurial endeavors. Companies are realizing that it's important to encourage and preserve the spirit that made the acquired company successful in the first place—and that doing that requires the entire enterprise to think more entrepreneurially. If you're going to be successful, you need to understand, embrace, and help spread that way of operating. An entrepreneurial mind-set is a crucial building block of success.

"Entrepreneurs are as valuable in running a business or a university as they are in starting a new venture," says Sam Zell.

Be True to Your Genes as a Manager

Ann Rhoades tells a story from her days as VP of People at Southwest Airlines that demonstrates how having a disconnect between who you are and how you treat people can backfire. A senior executive known for his oversized ego had been told he needed to improve his people skills:

> "He had an arrogance. He was a brilliant person technically, and he was known for it every place he's been, but he thought he was better than every living soul who worked for him—and he showed it everywhere. He turned people off. This group really respected his experience, respected his background; they had heard about how great he was. But I knew culturally he would never, ever complement them. It would always be how much better he was, and it just didn't work. It was 'Well, I did that,' never 'You're doing a great job.' I said, 'It's so simple. If you're that technically brilliant and you know you need these guys, you better start acting like you need 'em.' But it was so phony when he would try to do it. They'd come in to me and say, 'What did you do, talk to him yesterday?'"

Instead of genuinely understanding and acknowledging the contributions of others, the exec simply tried to paste a different personality over his own. Unfortunately, personality veneers are transparent. The real one always shows through. If he couldn't figure out a way to help himself truly believe he needed others and convey that belief in his own style, he needed to find a culture that fit his style better.

As I've said, anyone can have the Nice Guy Success Promoter gene. If you really can't bring yourself to be a Nice Guy, you probably either need to find a position in which integrity and humanity are less important (good luck!) or partner with someone in your organization who can provide those skills and is patient enough to put up with and camouflage you. If you're lucky enough to find people like that, pay whatever they ask—and just stay out of their way.

Think Like a CEO

Even if you're not a CEO, you can think intrapreneurially by making new strategic initiatives a serious step to advancement. Make clear why they're important, even if an individual initiative fails. If you want people to understand the value of a project, be prepared to put top talent on it. And don't punish unsuccessful attempts at individual intrepreneurial projects; learn from them.

Manage Up

Linking your intrapreneurial vision to that of the company or CEO's vision and values is one of the quickest ways to forward that vision. After all, who wants to say they're not interested in something that's clearly aligned with the stated corporate goals? The other reason managing up is valuable is that it requires an understanding of the company beyond your division. You cannot be intrapreneurial or innovative in a corporate structure by acting alone. You need a network of aligned people. Understanding those other internal markets tells you what information is needed by the people you need to convince. Think of each one of the other divisions as a kind of venture capitalist; the "capital" they're investing is their division's time, resources, and staff. Leverage your network. If you don't have authority or credibility, borrow it. Figure out who else in the organization could help you lobby for your project and why they can benefit from helping you.

Scan the Horizon

It's just as important for an intrapreneur as for an entrepreneur: Identify trends that will have an impact three, five, ten years from now. Treat your group's immediate tasks just as you did the picture of yourself in your own evolving vision. Concentrate on realizing that picture as fully as possible while recognizing that it's only one of a series of pictures that will appear over a longer career time line. Understand clearly what you must do each step of the way to develop your picture of intrapreneurial success for your organization.

Stay on Forward Focus

Like an entrepreneur, an intrapreneur will reach roadblocks or have projects that don't work out. When that happens, having an entrepreneur's resilience can keep a setback from defining a career. A corporation may have even more ability than an individual entrepreneur to find other uses or markets for a failed experiment. It may just be a matter of finding the right advocate in the company who can help you do that. That corporate cushioning is precisely the reason many near-entrepreneurs never escape the mother ship. If that's you, why not make use of it? Keep advancing innovative, entrepreneurial ideas that will grow your organization more rapidly than is possible without them. Eventually, as long as they are aligned with the CEO's leadership vision, one of your ideas will be given life. Even if your ideas don't fly, you're continually challenging yourself and others to think innovatively.

Entrepreneurial ventures can fail. Entrepreneurial thinkers can't. Unlike the Bill Gateses or Michael Dells of the world, they may not succeed at what they initially set out to do. They may not succeed in the time frame they and others expected. They may not succeed the next time, either. They may even fail several times before something hits.

But truly entrepreneurial personalities are unstoppable in support of a vision—even if that vision gets tweaked and refined. At some point, the individual, the idea, the circumstances, the resources will align to produce success. Why am I so confident in saying that? Because a born entrepreneur doesn't stop until that happens—and usually not even then. Entrepreneurs have an insatiable appetite for growth, for ideas, for innovation, for creating, for failing, and for succeeding. Failure, to an entrepreneur, is merely a pit stop on the way to ultimate success.

"The definition of a jerk is somebody who reaches his goals," says Sam Zell. "You should always be testing your limits."

HELPING OTHERS EXPRESS THEIR OWN SUCCESS GENES

A friend recently told me about seeing a human-resources Web site that talked about improving a company's "highering practices." As a typo, it's funny, but it's also quite appropriate. Part of thinking like an entrepreneur is putting people in positions that improve their chances of success. Remember I talked earlier about an entrepreneur being an integrator? That's even more true for an intrapreneur. You're helping to integrate people with the work that best matches their innate abilities. That increases their chances of achieving higher positions and doing their highest and best work. In other words, you're "highering" them.

Understanding the innate strengths and weaknesses of the people who work for you promotes that. I mentioned earlier that inherited personality traits such as the ones we've been discussing tend to remain stable over time. That means leaders who don't consider those traits when making training, hiring, and promotion decisions and later have a problem with a difficult employee may also find that the problem is equally difficult to eradicate.

There's another reason for a leader to think about a person's inborn personality. The impact of genes tends to be most obvious when the environment is most equal. The more similar a population's backgrounds, educational levels, social status, and upbringing, the more clearly genes stand out as a differentiator. If twenty people eat exactly the same food in the same amounts and exercise the same amount, the ones who will put on weight the quickest are the ones whose genes are predisposed to trigger weight gain. It's not a great leap from that to looking at, say, a group of engineers with similar backgrounds and seeing that gene-influenced personality traits may affect the individual level of success, at least within that group.

But as I've said before, that doesn't mean environment isn't important. As leaders, we can still help people unlock their own DNA of success by providing a work culture that helps others express their own genes maximally and productively. By definition, that will be an environment that's flexible, adaptable, and respectful of diverse skills and personalities. It will be collaborative, itself entrepreneurial and conducive to innovation from anyone. Remember the "forager bees" I mentioned earlier in this chapter? Even though their genes accurately predicted whether they'd grow up to be foragers or hive workers, their environment still affected their behavior. When older forager bees were removed from the hive, the younger bees started foraging earlier. Researchers concluded that the bees' genetic instructions were responding to changes in their environment—the need to get out there and bring home the pollen. Genes may influence a person's natural inclinations, but leaders can still create an environment that encourages thinking entrepreneurially, expressing what's really natural for that person.

Hire from the Inside Out

It's easier to equip the right personality with skills than it is to take someone with the right skills and reshape his or her personality to fit a given role. You can alter skills, but not genetic makeup. Analyze a job not only in terms of the work but the personality that will promote success in the role.

"At JetBlue, we wanted a very, very different type of flight attendant," says Ann Rhoades. "We would ask, 'Give me an example of a time you had difficulty getting to Yes for a customer.' If they said, 'I don't do that because it says on page twenty-nine of the handbook I can't do that,' they're never going to work out. For managers, we would ask them for an example of when they had a tough time with someone who worked for them and how they handled it. I want winners, but I don't want them to say, 'I fired them.' I also don't want them to say, 'I did what they told me to do; I gave them thirty days' notice, I gave written notice.' I hate that. I want them to understand what's wrong, try to develop the people, and then if they can't, say, 'Let's get out of here.' I want them to consistently make tough decisions using common sense, not a manual."

Use Diversity to Help the Company Evolve

I think there are enormous opportunities in marketing specifically to women—opportunities that will grow even greater in the future. One of the reasons I see those opportunities is because I have the chance to work with a large number of incredibly talented women. Diversity of gender, diversity of ethnic background, diversity of age groups—all provide new perspectives that can broaden your horizons. I find that I tend to hire women for positions of leadership. It's not that I exclude males by any means; I hire a lot of male leaders as well. But often I find that an equally competent female candidate for a job has a broader, deeper, more compelling understanding of a market that I feel needs to be served.

Researchers have found fifty-four genes that seem to affect differences in the way the brains of male and female mice develop. Eighteen of those genes seem to get expressed more in male mice; thirty-six get expressed more in females.[6] (And remember, the genes of mice and men differ by only about 2 percent.) I'm not about to wade into the debate over genetic differences between men and women except to say *"Vive la difference!"* I think any differences only make for a richer world, and any company that doesn't take advantage of what diversity offers is evolutionarily challenged—not to mention evolutionarily backward.

Remember too that entrepreneurial thinking requires integrating many different skills. Every good leader does the same thing in terms of putting together a team. Too many forget to balance their abilities with those of others; they want people just like them. Making an active effort to increase diversity on your team is thinking like an entrepreneur who has to make sure all capabilities are covered, all resources complementary.

One obstacle to making diversity a priority is getting people in core management to accept the idea that it's needed or valuable. How do you deal with that? By proving that you're right. At Harrison & Star, some of my partners from time to time would challenge me, asking, "Why are we hiring so many women? Shouldn't we have men in these roles?" For me, it was part of a POHEC experiment. I had assessed how the women I saw in biz were doing. My hypothesis was that we needed to populate the agency with more women. Often, they did things in a way that I felt served our clients best, and our clients themselves were hiring more women in what had once been male roles. Also, I felt we were going to be able to appeal to more people because we would be creating different kinds of client relationships and have a different understanding of the market we were serving—or creating—for our clients. I proved my hypothesis to my partners when they saw that our agency was growing incredibly rapidly because our client service was unmatched. Again, that's not to say we hired women exclusively; we certainly had our fair share of very talented, very loyal men at H&S. I believe the deliberate balance between competent females and males in our agency was one of the reasons for our success in the early years.

But using diversity to help the organization evolve isn't only about women or minorities. Remember our discussion in Chapter 1 about the different types of CEOs? There are entrepreneurial CEOs, maintenance CEOs, turnaround CEOs, growth CEOs, strong leader CEOs, visionary and innovative CEOs, and probably a lot of others. I have a theory that I've been giving some thought to. We know you can't change your inherited genetic makeup. That makes it difficult, if not impossible, to change a person's innate personality, his management style, or her entrepreneurial leadership style. If that's true, should the same individual lead an organization for an indefinitely long period of time? Or should that person hold the post for as long as his or her leadership style and attributes align with the needs of the corporation?

Human DNA may not change, but corporate DNA does. As the corporation evolves, its DNA changes and its leadership needs change. Different phases require different structural and leadership abilities. For example, a newly formed company will do well under the original entrepreneur for a while. If it's successful, eventually it will probably need a different kind of leader with different kinds of skills. The CEO must, then, change to embrace the growth needs of the corporation—and that may mean a change in the individual who fills that role. It doesn't mean the original CEO is no longer effective. It just means he or she may not be the best possible CEO at that time for that organization.

I think CEOs need to be traded out and moved around just as we do with other levels of employees, matching their innate skills with corporate needs. It provides a new growth opportunity not only for the CEO but for the corporation as well.

Train from the Inside Out

The more entrepreneurial your environment, the more jobs will tend to evolve around the people who hold them. If you're trying to encourage an entrepreneurial climate, try to develop people's core strengths and let those strengths help shape their role rather than trying to fit people into restrictive job descriptions. W. L. Gore, the makers of Gore-Tex, hires new employees for what the company calls a "commitment" instead of a specific job. Teams are put together based on specific opportunities, and leaders tend to emerge naturally. Each new associate is assigned a sponsor who helps the new person understand that commitment and identify assignments that take advantage of his or her skills to produce an early success. The sponsor also helps the individual move from team to team, matching the person's skills to the right projects. The company believes that strategy tends to attract, produce, and nurture entrepreneurial self-starters.

When Debbi Fields Rose began hiring people to sell her cookies, she would audition them. She coined the three Ss: Sampling, Selling, and Singing. First, she asked them to taste the cookies. ("If they ate them and loved them, I knew I'd never have to write a sales manual. People will sell a product they love.") Once she knew they loved the product, she would arm them with a tray of cookies and ask them to take to the streets and give cookies away for potential customers to try—the only way she knew that would grow the business without advertising. She calls it the "Try and Buy" method: "I had to know this was something they could do." Last but not least, she would ask if they would mind singing out loud her favorite song: "Happy Birthday to You." Why? "Everybody knows it, and I was looking for the person who would go out of their way to make a customer smile and be willing to build a company—the 'I can' people."

You can train somebody to sing "Happy Birthday to You," but you can't train them to like doing it. That's training from the inside out.

Help Imprint Success

Some companies believe in trial by fire for new employees. I'm not sure that's the best approach. Creating early wins can set up a pattern of success that can have long-lasting impact. Launch new employees in situations that give their natural strengths an opportunity to shine.

Help them understand what you perceive as those strengths and how to take advantage of them. In some cases, it may be useful to screen for hidden traits—not to disqualify people from certain jobs but to help uncover valuable aspects of their personality that you as a manager can help them unlock.

Lead by Example

What you focus on, your organization will focus on. If you demonstrate that you value evolution, risk taking, and opportunity seeking, the organization will, too. Create a climate that focuses on capitalizing on opportunity.

That's how American Airlines innovated under Robert Crandall. At first glance, Crandall might seem to be anything but an entrepreneur. However, his tenure as chairman and CEO of American Airlines was marked by multiple highly entrepreneurial projects. He created Super-Saver fares, which launched deep discounting for advance-purchase tickets. He led the development of the first yield-management system for airlines, which maximizes revenue and is now an industry standard. He created AAdvantage, the first frequent-flyer program. All are entrepreneurial in spirit.

"We had hundreds of ideas we funded that didn't work. We terminated them before they became a tremendous problem. At one point someone had the idea that we could set up a Web site within the SABRE structure just for organizing meetings. We set up the site and did some experimentation. What we found was that the people who run hotels and meeting venues—people who presumably had an interest in keeping the database up to date—wouldn't do it. And if the database wasn't up to date, meeting planners wouldn't use it. We took it far enough to know that it wasn't going to work and then we killed it—before we did ourselves any major damage. Any decent corporation should be looking for those ideas. Our position was, 'If you've got a new idea, come talk to me about it.' If it's halfway sensible, we'll invest some money, do some analysis. If the analysis suggests that the idea's a good one, we'll go with it. If it doesn't work, you don't go back to the proposer and say 'This doesn't work. You're toast.' If you want to be a leader, you've got to provide resources for idea advocates. And you have to provide encouragement by saying to the folks whose first idea didn't work, 'Okay, bring me another idea.'"

Encourage Gene Expression by Transmitting Information

People's success genes have a greater chance of getting expressed if they understand how their abilities can help further the company's goals. But for them to be able to think entrepreneurially, a leader has to help them understand what the company is trying to do and why.

The father of Harley-Davidson's Rich Teerlink was an entrepreneur in the tool-and-die business. Teerlink says his dad made a point of walking in the back door every day and talking to the guys on the presses: "I asked him one time why he did that. He said, 'Here's where the action is. It's not in the office.' I think if you try to create awareness about what the biz is attempting to do, people will understand and they'll want to come along. You'll give them a purpose. Then the challenge is how do you create the opportunities for them? How do you see they have the right kinds of training and development? That's where most organizations really miss the boat. They're big on big speeches and things of that sort, but then they don't hold people personally accountable. The only way to hold people personally accountable is to have them set their own goals. They only set their own goals well if they understand what's going on. If they start setting their own goals, they get more involved."

There are limits to what you can do, of course. How far you can encourage people depends in part on *their* genes. But your success as a leader will depend in part on how well you're able to uncover people's innate abilities and match them with opportunities that give them a chance to be successful.

TWELVE RULES FOR EXPRESSING THE "NICE-GUY" GENE

There are some things that seem to work regardless of whether you head your own company or are an intrapreneur. By and large, they're independent of personality or genetics. They're a kind of bottom line for dealing with other people. They work inside or outside your company. They apply to people who work for you, with you, and above you.

1. Don't Walk on Other People, but Don't Let Them Walk on You

Be respectful to a fault, but also respect people enough to demand the best of them. "The successful executive has as his or her objective getting people in the organization to do better than they know how, getting them to stretch themselves," says Al Neuharth. "How you do it depends on how you as the leader can figure out what it is that will motivate the people you're trying to motivate."

2. Respect the Big Idea in Everyone

Another practical reason for being a Nice Guy is that you never know who's going to provide you with something that could lead to your next success. It might be a mistake, a piece of info, an opinion, a personal contact, an inspirational quotation. Your next entrepreneurial success might come from the most unexpected person—mine came from my grad-school adviser—but only if you're listening for the big idea in everyone.

3. Own Everything

Accept responsibility for your mistakes as well as your successes. You're not fooling anybody when you try to pass the buck. Don't lie—not even a little white lie.

4. Never Let 'em See You Sweat

Nobody cares about your problems. They care about their problems. Focus on their problems—both today's and the ones you can anticipate down the road—and help them solve them.

5. Keep It Simple

Aside from any ethical questions, honesty is less trouble long term. You don't have to worry about remembering what you said when to whom and why. Oh, you might be able to get away with shading the truth for three or four days. But truly successful people are too busy to worry about constantly having to try to remember how to cover their tracks. Being honest means there are fewer things to keep track of. You've got enough stuff on your plate without worrying about keeping your lies straight. Do yourself a favor. The truth is simply easier.

6. Never Think in Terms of "So What Have You Done for Me Today?"

It's not what you or someone else has done today. It's what you can do over the lifetime of the relationship to make a positive difference. It's knowing that you can be relied upon all the time. You don't have to hit a home run every time you get up to bat. You just gotta hit the ball where it makes a difference.

7. More Is Less

The more you try to impress somebody, the less you usually do. People's built-in BS detectors have been refined over the last few years. Believe me, humility with integrity is better than false ego every time.

8. Live Your Word Consistently

Consistency may be the hobgoblin of little minds, but not when it comes to how you treat people. Match your actions to your words, and let your word be your bond consistently. It's like brushing your teeth: brushing seven times harder once a week doesn't give you the same benefit as doing it every day. Don't reinvent yourself around different people. The art of persuasion is all about trust. Trust is all about credibility, and credibility demands consistency. Be nice consistently.

9. Don't Lie: Fix What's Causing You to Think You Need to Lie

A lie is often an attempt to cope with or cover for a bad business practice. If you have to lie, there's probably something wrong with the way you're doing business that underlies it. For example, if late payments from customers are causing you to worry about missing payroll, reexamine your billing practices instead of shuffling money around by not paying the premiums on employees' health insurance. Fix the problem with your business; don't lie about it.

But what if the person asking you to lie is your boss? That should never happen. If it does, find another boss quickly. You'll do yourself no favors in the long term if you don't. Plenty of entrepreneurs got their start for just that reason. And don't ask someone else to do something you'd be uncomfortable doing.

10. Never Forget to Thank, Congratulate, or Acknowledge People for Their Efforts

Knowing your own power means not needing to abuse that power. Take responsibility; hand off a lot of the credit. And never be too big to get your hands dirty, or to say "Thank you."

11. Keep Your Door and Your Heart Open

People want in. Be an audience; be approachable. Temporarily suspend judgment about wrong and right if you really want to hear what someone's saying. Be empathetic to understand, and be sympathetic to be human.

12. Never Stand in the Way of Balance

One of the people who works for me came into my office a week after I hired her. Her husband's brother had died, and she said, "I feel terrible about this, but I really feel I should go home with him for the funeral." I said, "Why are you even asking me? Your family always comes first. Stay as long as you need to. And don't worry about anything here; we'll fill in for you." I'll say it again: People don't leave companies, they leave bosses. Attracting and retaining talent means letting people stay people.

THE LAST WORD

Time and again over the years, I've noticed that the most successful people have been those who have picked environments and challenges that suited their personalities. They don't adapt to their environments; they choose or create environments that suit who they are to begin with—or who they envision themselves as becoming. They don't work at who they are; they work who they *are*. They wrap the environment around themselves instead of the other way around.

Just because you may not feel you were born an entrepreneur doesn't mean you can't think like one. I'm not presenting a single recipe for success. The human DNA that we all share is made up of anywhere from 20,000 to 30,000 genes. The way they're combined and expressed produces nearly limitless variations. That makes each of us unique. No single formula can prescribe a path to success for everyone—one formula, one person. *What I hope this book will do is help you see the formula for* your *success.* The extremely successful people in this book used their native abilities to create an environment for themselves that both reinforces and takes advantage of those inherited abilities. Hearing their stories can help you begin to think like an entrepreneur. These successful people started out just like you and me. They understood who they were and capitalized on every gene in their bodies. They developed a series of career-expanding pictures and lived full-bore into them.

You can, too, by understanding what you were given, by envisioning your picture of success, and by creating your plan for realizing that picture. In doing that, you're engineering yourself to achieve the success that's genetically right for you.

NOTES

Chapter 1

1. "Genes, Evolution and Personality," Thomas J. Bouchard Jr. and John C. Loehlin. *Behavior Genetics*, May 2001.
2. "Passing On Privilege: Resources Provided by Self-Employed Parents to Their Self-Employed Children," Howard E. Aldrich, Linda A. Renzulli, and Nancy Langton, *Research in Social Stratification and Mobility,* 1998. "The Career Dynamics of Self-Employment," Glenn R. Carroll and Elaine M Mosakowski, *Administrative Science Quarterly,* December 1987. "Self-Employment, Family Background, and Race," Michael Hout and Harvey Rosen, *Journal of Human Resources*, Fall 2000. "Financial Capital, Human Capital, and the Transition to Self-Employment: Evidence from Intergenerational Links," Thomas Dunn and Douglas Holtz-Eakin, *Journal of Labor Economics*, April 2000.
3. *The Language Instinct*, Steven Pinker (Perennial Classics) pp. 327–328.
4. "Happiness Is a Stochastic Phenomenon," David Lykken and Auke Tellegen. *Psychological Science*, May 1996.
5. "Interacting Effects Between the Serotonin Transporter Gene and Neuroticism in Smoking Practices and Nicotine Dependence," C. Lerman, N. E. Caporaso, J. Audrain, D. Main, N. R. Boyd, and P. G. Shields. *Molecular Psychiatry*, March 2000.
6. "Association of Anxiety-Related Traits with a Polymorphism in the Serotonin Transporter Gene Regulatory Region," K. P. Lesch, D.

Bengel, A. Heils, S. Z. Sabol, B. D. Greenberg, S. Petri, J. Benjamin, C. R. Muller, D. H. Hamer, and D. L. Murphy. *Science*, November 1996.

7. Based on information from the Human Genome Project Information Web site, www.ornl.gov.

8. "Role of Genotype in the Cycle of Violence in Maltreated Children," Caspi et al. *Science*, August 2, 2002.

9. "Behavioural Abnormalities in Male Mice Lacking Neuronal Nitric Oxide Synthase," Randy Nelson, Gregory Demas, Paul Huang, Mark Fishman, Valina Dawson, Ted Dawson, and Solomon Snyder. *Nature,* November 23, 1995.

10. "A Comparison of Whole-Genome Shotgun-Derived Mouse Chromosome 16 and the Human Genome," Mural et al. *Science*, May 31, 2002.

11. "Genes, Evolution and Personality," Thomas J. Bouchard Jr. and John C. Loehlin. *Behavior Genetics*, May 2001.

12. "The Determinants of Leadership: The Role of Genetic, Personality, and Cognitive Factors," Richard Arvey, Maria Rotundo, Wendy Johnson, and Matt McGue. Available from the IDEAS online database http://ideas.repec.org/p/hrr/papers/1302.html.

13. Interview with Richard Branson and his mother, Eve Branson, for the documentary *Lemonade Stories,* written, produced, and directed by Mary Mazzio.

14. Interview with Arthur Blank and his mother, Molly Blank, for the documentary *Lemonade Stories,* written, produced, and directed by Mary Mazzio.

15. Interview with Tom Scott and his mother, Jane Scott, for the documentary *Lemonade Stories,* written, produced, and directed by Mary Mazzio.

16. Based on 1986 and 1997 studies by Paul Costa and Robert McCrae, quoted in McCrae's chapter "Emotional Intelligence from the Perspective of the Five-Factor Model of Personality" in *Handbook of Emotional Intelligence*, edited by Reuven Bar-On and James D.A. Parker.

17. "Imprinted Genes Suggest Your Cortex May Derive from Your Mother," Gail Vines. *New Scientist*, May 3, 1997.

18. "Genes, Environment and Personality," T. J. Bouchard Jr. *Science,* June 17, 1994.

19. "Growing Up, Growing Apart: A Developmental Meta-Analysis of Twin Studies," K. McCartney, M. J. Harris, and F. Bernieri. *Psychological Bulletin,* March 1990.

20. Though they use the OCEAN terminology for the five dimensions of personality, the questions on this quiz are not in any way associated with or drawn from the more formal NEO PI-R™ personality measurement tool developed by Robert McCrae and Paul T. Costa. The quiz also is not intended as a medical diagnostic tool or as a substitute for medical advice.

Chapter 2

1. *The Biology of Business: Decoding the Natural Laws of Enterprise,* John Henry Clippinger. (Jossey-Bass Publishers, 1999), p. 52.

2. "Instant Recognition: The Genetics of Pitch Perception," Peter K. Gregersen. *American Journal of Human Genetics,* February 1998.

3. "Hostility Differentiates the Brain Metabolic Effects of Nicotine," Dr. Steven Potkin and James H. Fallon. *Cognitive Brain Research,* January 2004.

4. "Partial Deletion of the cAMP Response Element-Binding Protein Gene Promotes Alcohol-Drinking Behaviors," Subhash C. Pandey, Adip Roy, Huaibo Zhang, and Tiejun Xu, *Journal of Neuroscience,* May 26, 2004. Also, "The Genetic Basis for Smoking Behavior: A Systematic Review and Meta-Analysis," Marcus Munafo, Taane Clark, Elaine Johnstone, Michael Murphy, and Robert Walton, *Nicotine & Tobacco Research,* September 2004.

5. "Genes Harbor Clues to Addiction, Recovery," Tracy Hampton. *Journal of the American Medical Association,* July 21, 2004.

6. "Nature's Clone," Roderick Angle and Jill Neimark. *Psychology Today,* July/August 1997.

7. "Homer Proteins Regulate Sensitivity to Cocaine," Karen K. Szumlinski, Marlin H. Dehoff, Shin H. Kang, Kelly A. Frys, Kevin D. Lominac, Matthias Klugmann, Jason Rohrer, William Griffin III, Shigenobu Toda, Nicolas P. Champtiaux, Thomas Berry, Jian C. Tu, Stephanie E. Shealy, Matthew J. During, Lawrence D.

Middaugh, Paul F. Worley, and Peter W. Kalivas. *Neuron*, August 5, 2004.

8. "Association Study of the Epac Gene and Tobacco Smoking and Nicotine Dependence," X. Chen, B. Wu, and K.S. Kendler. *American Journal of Medical Genetics*, August 15, 2004.

9. "Genetic Clues to the Molecular Basis of Tobacco Addiction and Progress towards Personalized Therapy," Robert Walton, Elaine Johnstone, Marcus Munafo, Matt Neville, and Sian Griffiths. *Trends in Molecular Medicine*, February 2001.

10. "Patterns of Brain Activity Associated with Variation in Voluntary Running Wheel Behavior," Justin S. Rhodes, Theodore Garland Jr., and Stephen C. Gammie. *Behavioral Neuroscience*, December 2003.

11. "Viral Gene Therapy Makes Males More Faithful and Friendly," Erica Klarreich, *Nature*, June 17, 2004.

12. "Nature's Clone," Roderick Angle and Jill Neimark. *Psychology Today*, July/August 1997.

13. "Periadolescent Mice Show Enhanced Delta FosB Upregulation in Response to Cocaine and Amphetamine," Michelle Erlich, John Sommer, Edwin Canas, and Ellen Unterwald. *Journal of Neuroscience*, November 1, 2002.

14. "Genetic Enhancement of Learning and Memory in Mice," J. Z. Tsien et al. *Nature*, September 1999.

Chapter 3

1. "Role of Genotype in the Cycle of Violence in Maltreated Children," A. Caspi, J. McClay, T. E. Moffitt, J. Mill, J. Martin, I. E. Craig, A. Taylor, and R. Poulton. *Science*, August 2002.

2. "Genetic and Environmental Processes in Young Children's Resilience and Vulnerability to Socioeconomic Deprivation," J. Kim-Cohen, T. E. Moffitt, A. Caspi, and A. Taylor. *Child Development*, May 2004.

3. *Dictionary of Biographical Quotations*, Richard Kenin (Knopf, 1978), as quoted on Anecdotage.com.

4. Interview on *Now with Bill Moyers*, aired on March 12, 2004.

Chapter 4

1. "Are You a Risk Taker?" Marvin Zuckerman. *Psychology Today*, November/December 2000.
2. "Attention-Deficit Hyperactivity Disorder Related to Advantageous Gene," Dr. Robert K. Moyzis et al. *Proceedings of the National Academy of Sciences of the United States of America*, January 8, 2002.
3. "Politics of Biology: How the Nature vs. Nurture Debate Shapes Public Policy and Our View of Ourselves," Wray Herbert. www.depressionisachoice.com/essays/biology.htm.
4. "Politics of Biology: How the Nature vs. Nurture Debate Shapes Public Policy and Our View of Ourselves," Wray Herbert. www.depressionisachoice.com/essays/biology.htm.

Chapter 5

1. "Work Values: Genetic and Environmental Influences," L. M. Keller, R. D. Arvey, T. J. Bouchard, N. L. Segal, R. V. Davis. *Journal of Applied Psychology*, February 1992.
2. "Genetic and Environmental Influences on the Continuous Scales of the Myers-Briggs Type Indicator: An Analysis Based on Twins Reared Apart," T. J. Bouchard Jr. and Y. M. Hur. *Journal of Personality*, April 1998.
3. "Evidence from Turner's Syndrome of an Imprinted X-Linked Locus Affecting Cognitive Function," D. H. Skuse et al. *Nature*, June 12, 1997.
4. "Intuition, Women Managers and Gendered Stereotypes," J. Hayes, C. W. Allinson, and S. J. Armstrong. *Personnel Review*, April 1, 2004.
5. "Unemployment Alters the Set Point for Life Satisfaction," R. E. Lucas, A. E. Clark, Y. Georgellis, and E. Diener. *Psychological Science*, January 2004.
6. "Happy Is as Happy Does," a paper presented by Dr. David T. Lykken at the American Psychological Society's Presidential Symposium, May 24, 1997.
7. "DNA Targeting of Rhinal Cortex D2 Receptor Protein Reversibly Blocks Learning of Cues That Predict Reward," Zheng Liu, Barry J. Richmond, Elisabeth A. Murray, Richard C. Saunders, Sara

Steenrod, Barbara K. Stubblefield, Deidra M. Montague, and Edward I. Ginns. *Proceedings of the National Academy of Sciences*, August 9, 2004.

Chapter 6

1. "Genetic Influence on Perceptions of Childhood Family Environment: A Reared-Apart Twins Study," Y. M. Hur and T. J. Bouchard. *Child Development*, 1995. Also, "Transmission of Social Attitudes," N. G. Martin, I. J. Eaves, A. C. Heath, R. Jardine, I. M. Feingold, H. J. Eysenck, *Proceedings of the National Academy of Science*, 1986.
2. "The Heritability of Attitudes: A Study of Twins," J. M. Olson, P. A. Vernnon, J. A. Harris, and K. L. Jang. *Journal of Personality and Social Psychology*, June 2001.
3. *The God Gene,* Dean Hamer. (Doubleday, 2004).
4. "Hoxb8 Is Required for Normal Grooming Behavior in Mice," J. M. Greer and M. R. Capecchi. *Neuron*, January 3, 2003.
5. "Allelic Variation in 5-HT Receptor Expression Is Associated with Anxiety- and Depression-Related Personality Traits," A. Strobel et al. *Journal of Neural Transmission*, December 2003.
6. "Interaction Between the Serotonin Transporter Gene and Neuroticism in Cigarette Smoking Behavior," S. Hu, C. L. Brody, C. Fisher, L. Gunzerath, M. L. Nelson, S. Z. Sabol, L. A. Sirota, S. E. Marcus, B. D. Greenberg, D. L. Murphy, and D. H. Hamer. *Molecular Psychiatry*, March 2000.
7. "Emotional Intelligence from the Perspective of the Five-Factor Model of Personality," Robert R. McCrae, *Handbook of Emotional Intelligence*, edited by Reuven Bar-On and James D.A. Parker, p. 266.
8. Personality, Stress, and Coping Section, http://www.grc.nia.hih.gov/branches/lpc/pcosta.htm, Paul T. Costa Jr., Laboratory of Personality and Cognition, National Institute on Aging.

Chapter 7

1. "Genes, Evolution and Personality," Thomas J. Bouchard Jr. and John C. Loehlin. *Behavior Genetics*, May 2001.

2. "The Determinants of Leadership: The Role of Genetic, Personality, and Cognitive Factors," Richard Arvey, Maria Rotundo, Wendy Johnson, and Matt McGue. Available from the IDEAS online database http://ideas.repec.org/p/hrr/papers/1302.html.
3. "Personality and Leadership: A Qualitative and Quantitative Review," T. A. Judge et al. *Journal of Applied Psychology*, August 2002.
4. "Genes, Evolution and Personality," Thomas J. Bouchard Jr. and John C. Loehlin. *Behavior Genetics*, May 2001.
5. "A Behavior Genetic Investigation of the Relationship Between Leadership and Personality," Andrew M. Johnson, et al. *Twin Research*, February 2004.
6. "How Are Entrepreneurs Different?" Tom Eckmann, *The Venturer Newsletter*. Interview with Carl Robinson, Ph.D. Advance Leadership Consulting.
7. "Canon, Lone Wolf," Bob Johnstone. *Wired*, October 1994.

Chapter 8
1. "The Genetics of Cognitive Processes: Candidate Genes in Humans and Animals," by K. I. Morley and G. W. Montgomery. *Behavior Genetics*, November 2001.
2. Entry on "Intelligence," Douglas K. Detterman, B.A., Ph.D. Microsoft Encarta Online Encyclopedia.
3. "Familial Studies of Intelligence: A Review," T. J. Bouchard and M. McGue. *Science*, April–June 1981.
4. "Structural Brain Variation and General Intelligence," R. J. Haier, R. Jung, R. Yeo, K. Head, and M. T. Alkire. *NeuroImage* (available 7/15/04 online).
5. "Genetic Influences on Brain Structure," Paul Thompson et al., *Nature Neuroscience*, November 5, 2001. Also, "Neurobiology of Intelligence: Science and Ethics," Jeremy Gray and Paul Thompson, *Nature Reviews Neuroscience*, June 2004.
6. "Drug Discovery in Alzheimer's Disease," Tim Tully, Josh Dubnau, Roderick Scott, Rusiko Bourtchuladze, and Scott Gossweiler. *Journal of Molecular Neuroscience*, August–October 2002.
7. "The BDNF Val66met Polymorphism Affects Activity-Dependent

Secretion of BDNF and Human Memory and Hippocampal Function," M. F. Egan, M. Kojima, J. H. Callicott, T. E. Goldberg, B. S. Kolachana, A. Bertolino, E. Zaitsev, B. Gold, D. Goldman, M. Dean, B. Lu, and D. R. Weinberger. *Cell*, January 24, 2003.

8. "Good Genes Count, but Not Only Factor in High IQ," Sharon Begley. *The Wall Street Journal*, June 20, 2003.

9. "Behavioral Genetics of Cognitive Ability: A Life-Span Perspective," M. McGue, T. J. Bouchard Jr., W. G. Iacono, and D. T. Lykken; in *Nature, Nurture and Psychology*, edited by R. Plomin and G. E. McClearn; American Psychological Association, 1993. Also, "Substantial Genetic Influence on Cognitive Abilities in Twins 80 or More Years Old," Gerald E. McClearn, Boo Johansson, Stig Berg, Nancy L. Pedersen, Frank Ahern, Stephen A. Petrill, Robert Plomin, *Science*, June 6, 1997.

10. "Understanding the Nature of the General Factor of Intelligence: The Role of Individual Differences in Neural Plasticity as an Explanatory Mechanism," Dennis Garlick. *Psychological Review*, January 2002.

11. "Decreased Memory Performance in Healthy Humans Induced by Stress-Level Cortisol Treatment," J. W. Newcomer et al. *Archives of General Psychiatry*, June 1999.

Chapter 9

1. "Phenome Fellow," Jonathan Shaw. *Harvard Magazine*, January–February 2003.

Chapter 10

1. "Outsourcing Not a Problem: Bernanke," Rex Nutting, CBS Marketwatch.com, March 30, 2004.

2. "A Few Bad Apples? An Exploratory Look at What Typical Americans Think About Business Ethics Today," Steve Farkas, Ann Duffett, and Jean Johnson for the Kettering Foundation and Public Agenda, January 2004.

3. "Nature vs. Nurture: Are Leaders Born or Made? A Behavior Genetic Investigation of Leadership Style," A. M. Johnson, P. A. Vernon, J. M. McCarthy, M. Molson, J. A. Harris, K. L. Jang. *Twin Research*, December 1998.

4. "Considering the Role of Personality in the Work-Family Experience: Relationships of the Big Five to Work-Family Conflict and Facilitation," Julie Holliday Wayne, Nicholas Musisca, and William Fleeson. *Journal of Vocational Behavior*, February 2004.

5. "A Behavior Genetic Investigation of the Relationship Between Leadership and Personality," A. M. Johnson, P. A. Vernon, J. A. Harris, and K. L. Jang. *Twin Research*, February 2004.

6. "Personality and Leadership: A Qualitative and Quantitative Review," T. A. Judge, J. E. Bono, R. Ilies, and M. W. Gerhardt. *Journal of Applied Psychology*, August 2002.

7. "Five-factor Model of Personality and Transformational Leadership," T. A. Judge and J. E. Bono. *Journal of Applied Psychology*, October 2000.

8. "Nature vs. Nurture: Are Leaders Born or Made? A Behavior Genetic Investigation of Leadership Style," A. M. Johnson, P. A. Vernon, J. M. McCarthy, M. Molson, J. A. Harris, K. L. Jang. *Twin Research*, December 1998.

Chapter 11

1. "Gene Expression Profiles in the Brain Predict Behavior in Individual Honey Bees," C. W. Whitfield, A. M. Cziko, and G. E. Robinson. *Science*, October 20, 2003.

2. "The Determinants of Leadership: The Role of Genetic, Personality, and Cognitive Factors," Richard Arvey, Maria Rotundo, Wendy Johnson, and Matt McGue. Available from the IDEAS online database http://ideas.repec.org/p/hrr/papers/1302.html.

3. "The Five-Factor Model of Personality: Assessing Entrepreneurs and Managers," B. R. Envick and M. Langford. *Academy of Entrepreneurship Journal*, volume 6, no. 1, 2000.

4. "Psychological Predictors of Entrepreneurial Success," E. Schmitt-Rodermund. Available from http://www2.uni-jena.de/svw/devpsy/projects/download/untern3.pdf, 2001.

5. "Risk Propensity and Personality," N. Nicholson, M. Fenton-O'Creevy, E. Soane, and P. Willman. London Business School, Open University Business School, and Said Business School

Oxford, 2002. Available from
http://facultyresearch.london.edu/docs/risk.ps.pdf.

6. "Sexually Dimorphic Gene Expression in Mouse Brain Precedes
Gonadal Differentiation," P. Dewing, T. Shi, S. Horvath, and E.
Vilain. *Molecular Brain Research*, October 21, 2003.

PARTICIPATING
EXECUTIVES

I'd like to thank the following entrepreneurs and business leaders for sharing their personal stories and giving so generously of their time and expertise. Their life and business stories each reflect an inborn DNA of success.

John Bogle Jr.	Founder/President, Bogle Funds
John Bogle Sr.	Founder, former Chairman/CEO, Vanguard Funds
	President, Bogle Financial Markets Research Center
Herman Cain	Former Chairman, Godfather's Pizza
Carlos de Cespedes	Co-founder, Chairman/CEO, Pharmed Group
Victoria Chacon	Founder/President, Victoria Chacon Cleaning Services
	Founder/President, Victoria Chacon Temporary Services
	Founder/President, *La Vision de Georgia* newspaper

Marcelo Claure	Founder, Chairman/CEO, Brightstar
Robert Crandall	Former Chairman/CEO, American Airlines
Pat Croce	Founder, Sports Physical Therapists
	Former President, Philadelphia 76ers
	Host, *Pat Croce: Moving In*
David Gardner	Co-founder, The Motley Fool
Barry Gibbons	Former Chairman/CEO, Burger King
Thomas Kinnear	Professor/Managing Director, Zell Lurie
	Institute for Entrepreneurial Studies
Kay Koplovitz	Founder, Koplovitz & Co.
	Founder/former Chairman/CEO, USA
	Networks
Bernard Marcus	Co-founder, former Chairman/CEO, Home
	Depot
TiTi McNeill	Founder, President/CEO, TranTech
Al Neuharth	Former Chairman/CEO, Gannett Co., Inc.
John Patrick	Former Vice-President of IBM for Internet
	technology
Ann Rhoades	Founder/President, PeopleInk
	Former Executive VP, JetBlue
Debbi Fields Rose	Founder/former Chairman, Mrs. Fields
	Cookies
Rich Teerlink	Former Chairman/CEO, Harley-Davidson
Peter Ueberroth	Chairman, Ambassadors International
	U.S. Olympic Committee chairman
	Former Chairman, Major League Baseball
Sam Wyly	Founder, Ranger Capital Group
	Chairman, Michael's Stores
Sam Zell	Founder, Chairman/CEO, Equity Group
	Investments LLC

INDEX

addictions
  D2 dopamine receptor and, 34
  DRD4 gene and, 74
  Epac gene and, 34
  genetic predisposition to, 5, 7, 28
  "Homer" gene and, 34
  "marathon mice" experiment and, 35–36
  self-quiz, "Are You Addicted to Success?," 35
  to success, xvii, 27–41
  teenagers and, 39–40
  twin studies, 28, 34
ADHD (Attention Deficit Hyperactivity Disorder), 72–74, 77
advisors, panel of, 78–79, 79
Agreeableness
  career choices and, 11, 200
  co-operation, 148–50, 200
  corporate setting and, 200
  entrepreneurial personality and, 21, 24
  Extroversion with, 185
  as genetic trait, 11–12, 20–21
  low vs. high degree of, 12, 20–21, 193
  picking business partners and, 177, 180

Power Pair with Extroversion, 24, 184–85, 187
  See also Nice Guys
alcoholism
  brain chemicals and, 33
  genetic predisposition to, 5, 28
American Airlines, xix, 9, 85–86, 210–11
  AAdvantage, 86, 94–95, 210
  SuperSaver fares, 210
anxiety, genetic predisposition to, 7
Apollo 13 (film), 79
Armstrong, Philander Bannister, 2
attitude
  Barry Gibbons on, 140
  and focus, genetic predisposition to, 93–95, 101
  John Bogle, Sr., on, 139
  obstacles and, 35, 36, 38–40, 43–46, 59, 112, 123, 139–40
  optimism, 64, 93
  pessimism and Neuroticism, 112, 140
  reboot your memory and, 140
  rejection and, 124–27
  self-awareness, ego, and, 158, 202
Attitude LLC, 87